The Crafting of
Absalom and Achitophel
Dryden's "Pen for a Party"

He who draws his Pen for one Party must expect to make Enemies of the other.... But ... if I happen to please the more Moderate sort, I shall be sure of an honest Party.
—John Dryden

Our last redress is dint of verse to try,
And *satire* is our Court of Chancery.
—John Dryden

The Crafting of
Absalom and Achitophel

Dryden's "Pen for a Party"

W. K. Thomas

Canadian Cataloguing in Publication Data

Thomas, W. Keith, 1927-
    The crafting of Absalom and Achitophel

Includes index.
ISBN 0-88920-059-9

1. Dryden, John, 1631-1700.   Absalom and
Achitophel.   I. Title.

PR3415.A25T46   821'.4   C77-001787-8

Copyright © 1978
Wilfrid Laurier University Press
Waterloo, Ontario, Canada
N2L 3C5

ACKNOWLEDGEMENTS

The bulk of the research for this study was done at the Huntington Library in San Marino, California. There the pamphlet collection in particular, and especially that part of it originally acquired by Narcissus Luttrell, proved of inestimable aid. So it is with a sense of double obligation, for permission to use the library and for the most courteous hospitality extended to me in that Eden of the West, that I wish to thank Mr. James Thorpe, the Director, and his admirable staff.

Supplementary work was done at the Houghton Library at Harvard University, for whose courteous assistance I should like to thank the Director and staff, and through the Interlibrary Loan office of the University of Waterloo, where I am greatly indebted to Mrs. M. E. Pletch and her assistants.

To the Canada Council go my thanks for its grant in aid of research that made my study possible. To that Council and to the Humanities Research Council of Canada go my further, even greater thanks for their assistance in publication, for this book has been published with the help of a grant from the Humanities Research Council of Canada, using funds provided by the Canada Council.

Parts of this book appeared, in somewhat different form, in articles of mine published in *The Explicator*, *The Philological Quarterly*, and the *Revue de l'Université d'Ottawa*, to the editors of which I am grateful for permission to reproduce.

Nor does my indebtedness end here, for without the multitudinous work, done by scores of scholars with loving care, on Dryden, the Exclusion Crisis, and related subjects, I should of course not have been able even to begin this study. It is a privilege to be able to walk on the road they have made and to extend it, perhaps, a cubit further. To the anonymous consultants of the Humanities Research Council of Canada I am especially indebted, for, owing to the suggestions they made, I have been able to strengthen the presentation of my argument, so that the direction in which the possible extension by a cubit proceeds may be seen more clearly.

University of Waterloo   W. K. T.
Waterloo, Ontario, Canada

CONTENTS

1

THE OCCASION PROMPTS

Among the many parallels of poetry and painting, the fate of Rembrandt's *Night Watch* has particular interest for students of literature. For generations his painting appeared so dark and gloomy that it came to be called *Night Watch*, even though it was originally entitled *The Company of Captain Frans Banning Cocq*. Actually it was obscured by many layers of dust and grime, and when in 1947 the painting was restored by experts, there appeared a flood of richly varied colour suffusing the whole. With the colour was revealed also something that had been lost even to the imagination: the original structure of the whole. What was before a meaningless hodge-podge of figures became a meaningful interplay of geometric forms, of light and dark, and of configurative movements, all coming to a point (not realized before) on the soldiers in the middle of the painting, who now stride out to meet the viewer.

An even more startling discovery was made when a painting by the Spanish artist Ribalta, called *Christ Bearing the Cross*, was restored. Suddenly out of complete darkness emerged a major figure, kneeling at the side of Christ. Even his existence had not been guessed at before, but now both he and the true nature of the painting have been presented to our generation in the way in which they appeared to the painter's contemporaries.

Dryden's verbal masterpiece, *Absalom and Achitophel*, has been, for most readers, in much the same kind of situation. For generations it has been known, but rather dimly. Readers have read as allegory the Biblical names of David, Absalom and Achitophel; they have recognized the many allusions to Milton's epic poems; and they have relished the verbal pyrotechnics of the gallery of satiric portraits. But, because a considerable portion of the poem has remained in comparative obscurity, they have spoken of its genre as uncertain and its structure as broken, and for the same reason they have missed altogether many of the finer points of literary skill. Curiously, this half-way approach has found support from certain critics, who appear to argue that it is sufficient for us of the twentieth century to bring to the poem only what we already know from the twentieth century, and to respond to the poem as if it had been addressed to our peculiar predilections in the first place.[1] I cannot help thinking that such an attitude is like being content with viewing *Night Watch* when it was all grimy, when the dust of centuries had got between us and the original.

If You Stand Closer

Fortunately certain other scholars have devoted much effort to making it possible, for those readers who will follow them, to penetrate the obfuscations and distortions of intervening time and to stand closer to the original, seeing the poem in more of its own light and on more of its own terms.[2] What appears before those readers' eyes as they approach closer to the poem is as exciting as what appeared when the veil of time was removed from the paintings of Rembrandt and Ribalta.

In fact, the closer one is able to stand before Dryden's poem, the more it surges with artistic vitality. The King who is described at the beginning as scattering his Maker's image through the land, in a most

---

[1] E.g., W. O. S. Sutherland, Jr.: " ... The modern reader should not think of Shaftesbury ... as the simple target of the poet's disapproval. The poet may think that way, but the modern reader should not. The man Shaftesbury is immaterial. It is the values symbolized by the man that constitute the poet's object" (*The Art of the Satirist* [Austin, Texas: University of Texas Press, 1965], p. 19). Somewhat similarly, Bernard N. Schilling apologizes for the "topicality" of *Absalom and Achitophel*, its being "contaminated by history," and asserts that "The distance that *Absalom and Achitophel* carries us in its moral allegory beyond a contemporary historical reference is the measure of its greatness" (*Dryden and the Conservative Myth* [New Haven and London: Yale University Press, 1961], pp. 15, 128, 14). Even H. T. Swedenberg, Jr., who provides a vast amount of much appreciated background information in his edition of the poem, suggests that perhaps the "timeless" aspect of the poem is more important to the modern reader than the topical (*The Works of John Dryden*, Volume II, *Poems 1681-1684* [Berkeley, Calif.: University of California Press, 1972], p. 232). One suspects that by "timeless" is meant that which appeals to the latter part of the twentieth century.

[2] Sir Walter Scott, in his edition of the poem in Vol. IX of Dryden's *Works* (1808), provided much elucidative information, as have, more recently and most notably, E. S. de Beer in his article "*Absalom and Achitophel*: Literary and Historical Notes," *Review of English Studies*, 17 (1941), 298-309; George R. Noyes in his notes to the poem in *The Poetical Works of Dryden* (Boston: Houghton Mifflin, 1950 [1st ed. 1909]), pp. 956-63, 1054-57; Ian Jack in his *Augustan Satire* (Oxford: Clarendon, 1952), pp. 53-76; James Kinsley in his article "Historical Allusions in *Absalom and Achitophel*," *Review of English Studies*, n.s. 6 (1955), 291-97, and in his edition of Dryden's poetry (Oxford: Oxford University Press, 1958), pp. 1877-1903; Elias F. Mengel, Jr., in his editing of *Poems on Affairs of State*, vol. 2 (New Haven and London: Yale University Press, 1965), esp. pp. 453-93; Earl Miner in his book *Dryden's Poetry* (Bloomington and London: Indiana University Press, 1967), pp. 106-43; and, as mentioned, H. T. Swedenberg, Jr., in his California edition of the *Works*, II, 209-85.

libertine manner, is, in the progress of the poem, so carefully re-shaped (reconditioned, as it were) that by the end he emerges as a credible vice-regent of God. Individual lines can explode with power. For example, when speaking of the Popish Plot, Dryden refers to it as "With Oaths affirm'd, with dying Vows deny'd" (line 111).[3] When each of an estimated thirty-five people was charged with complicity in the Plot, each was found guilty and sentenced to execution on the strength of false evidence, given under oath, by a group of rogues who made their living, and secured their power, by lying these people to death. Many of those thirty-five, when they ascended the scaffold and faced the executioner's blindfold, vowed, knowing that in a few seconds they would meet their Maker, that they were innocent. These two sets of dramatic scenes, in the courtroom and on the scaffold, so tense with injustice and tragedy, are compressed into that one, balanced line: "With Oaths affirm'd, with dying Vows deny'd." Nor is verbal dexterity all that appears when the dust is removed. Wondrous things can be seen going on with the various characters. In the person of Slingsby Bethel, for instance, we see Dryden taking an insignificant little sheriff who talked too much, and making of him a most effective weapon with which to afflict the King's enemies, time and time again. Even the original Samson had done no better with the jawbone of an ass. Furthermore, a new character may possibly emerge—as did with Ribalta's painting—in the person of Agag, but more of that later. Perhaps most importantly, when more of the grime is cleared away, the poem can be seen as a whole—literally—complete, not broken-backed, but integrated, and highly persuasive.

As the reader will have inferred, this present study of the poem seeks to incorporate the work of restoration that has already been done by other scholars, and also attempts to guide the reader past even further obscurity, so that a still larger portion of the structure, still more about the cast of characters, and a still greater number of its fine nuances and subtle complexities may be seen and appreciated.

Dryden himself has given us a key to a greater understanding of the poem. In his prefatory remarks to the poem he made it clear that he was writing in the midst of a pamphlet warfare that was raging between Tories and Whigs over an issue that threatened the nation with civil war. He himself wrote to help prevent that war by assisting the Tories, drawing his pen on behalf of that particular party to the dispute and addressing himself to "the more Moderate sort," the Restoration equivalent to our uncommitted voters. In composing his poem, Dryden had

[3] The text used is that of the first issue of the first edition, with three exceptions: the long "s" is replaced by round "s," typographical corrections are made in accord with the text provided by V. A. Dearing in the California *Works*, vol. II, and line numbers are inserted in brackets.

available to him what was public knowledge about the various persons concerned in the dangerous dispute, and there is reason for believing that he probably had read most of what had already been written about these persons in the pamphlet warfare. By comparing Dryden's poems with many of these other pamphlets, we can see him carefully selecting his material from the mass that was available to him and then, in the light of the strategies other writers had used successfully and unsuccessfully, choosing his own strategies astutely and shaping his material so as to implement them.

Nor is a key the only thing Dryden has given us. He placed on the title page of his poem a motto drawn from a passage of Horace's that begins with the famous phrase—particularly appropriate for us—"Ut pictura poesis" (A poem is like a picture).[4] The phrase Dryden selected reads, in translation, "If you stand closer, it will charm you more"—certainly an invitation to read closely, looking, presumably, for recurring motifs and images and exploring the implications both of what is said and what is left unsaid. Altogether, by tracing Dryden's selection and manipulation of materials, we can come fairly close to reading the finished poem in the way his more knowing contemporaries would have read it (and they are, of course, the people for whom it was written); and by accepting his invitation to stand closer, we can also come fairly near to observing the process of poetic creation itself, as Dryden crafts his poem so as to weave his charm.

Before we begin, however, most readers of this study will need to have sketched in a background of the reasons why Dryden's poem came into being in the first place, and why it contained the cast of characters and catalogue of crimes it did. If the reader should already be conversant with this background, he may of course prefer to skip the rest of this chapter and jump ahead to Chapter 2—or he may wish to refresh his memory with a quick skimming. Those who are not conversant with the background, however, will probably find it helpful, even needful, to become acquainted, in a preliminary way, with the people, the events, and the attitudes that are reflected in the poem—especially with the attitudes, some of which may well seem more than a little strange.

Who Should Rule?

The political crisis which gave rise to *Absalom and Achitophel* was concerned, basically, with the question "Who should rule England?" Should the King, in the person of Charles II, rule, or should Parlia-

---

[4] "Ars Poetica," ll. 361-62, in Horace, *Satires, Epistles and Ars Poetica*, tr. H. Rushton Fairclough, Loeb Classical Library (London and Cambridge, Mass.: Heinemann and Harvard University Press, 1970), pp. 480-81.

ment? More critical even was the related question of who, after Charles had died, should succeed to the throne, the legal heir (who was Charles's brother, James) or someone appointed by Parliament? If it were the latter, the effective ruler of the country would consequently be, not the King, but Parliament.

Most readers of today are the philosophical heirs of the political revolution in which this particular crisis constituted one of the early battles, and so most would assume that it would have been a good thing for Parliament to rule. Dryden, however, took the other side in the issue and did his best to persuade his uncommitted readers to support the King. Since those readers would not have found it unreasonable for him to do so, there is evidently a large difference between the political assumptions held by most people today and those held by many in Dryden's day. For this reason, if we are to understand how Dryden sought to work on his readers' minds, we have to disengage our own political assumptions and approach the situation in his day as objectively as we can.

As one would expect, there were a number of reasons for Dryden to support the King. For centuries the control of the government had rested, not with Parliament, but with the King and his ministers: it seemed that this had always been the situation—except, of course, for the years of the Commonwealth and its military dictatorship, an exception that proved how desirable the usual had been.[5] The King had been and once more was the active head of government, combining the functions of the twentieth-century British monarch and Prime Minister, and resembling the American President in his powers, except for the fact that the King came to his office by hereditary right. Charles II chose, appointed, and dismissed his ministers and advisers as he alone saw fit, for the ministers of the crown were then responsible, as their name implies, not to Parliament as now, but to the crown—the King himself. They supervised the executive branch of the government, operating through various boards and committees, and put into action the King's desires.

What then was the role of Parliament? It was of course the legislative branch of government. Laws were made by Parliament, which included the King in one of his roles. Usually a bill would be introduced into Parliament by one of the King's ministers, passed by the House of Commons and then the House of Lords, and finally pronounced law by the King (saying, "Le roi le veult"). The King could always and on occasion actually did refuse to accept a bill; instead he

---

[5] For a general survey of the political structure and activity in the reign of Charles II, see Sir George Clark, The Later Stuarts, 2nd ed. (Oxford: Clarendon, 1955), and David Ogg, England in the Reign of Charles II, 2nd ed., 2 vols. (London: Oxford University Press, 1956).

set it to one side and it never became law—a most effective form of veto. In theory anyone in either House could introduce proposed legislation, but in Charles II's reign—up to 1678—this rarely happened: it was usually the ministers who did the introducing—then as now. In addition to contributing to the legislative role of Parliament, the House of Commons had had for centuries and still had one very important control. All tax money raised inside the country and going to the King had to be approved by the House of Commons. The House could refuse—it could, for instance, refuse to allow the money needed to raise a certain regiment or to build a certain number of ships for the navy —and for this reason in particular the King felt obliged to try to retain control of a majority of votes in the House of Commons, sometimes by using bribes and the gift of pensions to various Members of Parliament.

As mentioned, succession to the throne depended on heredity, and in the years we are concerned with, 1678-81, a crisis arose over the succession. Since Charles had no legitimate children (although about a dozen illegitimate ones had survived to adulthood), the heir presumptive was his younger brother, James, Duke of York. James was openly and avowedly a Roman Catholic, and at the time of Dryden's writing *Absalom and Achitophel*, opposition to James's succession had come to a head.

That opposition was intimately connected with the theories of kingship then current.[6] Though at first glance it may appear that the King of England was a despot, he was really not: he was instead what was called a royal monarch. In theory there could be—and in the practice of other countries there actually were—two other kinds of monarch: despotic and limited. Some people in England feared that their royal monarch would become a despotic monarch, and some (a few) even wanted their royal monarch to become limited.

Under a despotic monarch the subjects held all their freedom and property in fealty from him: as he wished, he could take back either the freedom or the property (or both) from anyone at any time. The royal monarch, in distinction, was subject to the law of God and the law of nature. In addition he helped to make the statute law (through Parliament) and ruled by that law—as in fact he agreed to do in a clause of his coronation oath. But the royal monarch was still free to adjust the application of statute law as he saw fit, so as to ensure that the spirit of the law prevailed whenever it came into conflict with the letter: his concern, in other words, was that equity and justice be done. In times of crisis the royal monarch was also free to "resume" *absolute* control of

[6] The theories were set out by Sir Robert Filmer in his book *The Necessity of the Absolute Power of All Kings* (1648) in which he borrowed liberally from *La République* (1575) of Jean Bodin. The whole is summarized conveniently in Alan Roper, *Dryden's Poetic Kingdoms* (London: Routledge and Kegan Paul, 1965), pp. 67-69.

the country, just as western democracies have frequently suspended the operation of habeas corpus in times of national emergency. Distinct from both these kinds of monarchs, the limited monarch was strictly subject to the constitution and to the statute law. If he were thought to have broken the law, some other agency (such as a parliament) would determine whether in fact he had done so and what should be done about it. That agency was obviously superior to the monarch, and the monarch himself was in the very limited and inferior position of the Doge of Venice, who presided over what was in effect a republic. Charles II, to repeat, operated—in true, British fashion—between the two extremes, as a royal monarch. Dryden and other traditionalists thought that this was only right and just. But some others feared that he might become a despot, and some even sought to make him a limited monarch by establishing the supremacy of Parliament.

The fear of despotism arose largely from the influence which Roman Catholics had at court. We need to remember that in the seventeenth century religious differences provoked as much political animosity and strong, bitter feeling as they do today in Northern Ireland, and as do our own current conflicts elsewhere between capitalism and socialism, between white supremacy and black power. What fueled the fire in England was the indisputable fact that in all the Roman Catholic monarchies of the world, the king was absolute and despotic, and there were signs that Charles was falling under Roman Catholic domination. His Queen was Roman Catholic, his brother and potential successor was Roman Catholic, many of his mistresses were Roman Catholic, and many court officials were Roman Catholic. Some even suspected that Charles himself was a secret Roman Catholic, and they may well have suspected right, for, though always publicly professing to Anglicanism, Charles on his deathbed confessed himself a Roman Catholic and so may indeed have been one secretly for many years. Furthermore, his efforts to control the House of Commons looked like a movement towards absolutism. The King favoured many things French—drama, dancing, mistresses: did he favour the French form of government too? I personally have come across no record at all of the government's having invaded the personal liberty of anybody, but the fear continued in many people that, because of the obvious influence of Roman Catholics on the King and because he had available to him the services of his regiments of Guards (whom his opponents considered a standing army), the government could all too easily move towards absolutism.

This fear was intensified in relation to the Duke of York, the Roman Catholic heir to the throne. The English remembered all too well what had happened the last time a Roman Catholic had succeeded to the English throne. When Mary Tudor (Bloody Mary) had become

Queen, she speedily made England officially Roman Catholic, through her control of appointments to the church and government, and as a result caused a great deal of bloodshed. Many Englishmen feared a repetition, should James succeed to the throne.

It should be remembered, however, that, if a government is legitimate and functions fairly well, most of the citizens will be willing to put up with it. In fact it would be useful if we recognized three political categories into which the Englishmen of the time would have fitted. Presumably the largest number were apolitical, then as now, either ignoring the government or putting up with it and going on about their own business. There were then, on one side of the middle, those who consciously gave their support to the King, and on the other were those who just as consciously opposed the government and its policies. In fact this three-fold division is reflected in Dryden's note "To the Reader" with which he prefaced *Absalom and Architophel*: while recognizing that there were two parties in the dispute, he sought to please "the more Moderate sort," who, being "the least Concern'd," were evidently the third group, in the middle.

In a similar way we should recognize a three-fold division of religious (or sectarian) affiliation. At one extreme were the Roman Catholics, and at the other were those Protestant groups outside the Church of England whom the members of the Church of England referred to as Dissenters. The group in the middle were of course the Anglicans, the members of the Church of England, the official state church. There is no difficulty in seeing this three-fold division: what is difficult, however, is knowing how to use the term "Protestant," for, while some Anglicans considered themselves Protestants, others did not. At times, moreover, "Protestant" could be used to describe the Dissenters only, and at other times both the Anglicans and Dissenters together, as being distinct from, and opposed to, the Roman Catholics. In much the same way there was criss-crossing and overlapping with regard to political and religious allegiances. Most of the opposition to the government came, at this time, from the Dissenters, and most of the support for it came from the Anglicans and the Roman Catholics; but certainly there were some Anglicans who opposed the government and some Dissenters who supported it—and many of both groups, as well as of the Catholics, who neither supported nor opposed, but simply put up with it.

In view of this criss-crossing of allegiances, it was understandable that the political polemicists of the day should have sought new names for their opponents. Thus it was that the supporters of the King took the term *Whigs*, a short form of *Whiggamores* (the name for the Scottish covenanters, a Dissenting and anti-government group) and applied it to all their opponents, whether they were Dissenters or not. Similarly these Whigs took the term *Tories*, derived from the Irish *toraidhe* (out-law bog-trotters), and applied it first to the English Roman Catholic supporters of James and then to all people, regardless of what religious sect they belonged to, who supported the King and objected to the proposed exclusion of James. (Characteristically the English looked for their terms of abuse to their neighbouring kingdoms, the savages beyond the pale, the lesser breeds without the law.)

The name-calling and general controversy indicates that there had indeed developed a fair amount of opposition to the government of Charles II. But, in spite of the name *Whig*, there had not yet come into being an opposition *party*, just as there was not yet a government *party* (the "parties" Dryden spoke of in his prefatory note were not political parties: they were instead parties to the dispute). More important still, there was no concept at all of His Majesty's Loyal Opposition—in fact, opposition to the King bordered on being *dis*loyal. Nonetheless a spirit of opposition developed in various groups.

These groups were indeed various and varied, some of them providing added reasons why Dryden should have supported the King.[7] The old Presbyterians, the leftovers from the days of the king-killing Commonwealth, wanted to increase their power by having the Anglicans absorbed in a union of all the Protestant groups in England. The country opposition—those landed gentry who were against the government—gave some credibility to the opposition by wanting all the right things: honest administration, respect for the law on the part of the King's ministers, the dismissal of court favourites, the government's consultation with Parliament, the prompt redress of grievances, financial retrenchment, the furtherance of English trade, and the defence of the Protestant religion. In contrast were those few radicals who pursued the aims of the anarchical levellers and the republicans of the Commonwealth era: usually these radicals were of fairly humble origins and had no effective leadership.

Then there were the adventurers. Many of these, it appeared, opposed the government simply in hopes of being bought off by a pension or a place. The Duke of Monmouth, however, consistently followed the main chance: as the oldest, illegitimate son of Charles II—and a favourite with his father—he sought to make himself popular with those who opposed the influence of the Roman Catholics, for he thought that if the Duke of York were driven out, he might slip in as King. And lastly there was the Earl of Shaftesbury, the most formidable opponent the government had to face. He knew the country well and used his knowledge effectively. He wanted power for himself and for Parliament so that

[7] For a detailed study of these groups see J. R. Jones, *The First Whigs: The Politics of the Exclusion Crisis* (London: Oxford University Press, 1961), pp. 9-19, on which the following summary is based.

both might have a much larger say in government. To those who favoured an increase in the powers of Parliament—with a corresponding decrease in the King's powers—Shaftesbury appeared a hero, but in seventeenth-century Tory eyes he was a dangerous revolutionary trying to have Parliament usurp powers that were rightfully the King's. There were various leaders among the opposition groups, but by 1681, the year of *Absalom and Achitophel*, Shaftesbury had become preeminent among the leaders, largely because of his ability to provide efficient organization.

It should be noted that no one aimed at democracy. In fact one apologist for the King's opponents went out of his way to deny such an aim, saying that if a certain royalist pamphlet "would intimate that there had been any design for setting up a *democratic* government, in opposition to our legal monarchy, it is a calumny."[8] The opposition instead aimed at broadening the power base of government: each opponent of the government sought to have himself included in those who made the governing decisions for the country, but in no way tried to include anyone of a lower social status. They sought, not a democracy, but an oligarchy just large enough to include them.

What united these various groups—after a fashion, and made them Whigs to the Tories—was the fact that, unless other arrangements were made, the Roman Catholic Duke of York would succeed to the throne. Accordingly they joined together in an attempt to have James excluded from the succession. The old Presbyterians saw such an Exclusion as a means of safeguarding their Protestant religion, the "country" opposition saw it as a means of safeguarding the country's liberties, the radicals viewed it as a first step towards a more far-reaching reform, the self-seeking adventurers saw it as another opportunity for being bought off, Monmouth of course saw it as opening the way to his own succession, and Shaftesbury saw it as a means of making the King and his government dependent on Parliament—and him.

But however much the Whig opposition was united in their efforts to exclude James, they were anything but united as to who should take his place when Charles died. James had two adult, Protestant daughters, Mary and Anne, and if he were to die instead of being excluded, the succession would go to one of them—which one was not clear, for, though Mary was the older, the law did not prescribe primogeniture for females. The next in line, after the two daughters, was the Dutch William of Orange, the only nephew of Charles and James, who was also married to Mary, daughter of James. These three were all legitimate: there was also to be considered the handsome and dashing James, Duke of Monmouth, who was Charles's oldest son—illegitimate but the old-

---

[8] *A Just and Modest Vindication of the proceedings of the Two last Parliaments* ([London, 1681]), p. 44. (Ascribed variously to Sir William Jones and to Robert Ferguson.)

est. He had the triple advantage of being male, English, and Protestant—and as far as those who wished to make Parliament supreme were concerned, he had the further advantage of having no legal claim to the throne, so that if Parliament were to make him king, he would be very much subservient to Parliament. But it was not until very late in the Exclusion Crisis that any of the principal leaders of the opposition put forward Monmouth at all seriously as an alternative to James.

By that time it looked to many in England as if the country were on the brink of another civil war, similar to the one that less than forty years before had deposed and murdered the King, had caused immense anguish, and had produced a form of government from which the people had eventually turned in relief to a renewal of the traditional, kingly government, which now, paradoxically, was once again endangered.

The Crisis Deepens

Shaftesbury and the Whigs had secured ascendancy in the House of Commons. They had done so thanks to errors on the part of Charles, errors which had compounded the advantage the Whigs had derived from events that looked like a godsend to them. The charges which Titus Oates had made about there being a Popish Plot to kill Charles, bring James to the throne, and thereby subject England to despotic Roman Catholicism, had been believed by the Protestant populace of London, and when these charges had been parallelled by revelations of secret governmental dealings with France, something nearly akin to hysteria swept the capital. The Whigs had used this fear to make things difficult for government officials in the House of Commons, and Charles, understandably taking the advice of a senior counsellor, had dissolved Parliament and had called a new election. The counsellor and Charles had thought that they would secure a majority of supporters in the new Parliament. They were wrong: the opposite happened —the Whigs elected a majority in the House of Commons. Again we of the twentieth century must be careful not to jump to the conclusion we would if the election had been held in our own day: then, in distinction from now, the suffrage was very far from being universal; so the presence of a Whig majority in the House did not necessarily mean that the majority of Englishmen throughout the country supported the Whigs.

But one result in particular of the election proved very awkward to the King. The Whigs introduced into the House a bill to exclude James from succession to the throne (with no replacement stated), and it received second reading, approval in principle. Faced with the prospect of losing the struggle over who should rule, Charles promptly dissolved Parliament and called another election. That, too, however, produced a majority for the Whigs in the House of Commons; so Charles postponed calling the new Parliament into session.

At this point, in the summer of 1680, the Duke of Monmouth added to the urgency of the crisis by doing something which it was illegal for a subject to do: he made a progress through the West of England as if he were the monarch receiving the loyalty and obeisance of his subjects. He drew large crowds, being hailed as the Protestant Duke (James being the Catholic Duke) and greatly strengthening his position as a contender for the succession. On November 1 Charles allowed the new Parliament to meet. Immediately the Whigs re-introduced the Exclusion Bill. Charles offered alternatives whereby legal protection for the Protestant religion would be guaranteed and whereby even a regency would be established, with James enjoying the name of King only. But the Whigs pressed their advantage, and the Exclusion Bill passed the House of Commons. In the House of Lords, too, it might possibly have succeeded, so great was the Whig momentum, but there the presence of Charles during the debate and the persuasive oratory of the Earl of Halifax caused the Bill to founder. Parliament was deadlocked, split between a Whig House of Commons and a House of Lords in which the majority supported the King.

The battle over who should rule had reached a stalemate in Parliament, but that was not the only battlefield. In the law courts the Whigs had taken charge of the evidence being given against those accused of complicity in the Popish Plot: that evidence often appeared to implicate James himself and so appeared to provide further reason why he should be excluded from the succession. But in the courts, too, Charles and his supporters counterattacked, and the government now instituted proceedings against the false witnesses in the Popish Plot in an effort to prove their testimony false and to silence the accusations against James. In the courts, as in Parliament, the struggle had reached a stalemate. There remained a third battleground, the public press, in which the combatants sought to do directly what debaters in Parliament and witnesses in the law courts were doing indirectly: they sought to influence public opinion. On this battleground, likewise, the government had to win its fight. So in answer to the virulent attacks on the government which appeared anonymously from clandestine presses, the government increased its equally virulent and often anonymous replies.

Then everything came to a head. On 20 January 1681 Charles dissolved Parliament and called a new one, to meet at Oxford. By changing the place of meeting from London to Oxford, Charles did two things: he sought to remove the Parliamentarians from the influence of the Whiggish mobs in London and he dramatized the fact that the crown was in danger from attack as it had been when his father, Charles I (the Martyr King), had called Parliament to meet at Oxford. When Parliament met at the beginning of April, the Whigs again had a majority in the House of Commons and again reintroduced the Exclusion Bill. A story went about that Shaftesbury had offered to call off the attack if Charles would consent to the naming of Monmouth as his successor in the place of James: true or not, Charles did no such thing, and instead dissolved Parliament a week after it had opened. Unknown to all but a very few, he by then had secured a pension of his own: by secret agreement the King of France was to send him, covertly and over the next three years, £400,000—enough to allow Charles to continue his government without financial assistance from Parliament.

Having won the battle in Parliament by causing the battlefield to vanish, Charles turned to the law courts. On July 2, Shaftesbury was arrested and charged with high treason, with conspiring for the death of the King and the overthrow of the government. He was sent to the Tower to await his trial in the autumn. In the meantime the remaining battlefield was to be conquered. It had already been fought over by authors who had produced more than 500 pamphlets, ranging from prose to verse in form and from broadsheet to several pages in length, but all concerned with some aspect of the Exclusion Crisis and the threat of civil war. Dryden had himself entered the pamphlet warfare earlier, in the spring of 1681, to defend an official Declaration of the King that had been attacked by Whig pamphlets.[9] Now, in the summer of 1681, while the government was preparing its case against Shaftesbury, it can be taken for granted that Dryden, as a loyal supporter of the King and especially as poet laureate and historiographer royal, came to the conclusion that he should write again. Possibly he sought to influence the jury that would try Shaftesbury, but much more likely (since that jury would be packed with Whigs) he wished to persuade those Englishmen who were not yet committed to either side that they should support the King against the seditious attacks of the Whigs. In early November his poem *Absalom and Achitophel* appeared anonymously and at once drew attention.

[9] [John Dryden,] *His Majesties Declaration Defended: In a Letter to a Friend, Being an Answer to a Seditious Pamphlet, called A Letter from a Person of Quality to his Friend* . . . (London: T. Davies, 1681), available as Publication Number 23 of the Augustan Reprint Society, ed. Godfrey Davies (Los Angeles: Clark Library, University of California, 1950).

2

FIRST BLOOD

The Problem Father

The first problem Dryden faced in trying to persuade his readers to support the King against the Whigs was the King himself, Charles II. There were a number of reasons why the uncommitted Englishmen of the Restoration might feel less than sympathetic towards Charles.

For one thing, by the time of the Exclusion Crisis it was widely known that King Charles II was an inveterate lecher. Although married to his Queen, Catherine, he had a long succession of mistresses and paramours—and frequently a gaggle of them at any one period. To the more prominent and lasting of these he gave titles of nobility, and to most of the dozen or so of his children by them who survived to adulthood he also gave titles: six dukes, one earl, and four countesses.[1] At the height of the political crisis, when the Duke of Monmouth and his supporters were claiming that the Duke was in fact legitimate, Charles treated his subjects to the spectacle of the King of England (and temporal head of the Church of England) making the following public declaration in the *Gazette* (of 10 June 1680): "We... call Almighty God to witness, and declare upon the faith of a christian, and the word of a king, that there was never any marriage, or contract of marriage, . . . between us and . . . Mrs Walters, alias Barlow, the Duke of Monmouth's mother. . . ."

Charles was quite open about his amours: his court followed his example and so gained a reputation for lechery, luxury, and idleness. Samuel Pepys recorded as early as 1663 (in his *Diary* for Nov. 9th) that a friend had told him "how loose the Court is, nobody looking after business but every man his lust and gain; and how the King is now become besotted upon Mrs. Steward, that he gets into corners and will be with her half an hour together, kissing her to the observation of all

[1] For more details, see a biography, such as that by Adolphus William Ward, in *Dictionary of National Biography*, IV, 84-108.

the world. . . ."[2] On 27 July 1667 Pepys recorded the view held by the business community that the peace which the King had just concluded was "made only to preserve the King for a time in his lusts and ease, and to sacrifice trade and his kingdoms only to his own pleasures. . . ." All in all, Charles gave the impression that he was like Shakespeare's Mark Antony and would, repeatedly, brush aside important state business to indulge himself further with his latest Cleopatra. And when he did pay attention to state affairs, he gave the appearance of being subservient to the wishes of his mistresses, his favourites, and his brother—to the point even, on occasion, of sacrificing his loyal ministers when his Parliamentary opponents pressed hard, as Clarendon and Danby could attest.

This sensual self-indulgence, and the lechery in particular, had been seized upon by the King's enemies writing (anonymously and illegally) in the public press. The nickname they applied to him was "Rowley," the name of one of his own prize studhorses.[3] An early attack (1670) had presented him as insisting, above all, on having his mistresses:

> But whatever it cost I will have a fine whore,
> As bold as Al'ce Pierce and as fair as Jane Shore,
> And when I am weary of her I'll have more.[4]

A later attack, part of the pamphlet warfare over the Exclusion Crisis, called Charles a raree show (i.e., a peep show or, more likely, its manager), and concluded by referring to his contact with his French mistress and by inviting the readers to hunt down both him and James, as their father had been hunted down and killed:

> Haloo! the hunt's begun, with a hey, with a hey,
> Like father, like son, with a ho;
> Raree show in French lap,
> Is gone to take a nap,
> And successor has the clap,
> With a hey, trany nony nony no.[5]

(As can be seen, they played rough then—on both sides, for the author of this attack was hanged for it.)

Another source of antagonism towards the King was his association with Roman Catholicism. As mentioned earlier, he was sur-

[2] *The Diary of Samuel Pepys*, ed. Robert Latham and William Matthews, Vol. IV (London: Bell, 1971), p. 371. The next quotation is from Vol. VIII (London: Bell, 1974), pp. 354-55.

[3] Cf. Poems on *Affairs of State*, II, 173, 184, 343.

[4] "The King's Vows," reprinted in *Poems on Affairs of State*, vol. I, ed. G. de F. Lord (New Haven & London: Yale University Press, 1963), p. 161. Alice Perrers was a mistress to Edward III, and Jane Shore to Edward IV.

[5] Stephen College, "A Raree Show," reprinted in *Poems on Affairs of State*, II, 431.

rounded by several Roman Catholics, many of whom had an obvious influence upon him. Some members of the Court even suspected (perhaps rightly) that Charles himself was a Papist. Some feared, moreover, that he had entered into a secret understanding with Louis of France and was receiving subsidies from him. The truth, known to very few, far exceeded the suspicions, for on 1 June 1670 Charles had concluded the secret Treaty of Dover with Louis, whereby Charles agreed, when the time was right, to announce his personal conversion to Roman Catholicism and to seek to establish Catholicism in England—in return for several large subsidies and the use of 6,000 French troops to help convert England. Actually the time somehow never proved right, but Charles still collected the subsidies and usually followed a foreign policy favourable to Louis. Little of this was actually known by the public (just as well, for Charles's sake), but what was known was the constant presence about him of Roman Catholic influence, and this presence posed a problem for his defender.

Charles did have a quality that could have endeared him to his subjects. On occasion he could prove loyal. Though he broke his marriage vows shamelessly, he defended his wife when accusers sought to implicate her in the Popish Plot, and, although he could easily have done so, he steadfastly refused to divorce her, as many of his advisers urged him to, so as to marry a woman who could bear him children and thereby end the problem of succession. Similarly, throughout the whole of the Exclusion Crisis, although Charles offered various expedients which would have stripped his brother of kingly power, he steadfastly insisted that James be allowed to succeed to his hereditary right, even if in name only. Unfortunately, of course, much of the possible appeal of this loyalty, which Charles displayed on occasion, was dissipated, because the loyalty was directed to the two Roman Catholics in particular who, if they had only gone away, would have contributed greatly to the solving of England's problems.

Nor did much assistance come from any of the public defences of the King himself which had appeared in the pamphlet warfare. These simply ignored the King's lechery and other failings and chose rather to condemn the scurrilous attacks that had been made on his Sacred Majesty. Another kind of defence chose to attack the King's ministers as the ones responsible for the country's plight, but one, at least, of these "defences" glanced sideways at the King. The anonymous author of *The Character of an Ill-Court-Favourite* spoke of "those *soft Princes* . . . such as divide their time between the *Cup and the Bed*, and are more intent at the *Theatre* than the Councel Chamber."[6] Obviously

---

[6] *The Character of an Ill-Court-Favourite: representing the Mischiefs that flow from Ministers of State when they are more Great than Good* (London: 1681), p. 10.

Charles's lechery, laxity, and self-indulgence posed a serious artistic problem for Dryden.

A bold stroke was needed that could somehow turn Charles's lechery to good use—his other shortcomings could be dealt with later. Charles's lechery could of course always be used to emphasize the bastardy of Monmouth and to remind the reader that Monmouth was but one of over a dozen such bastards (so why should he be favoured over the others?). But could Charles's lechery itself be turned to something like a joke? Yes, through a witty comparison that had already been made between Charles and King David of the Old Testament. At least six pamphlets had already compared Charles to David, Monmouth to David's rebellious son Absalom, and Shaftesbury to the evil counsellor Achitophel.[7] These had all made the comparison seriously: Dryden saw how to make comic use of it, by fastening on the prolific aspect of David's engendering on various women, dutifully recorded by the author of the Second Book of Samuel. An argument could be made, so outrageously witty and funny, that the reader would laugh at the wit, pass over the lechery without judgement, and still be reminded of the illegitimacy of Monmouth.

So Dryden began:

> In pious times, e'r Priest-craft did begin,
> Before *Polygamy* was made a sin;

Note the "e'r": it does the work, intimating that pious times existed before (and only before?) the arts (really the skulduggery?) of priests began. Ostensibly such an intimation is the opposite of what the reader would expect, but actually it satisfies a latent desire no doubt present in many of Dryden's readers: to see a suave man of the world quietly establish his superiority over the clergy, who are not so much members of "priesthood" as practitioners of something much more depreciatory, "Priest-craft." And how neatly the thought is expressed, thanks to the ironic balance, the pause, and the alliteration. Wit is joined by historical point and substance in the second line: there was indeed a time when polygamy was an honourable institution, and it was only made a sin, arbitrarily, and that by "Priest-craft," in the practice of which there were applied to polygamy all sorts of unsympathetic and scurrilous names. Here is a test of true piety: how one regards polygamy, that practice which by any other name should be as fair.

---

[7] *Naboth's Vineyard* by John Caryll (1679) in which the comparison is implicit, *Absalom's Conspiracy* and *A Letter to His Grace the Duke of Monmouth* (both in 1680), and three in 1681: *An Answer to a Paper, Entituled, A Brief Account of the Designs of the Papists against the Earl of Shaftesbury*, *A Seasonable Invitation for Monmouth to Return to Court*, and *The Waking Vision; or, Reality in Fancy*. All the pamphlets were published in London.

> When man, on many, multiply'd his kind,
> E'r one to one was, cursedly, confind:

The Biblical implications are extended beyond "Priest-craft" and
"Polygamy" to a remembrance of God's command, "Be fruitful, and
multiply, and replenish the earth," which He made not only to Adam
and Eve but also to Noah and his sons (Genesis 1:28, 9:1). This remembrance, fraught with multiplicity and reinforced in the couplet by the
alliteration, somehow seems to require the employment of "many."
Then "e'r" again: ere one to one was confined—cursedly. That word
"cursedly," both in its choice and in its placing, appears to be deliberately ambiguous. As "execrably" it defines the sad new plight of being
confined; as "under a curse" it suggests that polygamy was part of
pre-lapsarian bliss; and as "by means of a curse" it implicates the
practitioners of priestcraft again, who enforce monogamy through the
power of their curses, especially that of excommunication. (All sorts of
anachronisms are inherent in such ambiguity, a point that will be discussed shortly.)

> When Nature prompted, and no law deny'd   [5]
> Promiscuous use of Concubine and Bride;

Not only God, in his command, "Be fruitful, and multiply," but also
Nature, which is of course the same in all times and all nations,
prompts polygamy. Only law, man-made law, priest-made law, denies
it. Can a person be blamed for doing simply what all-wise Nature
prompts? "Promiscuous" by a quirk of history is a booby trap for us,
for, if we read in it anything sexually censorious, we are much too
modern and wrong. As the OED indicates, it meant "without discrimi-
nation or method" and "without respect for kind, order, number." As
used in line 6, it merely indicates that concubines and brides could be
used without distinction, one being regarded as equally valid and per-
mitted as the other. Many leaders of Israel certainly used them in this
way, without distinguishing—except when it came to the legitimacy of
the offspring: the children born of concubines were not legitimate.
When the reader comes to realize, as he will a few lines later in the
poem, that all of this is to be applied to King Charles, he will at the
same time realize that the author, through his word "promiscuous," is
facetiously complimenting Charles for his liberal and generous overlooking of class differences in his choice of mistresses.

> Then, Israel's Monarch, after Heaven's own heart,
> His vigorous warmth did, variously, impart
> To Wives and Slaves: And, wide as his Command,
> Scatter'd his Maker's Image through the Land.   [10]

About these lines certain things in particular should be noted. A parallel is established in line 7 between God and Israel's monarch, who is soon to be identified as David, who in turn will soon be seen as parallel to Charles. The tremendous gap between David and God is closed as much as choice of diction can effect. Instead of David's name, Dryden uses a term for the office, and the most magniloquent term, "Monarch," further exalted by being associated with the Biblical Israel, God's chosen people. At the same time the word "God" is avoided and in its place appears "Heaven," the sky from which came the original command, "Be fruitful, and multiply." Implied of course is the concept of King as Vice-Regent of God, a concept only implied in line 7 so as to keep the tone light, but suggested a little less indirectly in line 10, where the particular point of the parallel is made: as God scattered his image through the land, so did his Vice-Regent. Such a suggestion is of course outrageous in overlooking the moral difference, especially when for David one reads Charles. But there are two modifications. One is serious: the parallel in line 8 suggests that, because the monarch's warmth was vigorous, it had to be imparted variously, and thereby the parallel appeals tacitly to the concept that variety of creation is a good in itself (and so complements, incidentally, the "promiscuous" use of concubine and bride). At the same time, of course, exaggeration is introduced so as to make the outrageous wit of the parallel between the monarch and heaven comic and therefore acceptable. "Variously" begins to suggest a rather large number, "wide as his Command" is certainly hyperbolic, and "scatter'd" completes the pattern of increasing comic exaggeration, for, not only does it indicate a very large number, but also it suggests a haphazard manner and hence (in prospect) the accidental nature of Monmouth's conception. (In addition, the meaning of scattering seed broadcast prepares for the image, soon to come, of a soil ungrateful to the tiller's care.) Finally in these lines the phrase "Wives and Slaves" should be noted. The "Concubine" of line 6, referring to a perfectly respectable occupation, has become in line 9 a "Slave," so that the low nature of Monmouth's birth may be subtly emphasized. And, although David had a number of wives, as well as concubines, Charles had only one wife: so that when the application of the phrase is made to Charles, it will be appreciated that it was to other men's wives that he imparted his vigorous warmth.[8]

Through his witty play on the concept of polygamy in these opening ten lines, Dryden has achieved at least two things. He has created in

---

[8] Professor Miner suggests that in these opening lines, by playing with ideas of Christian liberty put forth by Edward Stillingfleet and Gilbert Burnet, Dryden "provided a special wit" to those few of Charles' advisers who were privy to a discussion in 1662 as to whether it might be in accord with ecclesiastical law for the King to practise polygamy (*Dryden's Poetry*, pp. 115-21).

his reader the impression that the author, appearing anonymously in 1681, is a man to trust. He is obviously not an apologist for the clergy, of whatever stripe. If the reader suspects that King Charles is behind "*Israel*'s Monarch," it would also be obvious that the author is not a fanatic apologist for the King, for he does recognize the King's greatest failing—though he refers to it in a way that makes the reader laugh. Instead of being an apologist for anyone, he is obviously suavely independent, witty, and urbane; he is a man of the world, a spectator who observes with amused perception (which argues for accuracy) and writes with amusing insouciance (which invites continued reading). At the same time the Dryden behind this spectator has set up an intricate and complicated pattern of parallels all ready to be applied to someone, with a marvellously comic effect. The time has come to apply it.

> *Michal*, of Royal blood, the Crown did wear,
> A Soyl ungratefull to the Tiller's care:

The name *Michal* makes the application, for Michal was wife to King David, and since the author has chosen her, from all the wives of David, because of her royal blood and her barrenness, the parallel to Queen Catherine and through her to Charles is inescapable, for Catherine was daughter of the King of Portugal and her inability to produce an heir was what had brought about the Exclusion Crisis.

But something strange is going on. "Priest-craft," the arts of priests, must have begun at much the same time as the priesthood was instituted, but the Biblical David became king long *after* the priesthood had been instituted, not before, a fact of which Dryden's contemporary readers would be well aware.[9] Then there is the problem of Annabel. Before long we shall find that David gave to Absalom the charming Annabel as bride. But *Annabel* as a name is completely non-Biblical. What is Dryden doing? And really what is he doing with Michal? It is true that the Biblical Michal was of royal blood, but she was so by virtue of being a daughter of King Saul, and in *Absalom and Achitophel* the name Saul is used in line 57 to suggest Oliver Cromwell. Furthermore, the reason why the Biblical Michal "had no child unto the day of her death" (2 Sam. 6:23)—a phrasing that parallels Queen Catherine's situation—was that, when she rebuked David for "uncovering" himself

---

[9] It might be objected that by "Priest-craft" is meant rather the use of priestly policy and power so excessive that it was able to change non-religious customs, such as the polygamy mentioned in line 2, and hence that David reigned before *that* kind of "Priest-craft did begin." In reply it should be noted that priestly policy and power had been so strong in Israel before David that it had made the whole nation a theocracy, which had ended only with Saul, David's predecessor—a fact alluded to in lines 417-18 of the poem itself. This allusion of course raises another question: how could Dryden say in the opening lines that the David of the poem reigned before priestcraft and then in lines 417-18 of the same poem admit to the very opposite? The answer has to do with the changing nature of Dryden's construct, which will be discussed a little later on.

during a dance in front of the ark of the covenant, he became angry and presumably banished her from his bed—an explanation that does not parallel Queen Catherine's situation.[10] These difficulties arise from points of parallel Dryden has chosen to make: there could be in addition such interesting considerations as the two hundred foreskins that David paid for Michal (1 Sam. 18:27) and the fact that after giving Michal to David, Saul presented her as a wife to another man, from whom David eventually reclaimed her (1 Sam. 25:44 and 2 Sam. 3:13-15).

Have we to do with an allegory in which we should not press details too far, or have we to do with something different? Especially in view of Annabel, I suggest that what Dryden is constructing is not a direct parallel or allegory between his England and the Biblical Israel, but rather a fictitious, never-never land, whose existence and nature are signalled in the very first line: "e'r Priestcraft did begin." This fictitious construct is composed of hundreds of details, most of which are derived from the Biblical story of David and Absalom, but a significant number of which come from elsewhere, and the construct itself, rather than Scripture, then serves as the allegorical parallel for Restoration England.[11]

One advantage of such a construct is obvious: Dryden can put into it precisely what he wants to. He can take as central core the basic story of David, Absalom, and Achitophel and then add to it details from elsewhere. This he does with the name Annabel, obviously, and also with other events, such as the murder of Agag, which in the Bible are rather far removed from the story of David and Absalom. He is also at liberty, since it is his construct, to ask his reader to see in the Biblical names and characters he uses only those aspects that fit the parallel with Restoration England and to leave behind in the Bible, and out of the construct, those aspects that do not fit. When Dryden's partisan opponents replied to his poem, they did not grant him the independent existence of his artistic construct, but instead made rude noises over the various ways in which the supposed allegory did not fit, breaking down in its relation either to the Bible or to England. But we of a later and politically disinterested day can grant him his construct, espe-

[10] This interpretation of why Michal remained barren receives some support from Dorothea Ward Harvey, writing in The Interpreter's Dictionary of the Bible (Nashville and New York: Abingdon Press, 1962), III, 373: when Michal rebuked him, "David apparently retaliated by giving her 'no child to the day of her death'."

[11] With regard to Dryden's fictional construct, it is interesting to note that John Traugott, in his essay "The Rake's Progress from Court to Comedy: A Study in Comic Form," describes the world of Dryden's heroic tragedies as "a never-never land where there is no society, only terrible aggressions and violent longings almost free of personality"; similarly, the "world of manners comedy," he says, "is a sort of Hobbesian state of nature in the drawing room; the best artificer will win" (Studies in English Literature, 6 [1966], 392, 398).

cially when he has indicated its independent nature in the very first line.

Having made the application of his construct through the name *Michal*, and having, in typical Restoration manner, couched an indecent thought in a decent image, Dryden compared Michal to the other women with regard to barrenness and fecundity:

> Not so the rest; for several Mothers bore
> To Godlike *David*, several Sons before.
> But since like slaves his bed they did ascend,   [15]
> No True Succession could their seed attend.

"Godlike" comically exaggerates the Vice-Regency of God; "slaves," repeated, emphasizes the illegitimacy of the offspring; "several," also repeated, enlarges the comic exaggeration still further and emphasizes that Monmouth was simply one bastard of many. And note the word "ascend": it would be literally accurate for Charles's bed with, no doubt, steps beside it for ascending; and also of course it provides tonal elevation as well—each woman was a paramour, yes, but a royal paramour. Note, too, that Dryden's construct differs still further from the Biblical story, for the Biblical David had several legitimate sons who could have succeeded him (one of them—Solomon—of course actually did). But in Dryden's world all the royal sons are illegitimate. Of these there was one more noticed than the others (and his name could be spelled either "Absalom" or "Absolon"):

> Of all this Numerous Progeny was none
> So Beautifull so brave as *Absolon*:

What a superbly smooth transition. "This . . . Progeny" gathers up the preceding, while the words "all" and "Numerous" reinforce the multiplicity of bastards, and Monmouth is introduced as the member of the "Numerous Progeny" who is pre-eminent for his beauty and bravery.

That much praise Monmouth deserved, or almost that much.

The Bastard Son

Monmouth was born on 9 April 1649 of Lucy Walter, having been fathered, Lucy said, by Charles. There was later some question as to whether Charles was really the father.[12] At the time he might have got the child, Lucy had just been handed over to the uncrowned King by her keeper, Colonel Robert Sidney, who said, "Let who's will have her—she's already sped!"[13] (Whether by "sped" he meant syphilitic or pregnant is a moot point.) Paintings reproduced in Allan Fea's biog-

[12] As in "The Ghost of Tom Ross," *Poems on Affairs of State*, II, 251-52.

[13] Allan Fea, *King Monmouth* (London and New York: Lane, 1902), p. 5. Fea's book is the source for most of the information following on Monmouth.

raphy point to a kinship between Sidney and Monmouth. There is a strong resemblance between the two painted figures (done by different artists) in the cast of eyes, the length and shape of nose, the set of lips and mouth, the size and shape of chin, the length of the face and the contour of the cheek, and the general configuration of all these aspects. There is in fact much greater facial resemblance between Sidney and Monmouth than there is between Charles and Monmouth. But, tempting as the similarity is, we must hesitate to draw the facile conclusion. Facial resemblance is in itself not conclusive, and the obviously stylized manner of painting in the figures of both Sidney and Monmouth suggests that much of the painted facial resemblance may derive, not from actual resemblance, but from a fashion current in portrait-painting at the time. Certainly Charles accepted Monmouth as his own, and Charles did not accept all children imputed to him: one of the three children that the Duchess of Cleveland presented to him he refused to acknowledge, though he did accept the other two; so presumably Charles was not one to be hoodwinked in such matters.

Like the Biblical Absalom, Monmouth was a handsome fellow, and very successful with the ladies. Married by his father at the age of 14 to a wealthy bride, he in the same year contracted a liaison with the Duchess of Cleveland (then Lady Castlemaine), who was still his father's reigning mistress. In doing so, he was already acting Biblically, for Absalom, it is recorded, "went in unto his father's concubines" (2 Sam. 16:22). Four years later he found himself sharing the favours of a maid of honour to the Duchess of York with his uncle, the Duke of York, and also with the Earl of Mulgrave. In 1670 he and two other dukes murdered a beadle who had attempted to arrest them in a brothel, but no charges were brought, for Charles granted his "gracious pardon unto our dear sonne, James, Duke of Monmouth, of all Murders, Homicides, & Felonyes, whatsoever at any time before ye 28th day of Feb^ry last past, committed either by himselfe alone or together wth any other person or persons."[14] And early in 1680 it was rumoured that he had been carrying on an affair with the wife of Lord Grey, one of his closest supporters.

Monmouth had pretensions above his station. He persuaded his father to strike the word "natural" from the phrase "natural son" in the commission the King gave him as General. He had designed for him a coat of arms which not only had no bar sinister showing but also resembled very closely the coat of arms traditionally used by the Prince of Wales, the legitimate heir to the throne. And when he made his progress through the West of England—where he was hailed as the Protestant Duke (as distinct from his uncle the Catholic Duke)—he

[14] Quoted in Fea, p. 49.

allowed it to be reported that he had touched a girl for the king's evil and had cured her—a sure sign that he was a legitimate son of the King.

His intelligence, however, left something to be desired. His contemporary, the Comte de Gramont, after praising his manly beauty, remarked that his mind, in contrast, said not a word in his favour.[15] He became the tool or cully of the Earl of Shaftesbury in the Exclusion Crisis, and was referred to by the Tories as Perkin, after Perkin Warbeck of the fifteenth century who had claimed to be the son of Edward IV. When Monmouth joined in the debate on the Exclusion Bill in the House of Lords and spoke in favour of the Bill, because of the danger his father's life would be in if a Papist remained the successor (England one heartbeat from Rome), that father, listening to him and momentarily forgetting his indulgent affection for him, remarked, "C'est un baiser de Judas qu'il me donne"—It is a kiss of Judas that he gives me.[16] (The fact that Charles would speak spontaneously in French is interesting.)

All in all, Monmouth had, in a sense, set himself up for Dryden to cut the ground out from under him. But how gracefully Dryden does it.

He has just tied him in firmly with all the other bastards but at the same time has appeared to compliment him:

> Of all this Numerous Progeny was none
> So Beautifull so brave as *Absolon*:

Further integration is made with the preceding lines, especially with the concept of the Vice-Regent who practised the Divine Right of Kings (to scatter his Maker's image):

> Whether, inspir'd with some diviner Lust,
> His Father got him with a greater Gust;   [20]
> Or that his Conscious destiny made way
> By manly beauty to Imperiall sway.

Note that while Dryden appears to be continuing his praise, he is at the same time actually undercutting. As an alternative to Charles's responsibility for Monmouth, Dryden suggests Monmouth's own, in "his Conscious destiny," and, while repeating the Duke's beauty, suggests that Monmouth used that beauty (rather than anything else) to make his approach to "Imperiall sway." The beauty introduced earlier has here been elaborated on; now for his bravery:

> Early in Foreign fields he won Renown,
> With Kings and States ally'd to *Israel*'s Crown:

[15] Anthony Hamilton, *Memoirs of the Comte de Gramont*, tr. Peter Quennell, ed. C. H. Hartmann (New York: Dutton, 1930), pp. 297-98.

[16] Francis S. Ronalds, *The Attempted Whig Revolution of 1678-1681* (Urbana, Ill.: University of Illinois, 1937), p. 123n, referring to P.R.O. Trans. 3/147, 28 Nov. 1680.

> In Peace the thoughts of War he could remove,   [25]
> And seem'd as he were only born for love.

Dryden here alludes graciously to Monmouth's having commanded the English army fighting with France against the Dutch in 1672, and with the Dutch ("States") against France in 1678, but at the same time what was billed as bravery in line 18 has by line 23 become "Renown"—and there is a difference. In addition, the next couplet is rather ambiguous: "only born for love" appears to compliment Monmouth on how natural it was for him to love and to be loved, but at the same time suggests that this is where his true nature lies, rather than in bravery, and it also glances (through the concept of "love-child") at his bastardy again. The same ambiguity continues in the following lines:

> What e'r he did was done with so much ease,
> In him alone, 'twas Natural to please.
> His motions all accompanied with grace;
> And *Paradise* was open'd in his face.   [30]

Apparent praise, again, for Monmouth's graceful appearance and actions, but, again, it is undercut. If it was "Natural" for him to please, it was not by act of will that he pleased others; so where was the merit? The emphatic positioning of "Natural," in the midst of this context of illegitimacy, could not fail to remind the reader that Monmouth was indeed the "natural son" of Charles. That same Charles was understandably pleased with his beautiful son who danced so well, and in mentioning Charles again, Dryden is able to begin his refutation of the charge that the King was much too lax in his government. Here, within the framework of domestic concern, is offered a reason for that apparent laxness: a fatherly indulgence.

> With secret Joy, indulgent *David* view'd
> His Youthfull Image in his Son renew'd:
> To all his wishes Nothing he deny'd,
> And made the Charming *Annabel* his Bride.

The "Youthfull Image" echoes the "Maker's Image" scattered "wide as his Command"—just to maintain the context. Especially since Charles saw his own youthful beauty (he actually had been good looking) reflected in his son, who can blame him for being indulgent? Is he not simply being a loving father? At the same time one wonders about the phrase "made the Charming *Annabel* his Bride": does it go beyond reflecting the fact that the marriage was arranged, as most aristocratic marriages were, and does the "made" suggest that the lady was so unwilling that Charles had to compel her? We have for some time been wondering what lay behind the beautiful exterior of Monmouth: perhaps Annabel (representing the Countess of Buccleuch) knew. And now we are made acquainted:

What faults he had (for who from faults is free?)   [35]
His Father coud not, or he woud not see.
Some warm excesses, which the Law forbore,
Were constru'd Youth that purg'd by boyling o'r:
And *Amnon*'s Murther, by a specious Name,
Was call'd a Just Revenge for injur'd Fame.   [40]

The irony which was, up to this point, implicit in that aspect of ambiguity which undercut the praise of Monmouth, now moves into the
open. The faults, excused with such seeming generosity, were such
that Monmouth's father could not, or would not, see them, but
everyone else could. No wonder, for they were "warm excesses" that
should have been subject to punishment by the law, and were not subject only because of Monmouth's privileged position, as witnessed by
the pardon granted him, a pardon probably alluded to in the phrase
"which the Law forbore." These excesses were "constru'd" something
less, but "constru'd" only: their actual nature remained what it was,
and is immediately illustrated by a murder, passed off by "a specious
Name," but murder still. Presumably the murder referred to is that of
the beadle, and he is given the name *Amnon* because that means "faithful" and the beadle was merely being faithful to his trust in arresting
Monmouth. That he had dared to injure the fame of a Duke by arresting
him was then used as the excuse for regarding his murder by Monmouth as "a Just Revenge."[17] How we have progressed in only a few
lines: from beauty and bravery through graceful motions to wishes,
which become faults turning to excesses and culminating in murder.
And still the appearance of compliment continues.

Thus Prais'd, and Lov'd, the Noble Youth remain'd,
While *David*, undisturb'd, in *Sion* raign'd.[18]

Monmouth has had everything his way, as long as Charles has been allowed to reign undisturbed, but Monmouth is so unintelligent that he
has been contributing to a major disturbance. That disturbance, however, should of course not be taken as a sign that anything is wrong
with the government itself:

But Life can never be sincerely blest:
Heaven punishes the bad, and proves the best.

Ever since the Book of Job it has been recognized that misfortune visited
upon a person, making his life less than "sincerely" (i.e., completely)
blessed, is not necessarily a sign of divine disfavour. It is true that God
punishes the bad with misfortune, but He also uses misfortune to prove

---

[17] Other interpretations have been offered for "*Amnon*'s Murther": they will be discussed later, in the part of Chapter 8 concerned with Dryden's use of Biblical names,
pp. 160-61.

[18] *Sion* is a variant spelling of *Zion*, the city of David (1 Kings 8:1).

(i.e., test) the best; so we poor mortals can never tell from a person's misfortune which purpose God has in mind. In this way, Dryden prepares to examine the nature and cause of the misfortune visited upon Charles, and so by another smooth transition glides towards his next topic.

By line 44 of his poem he has achieved one of the signal triumphs of his career. He has taken a very grave liability, Charles's lechery, and used it in such a way—in such a witty, outrageously funny way—that, not only would his contemporary readers be inclined to pass over the lechery (by laughing at the wit), but also they would come to feel that the odium for Monmouth's bastardy, properly belonging to Charles, has actually somehow come to rest more on Monmouth himself, who is, par excellence, a beautiful murdering bastard.

Dryden has drawn first blood and is now ready to take on a larger enemy.

(**Note:** The whole of *Absalom and Achitophel* is reproduced in the last chapter, so that passages quoted and referred to in the intervening chapters may be located within their context by consulting pages 175-213.)

3

GOD'S PAMPERED PEOPLE

Those Very Jews

When Dryden in line 45 turns to a larger group and writes, "The *Jews*, a Headstrong, Moody, Murmuring race," every edition (to my knowledge) that provides a gloss for "The *Jews*," identifies them as "The English." If in fact by "The *Jews*," Dryden meant "The English," then he is saying, in this line, that the nation as a whole is headstrong, moody, and grumbling (for "murmuring" then had that stronger meaning), which, on the face of it, is a rather strange thing for him to say. He is, after all, addressing himself to the moderates of the nation, and he will soon be speaking in favour of the King's supporters: is he likely to call either group headstrong, moody, and grumbling? He might, of course, be speaking with tongue in cheek or in mock self-depreciation ("We English are a curious lot"), but he might also be speaking seriously about a specific group within the nation. As he proceeds with his description, he provides distinguishing characteristics for his "Jews," and it will be interesting to see how seriously we should take them and whether they apply to the nation as a whole or to a certain, specific group within it.

Having introduced his "Jews" with their general characteristics, Dryden then focuses first on the distinguishing marks of their religion:

> The *Jews*, a Headstrong, Moody, Murmuring race,   [45]
> As ever try'd th'extent and stretch of grace;
> God's pamper'd people whom, debauch'd with ease,
> No King could govern, nor no God could please;
> (Gods they had tri'd of every shape and size
> That God-smiths could produce, or Priests devise.)   [50]

Grace, while joyfully accepted by all Christian members of the nation, was still, as is well recognized, a shibboleth of the Dissenters: it was grace descending by the will of God alone that converted and saved them, and set them off from the Papists and their fellow-travellers, the

Anglicans. Similarly, while all Christians would no doubt consider themselves the people of God, it was again the Dissenters who, believing themselves to be "the Elect," made a habit of referring to themselves as "the chosen people" (a phrase Dryden uses in line 88), "God's people," and "the Godly people." In fact the identification is made in an amusing parody of a petition which appeared in the Tory *Observator* for 25 June 1681. It read, in part, "We your Majesties Dissenting Subjects, . . . We the Godly People of the Land. . . . " What Dryden appears to have done is to take this other catchword of the Dissenters—God's chosen people—and to replace the usual epithet "chosen" with the more appropriate "pamper'd." Then there is the matter of the multiplicity of gods: "Gods they had tri'd of every shape and size." While the nation as a whole, since it contained within itself the various Dissenting sects, could be characterized as having many different concepts of God, it was of course those very Dissenting sects who were, pre-eminently, so characterized. The Roman Catholics had a common view of God, and by and large so did the Anglicans, but each of the Dissenting sects had its own, and their name was legion.

From the distinguishing marks of the religion of his "Jews," Dryden turns to the distinguishing marks of their political theory. He first denounces them as "*Adam*-wits," which Professor Swedenberg has explicated most happily: "Apparently a reference to those who, like Adam, could not be satisfied with the true freedom under God's law and wrongly yearned for more."[1] These "*Adam*-wits," these "*Jews*," "began to dream they wanted" (i.e., lacked) "libertie,"[2] and when they could find no record of any people who had been

> by Laws less circumscrib'd and bound,
> They led their wild desires to Woods and Caves,   [55]
> And thought that all but Savages were Slaves.

This phrasing evidently refers to the contract theory of government, whereby it was believed that civilized government began when the people of a nation appointed a king and voluntarily surrendered to him some of their liberties, for as long as he continued to rule well. This contract theory was abominated by the Tories, who held to a patriarchal view of government (that the King held his power from God),[3] and was in fact a distinguishing mark of the political views of the Whigs (many of whom were of course Dissenters). That this is the

[1] *Works*, II, 241.

[2] Since the earliest use the OED records of *want* with a noun object and meaning "desire" occurred almost 200 years after *Absalom and Achitophel*, it is most unlikely that *want* could mean "desire," as W. O. S. Sutherland, Jr., would have it (*The Art of the Satirist*, p. 40). Almost certainly it meant "lacked."

[3] That Dryden shared this patriarchal view can be seen in his dedicatory epistle of *All for Love* and in the prologue to *The Unhappy Favourite* (see *Works*, II, 226, 181-82).

theory implied appears certain in the following lines, where Dryden indicates that the "Jews" thought they themselves made and unmade Kings as they chose:

> They who when *Saul* was dead, without a blow,
> Made foolish *Isbosheth* the Crown forgo;
> Who banisht *David* did from *Hebron* bring,
> And, with a Generall Shout, proclaim'd him King: [60]

Here is indeed reflected the succession of de facto rulers of England: Oliver Cromwell (whom, it is implied, the Whigs thought they had made ruler—though in fact he had made his own way to power), then Oliver's son Richard (who was indeed forced to relinquish rule), and then Charles II, who had been crowned King of the Scots in 1651, returned to England in 1660, and was crowned King of England in 1661. But Dryden's point is made through the words "Crown" and "King": while in the Whig view the succession of rulers was as listed, in the Tory view, de jure and in fact Charles II had been King from the very moment, in 1649, when the head of his father, Charles I, had rolled from the block.

The presumption of the "Jews" in thinking that they were king-makers is made even clearer in the lines following:

> Those very *Jewes*, who, at their very best,
> Their Humour more than Loyalty exprest,
> Now, wondred why, so long, they had obey'd
> An Idoll Monarch which their hands had made:
> Thought they might ruine him they could create;   [65]
> Or melt him to that Golden Calf, a State.

The last phrase, "a State," should clinch the identification, for in this line, in view of the diminution from the "Idoll Monarch," the word "State" must have the meaning then current of "a republic" or a "non-monarchical commonwealth" (OED, meaning 28b); and among the English only a small number worshipped the concept of a republic and sought to make their country into one (or into another commonwealth), and that number was to be found within the Whigs.

Supporting this line of reasoning about "The Jews" being meant to reflect the Whig Dissenters is the identification made by Narcissus Luttrell, the most omnivorous collector of pamphlets in Dryden's day. He twice identified the phrase "Jews" on his copy of the poem (now in the Huntington Library), and each time he did so, at lines 338 and 607, he wrote "Fanaticks"—the most opprobrious term then used for the Dissenters.

These "Jews" Dryden distinguishes from two other groups, both of whom are likewise inhabitants of Israel. The "Jebusites," who are clearly meant to reflect the Roman Catholics (lines 85-125), are in a part of Absalom's speech set over against the Jews, with both groups being subjects of David, King of Israel:

> Were he a Tyrant who, by Lawless Might,
> Opprest the *Jews*, and Rais'd the *Jebusite*. . . .
>
> (ll. 337-38)

The third group mentioned are the "*Hebrew* Priests," evidently reflecting the Anglican clergy, who objected when the Jebusitic teachers extended their proselytizing activities from the Jews to the people at David's court (lines 126-29). When the various terms are viewed together, then, it would appear that in Dryden's fictitious construct the nation is composed of three groups. The nation itself is repeatedly called *Israel* (paralleling England), and the totality of its inhabitants are *Israelites*, as reflected in Absalom's speech when he says (lines 721-22),

> And, 'tis my wish, the next Successors Reign
> May make no other Israelite complain.

Within these Israelites are the three groups—the *Jews*, the *Jebusites*, and the *Hebrews*—who correspond to the three-fold division we have already seen within the English, of Whig Dissenters, Roman Catholics, and Tory Anglicans.[4]

The "sober part of *Israel*," the "moderate sort of Men" (we are told in lines 67-78), instead of agreeing with the "Factious Croud," fear a renewal of civil war as a result of their troublesome activities.

---

[4] The passage referred to (ll. 126-29) containing mention of Jebusites, Hebrew priests, and the Jews is one of two in which the use of the word "Jews" may appear to contradict the identification of Jews with the Whig Dissenters. The other passage should perhaps be examined first. In line 104 Dryden refers to "the *Jewish Rabbins*" and calls them the "Enemies" of the Jebusites. Since the Jebusites clearly reflect the English Roman Catholics, "the *Jewish Rabbins*" cannot, for one thing, mean *all* the English clergy (Anglicans, Dissenters, and Catholics), for Dryden would not be likely to say that *all* the English clergy were the enemies of *some* of the English clergy (the Catholics). The "*Jewish Rabbins*" may indeed reflect the learned members of the Anglican clergy alone (as recently suggested by Professor Swedenberg—*Works*, II, 242), but if so, one must either apply all the opprobrious things said about the Jews in lines 45-67 to those members of the Anglican clergy or see Dryden shifting the meaning of his terms. Admittedly such a shift could make "Jews" a variable term as in fact "Protestants" was, and here it could read, not simply the Dissenters as it reads earlier, but both the Anglicans and Dissenters together, as those opposed to Catholicism. But is there really any need to see the "*Jewish Rabbins*" as reflecting any group other than the Dissenting clergy? Such a reading would at least be consistent with the meaning of "Jews" earlier, and it would be further supported by the fact that, in the political situation of the day, Anglicans and Roman Catholics had to make common cause against the onslaught from the Whig Dissenters: consequently calling the "*Jewish Rabbins*" the "Enemies" of the Jebusites would parallel, not the position of the Anglican clergy with relation to the Roman Catholics, but that solely of the Dissenting clergy in their animosity to the Catholics.

The other passage referred to may be more complicated. In lines 126-29 Dryden wrote, referring to the Jebusites:

A Murmuring Race

And well might they fear such a result. The Whig Dissenters had whipped up a great deal of ferment by means of the frightening arguments they aimed against the Duke of York and his Tory supporters. They pointed to the three times within the preceding 130 years when Roman Catholics tried to convert England to Catholicism. Queen Mary, according to a twelve-page pamphlet entitled *An Account of Queen Mary's Methods for Introducing Popery* (1681), took the kinds of action which Charles's government had already taken (influenced by the Duke of York): after declaring religious tolerance (for the Roman Catholics), she packed a new Parliament, had it pass laws against Dissenters, made an alliance with a Catholic power abroad, and used money from that power to bribe members of the English Parliament. All this led to the reinstitution of Roman Catholicism and the burning of countless Protestants—as would, inevitably, the Duke of York's actions if he were allowed to become King. Another pamphlet, *A Brief History of the Life of Mary Queen of Scots* (1681), pointed out that in Elizabeth's reign, too, the Papists had sought to murder the Protestant monarch so that a Roman Catholic successor (Mary Stuart) would come to the throne and reintroduce Popery. References were made also to Guy Fawkes's Gunpowder Plot of 1605, which was designed by Papists in an effort to overthrow the Protestant government. And of course the English had before them, right then, the instance of the Popish Plot, designed, they said, to kill the King and reintroduce Popery through his successor.

> Their busie Teachers mingled with the *Jews*:
> And rak'd, for Converts, even the Court and Stews:
> Which *Hebrew* Priests the more unkindly took,
> Because the Fleece accompanies the Flock.

In considering whether the names *Jebusites*, *Jews*, and *Hebrews* here reflect the three religious groups of Roman Catholics, Dissenters, and Anglicans, we could again explore the various combinations and permutations of interpretations resulting from the various conceivable readings of *"Jews"* and *"Hebrew* Priests." But fortunately the word "Fleece" provides a short cut. Undoubtedly the most valuable fleece (in terms of influence as well as money) would be found in the Court. Very few Dissenters were at Court, and the Roman Catholics already there would not be subject to proselytizing by Roman Catholics; consequently the fleece would belong for the most part to Anglicans. So the *"Hebrew* Priests" who took unkindly to the attempts at proselytizing were probably Anglican clergy. The remaining problem then is whether "the Court and Stews" are part of the larger group *"Jews,"* in which case *"Jews"* would have to be read as Anglicans or the combination of Anglicans and Dissenters, and Dryden would have shifted the meaning of his term. But the word "even" suggests that the Jebusites, having mingled with the *"Jews,"* then went *beyond* them, to "the Court and Stews," to both social extremes beyond the *"Jews."* These *"Jews,"* being in the middle socially, would again parallel (as before) the Whig Dissenters, who, for the most part and especially in London, were in the middle social class. At the Court were the Tory Anglicans, bearing their precious "Fleece" and enjoying a court that, because of its aristocratic membership, could be distinguished socially from the "Stews," the brothels of London, and at the same time, because of its sexual licentiousness, could be identified with them morally.

To their accounts of past history the Whigs added lurid prophecies of the future. In various pamphlets forecasts were made of burning and rape, murder and pillage, if the Papists should come to power, because the Papists (all of them) were commanded by the Pope to try to convert heretics and, if unsuccessful, to kill them.[5] Many references were made to the massacre of the Protestants in France on St. Bartholomew's day in 1572: although the proportions of Catholics to Protestants were more than reversed in the two countries (there being fewer than one Catholic to nine Protestants in England—if Anglicans could be counted as Protestants), many Whig pamphlets assured the Protestants of England that they faced the same kind of massacre as befell their brothers in France. Those Anglicans who did not agree with the Dissenters were, if not Papists outright, "Popishly affected"—just as those liberals in the twentieth century who did not agree with Senator Joseph McCarthy's hunt for Communists were themselves either Commies or fellow-travellers.

In view of these arguments presented by the Whigs, it is understandable that the Tories, for whose party Dryden wrote, were suspicious about their aims. Were those aims simply, as many of them protested, to protect the King's person and the subjects' liberty? The Tories thought not, and charged the Whigs with trying to seize control of the government.[6] This the Whigs sought to do in a number of ways. Inside Parliament, when the King asked for the money he needed to do such necessary things as send an expedition to relieve British troops sorely pressed in Tangier, they refused and said that they would continue to refuse until he acceded to their demands. Outside Parliament, they packed juries in London with Whig supporters so that any Whigs charged with criminal offenses would get off. If they kept up this kind of action long enough, they would force the King to do as they bid, and so they would become the effective rulers of the country and England would be back virtually in the days of the Commonwealth. As Dryden put it, they

> Thought they might ruine him they could create;
> Or melt him to that Golden Calf, a State.

That this view of their aims was not altogether erroneous is suggested by the remarks of a Whig member of Parliament who wrote, two years after the session of 1680, that in that session "he had been young and innocent, believing that his colleagues were really actuated by zeal

---

[5] E.g., [Charles Blount], *An Appeal from the Country to the City, for the Preservation of His Majesties Person, Liberty, Property, and the Protestant Religion* (London, 1679), *The Case of Protestants in England under a Popish Prince* (London: Janeway, 1681), *A Reply to Roger L'Estrange's Pamphlet* (London: Dew, 1681).

[6] See *Heraclitus Ridens*, no. 42 (15 Nov. 1681), and *Observator*, no. 5 (25 April 1681), no. 27 (25 June 1681), and no. 29 (2 July 1681).

against Popery, but that he had soon seen through them and, having had a bellyful, had deliberately refused election to the Oxford Parliament.''[7] One Tory pamphleteer put the matter succinctly in a fictional anecdote:

> A Gentleman coming t'other day from *London*, met with three or four... Protestant Dissenters, upon the Road, and enquiring, what News? one of them replyed, That the D[uke] of Y[ork] was dead: Then says the Gentleman, I hope people will be quiet and satisfied: Not so hasty, quoth one of the Company, we must have no Popish [i.e., Anglican] Bishop, no Popish Council, no Popish Guards, no Popish Clergy, no Popish Justices [of the peace], but the true Church setled, that His Majesty may be a glorious King.[8]

Behind such an anecdote was, of course, the basic Tory premise that government was kingcraft and belonged, not to Parliament (let alone the lowest branch of Parliament), but to the King.[9] That this anecdote, though fictional, was based on truth, can be seen in a pamphlet from the Whig side. The author of *An Appeal from the Country to the City*, when urging the nation to accept the Duke of Monmouth as successor, wrote:

> And remember, the old Rule is, *He who hath the worst Title, ever makes the best King*; as being constrain'd by a gracious Government, to supply what he wants in Title; that instead of *God and my Right*, his Motto may be *God and my People*. Upon the death of *Alexander* the Great, when there was so great a confusion amongst the Officers about choosing a Successor to the Empire, no other expedient could be found out to pacifie the uproar of the Multitude, but the choosing of King *Philip*'s illegitimate Son *Aridaeus*, who notwithstanding he was a man of reasonable parts himself, might (as they thought) perform that Office well enough, by the help of his wise Protector *Perdiccas*. [10]

Clearly the author, who had earlier praised Shaftesbury, had him in mind when mentioning *Perdiccas*, and the word "Protector" showed inescapably the Cromwellian role he would like to see Shaftesbury assume.

Not only was there serious danger from the Whigs in the inflammatory arguments they presented and in the aims they pursued, but also the actions they had already indulged in showed the kind of arbitrary tyranny they would press upon England if they were allowed to seize power. Inside the House of Commons they frequently spoke as if that House constituted the whole of Parliament instead of merely a

---

[7] J. R. Jones, *The First Whigs*, p. 158, referring to Bodleian, Firth MSS, c. 3. Lionel Duckett, 30 July 1683.

[8] *Heraclitus Ridens*, no. 2 (8 Feb. 1681).

[9] See, e.g., *Observator*, no. 4 (23 April 1681), quoting King James I on the respective roles in government of the King and the House of Commons.

[10] [Charles Blount], *An Appeal from the Country to the City*, pp. 25-26.

part,[11] and indeed as if it spoke for the whole of the British Isles instead of merely a part. Even though it was clear that the Scottish Parliament would confirm James's right to the succession (something they were to do officially in August of 1681),[12] the Whigs in the House of Commons at Westminster continued to press for his exclusion, in spite of the fact that, if in time James were to succeed in Scotland and someone else in England, war between the two nations would thereby become virtually inevitable.

With regard to affairs inside England, the Whigs in the House of Commons passed a resolution that anyone lending the King money "shall be judged a hinderer of the sitting of parliaments, and be responsible for the same in parliament."[13] What that threat meant can be seen from what they did to those who displeased them. When the Earl of Halifax was in large measure responsible for the House of Lords' defeating the Exclusion Bill, the House of Commons called on the King to dismiss the Earl from his "presence and councils forever" because of his "evil and wicked coun[se]ls."[14] Those lesser subjects who likewise crossed the will of the House of Commons the Whigs sentenced, without trial, to imprisonment in the Tower, and when one of these unfortunates appealed under the Habeas Corpus Act (which the Whigs themselves had recently been responsible for passing), the Whigs in the House of Commons took umbrage and said that they were above the Habeas Corpus Act—it applied only to lesser courts, outside Parliament.[15] In those lesser courts all judges and justices of the peace, the Whigs said in an address from the Commons to the King of 30 December 1680, had to be men of known affection to the Protestant religion, and in the same address they insisted that all deputy lieutenants in the counties and officers in the army and navy had likewise to be men of known affection to the Protestant religion.[16] What that repeated key phrase would have meant in practice can be seen in a particular Whig speech made when the House of Commons was debating a proposal to banish all "considerable Papists out of England." The proponent complained that the Court took

care to get the Protestant Papists into the administration of the government; they are encouraged, and true Protestants turned out. Next to Papists, I would consider to put out those popishly affected. When they are banished, next you

[11] See William Cobbett, *Parliamentary History of England*, vol. 4 (London: Bagshaw, 1808), col. 1175-1321.

[12] James Wright, *A Compendious View of the Late Tumults & Troubles in this Kingdom* . . . (London: Lownds, 1685), pp. 123-24.

[13] Cobbett, vol. 4, col. 1293-94.

[14] Cobbett, vol. 4, col. 1223.

[15] Cobbett, vol. 4, col. 1263-64.

[16] Cobbett, vol. 4, col. 1257-58.

may take into consideration how their estates shall be disposed of and how to breed their children. . . .[17]

Outside the House of Commons, many of the Whig actions were equally divisive and arbitrary. Throughout England the Whigs got various local councils to send petitions (which actually were illegal) to the King, urging him to heed the House of Commons and to agree to the Exclusion Bill.[18] When the Tories got other local councils to send "loyal addresses" to the King "abhorring" the subversive and illegal petitions, the Whigs complained that the Tories were not playing the game. A Whig grand jury in London even took it upon itself to indict the City of Norwich for its "loyal address," which the jury called a seditious libel.[19] Their tyranny could be religious as well as political. When a statue of St. Michael was erected in an Anglican church in London, they indicted the vestry of the church and had the statue burned—just as in the days of the Commonwealth.[20] Each year on November 17 (the date of Queen Elizabeth's birthday), and especially in 1681, the Whigs organized a Pope-burning procession in London. It comprised various groups of actors and floats depicting heinous crimes of the Catholics and carrying the effigy of the Pope himself, which was then burned to the accompaniment of general glee. In 1681 in particular, the Whigs saw to it that many thousands of people witnessed and participated in the procession.[21]

All in all, John Dryden could be forgiven for fearing that, if the Whigs were to succeed, there would inevitably be civil war again, with the return of the Commonwealth and all its religious and political tyranny. Understandably, then, it is this fear about the Whigs that Dryden seeks to communicate to his uncommitted countrymen.

The Factious Crowd

He does so in a number of ways, many of which, however, are understated. To begin with, he stresses the divisiveness of the Whigs. In the first passage dealing with the Whigs as a group, the one we have looked at for the identification of the "Jews" with the Whig Dissenters, Dryden first reminds the reader of how divisive the Dissenters are in their religion. They set themselves apart as "God's pamper'd people" and even

[17] Cobbett, vol. 4, col. 1241.

[18] See Jones, *The First Whigs*, pp. 115-20; Ogg, *England in the Reign of Charles II*, II, 602.

[19] Narcissus Luttrell, *A Brief Historical Relation of State Affairs from September 1678 to April 1714* (Oxford: Oxford University Press, 1857), I, 91.

[20] See Edmond Sherman, *The Birth and Burning of the Image called S. Michael* (London, 1681).

[21] Luttrell, I, 144.

within themselves they cannot agree on what kind of God they should worship. In their politics they think that they and they alone make and unmake kings and are even at liberty to remove the King (as they did before) and replace him with a republic. Their divisiveness extends so far, indeed, that they are not of the same mind for any length of time, for, as Dryden remarks in a later passage (lines 216-19),

> govern'd by the *Moon*, the giddy *Jews*
> Tread the same track when she the Prime renews:
> And once in twenty Years, the Scribes Record,
> By natural Instinct they change their Lord.

One can, in fact, begin in 1603, with James I's accession as the first of the Stuarts, and, proceeding in blocks of roughly twenty years, match the change of English rulers according to the Whig way of thinking: 1625, the beginning of Charles I's reign, allowed by the people, who proclaimed him; 1642, the beginning of the Civil War, which removed Charles I and overthrew the monarchy; 1660, the Restoration of the monarchy and the proclaiming of the former King's son, Charles II; and now 1681, the opportunity for removing Charles II and over-throwing the monarchy, again. Dryden may possibly have got his idea from a phrase in a pamphlet by the Earl of Halifax, who wrote, "I very much suspect we are grown weary of monarchy, and, with an incon-stancy natural to islanders, affect a change, though for the worse."[22] If Dryden did borrow, he put his loan to good use, for he has wittily worked out the details and extended the "inconstancy" to lunacy, showing most graphically how factious the Whigs are, even being un-able to hold to the same desire for more than twenty years.

The factiousness has been presented so far in a light tone, born of contempt rather than fear. But the seriousness of the danger posed by the factiousness is always at least implicit and comes to the surface in two passages in particular. When speaking of the Popish Plot, Dryden remarks that it had

> a deep and dangerous Consequence: [135]
> For, as when raging Fevers boyl the Blood,
> The standing Lake soon floats into a Flood;
> And every hostile Humour, which before
> Slept quiet in its Channels, bubbles o'r:
> So, several Factions from this first Ferment,   [140]
> Work up to Foam, and threat the Government.

As will be realized, to threaten the government meant, not, as now, to pose the possibility of turning one party out and putting another one in

---

[22] [Earl of Halifax], *A Seasonable Address to both Houses of Parliament concerning the Succession, the Fears of Popery, and Arbitrary Government* ([London], 1681), in *Somers' Tracts*, vol. VIII (London: Cadwell & Davies, 1812), p. 235.

(often Tweedledum and Tweedledee), but rather to threaten the over-throw of the legitimate government, probably in the midst of bloodshed, and its replacement with an oppressive cabal, as had actually happened in the 1640's. Who these factious people were, Dryden sketches in quickly. Some rebelled because they could not hope to rise to power otherwise, and some, having been thrown from power, were, like Milton's fiends, "harden'd in Impenitence." Others were even more dangerous:

> Some by their Monarch's fatal mercy grown,   [146]
> From Pardon'd Rebels, Kinsmen to the Throne;
> Were rais'd in Power and publick Office high:
> Strong Bands, if Bands ungratefull men could tye.

Since Clarendon was the only person who was in our sense "kinsman" to the throne, his daughter having married the Duke of York, and since Clarendon had never been a rebel, having instead served Charles even in his exile,[23] Dryden must have a peculiar meaning in mind for "Kinsmen." It appears to refer to the fact that the sovereign officially addresses each peer of the realm, above the rank of Baron, as "cousin."[24] Three men had been created peers higher than Baron since the Restoration, had been given high office, and still had gone into opposition to the King. Two of these had actually been royalist sympathizers during the Commonwealth, but since they had remained in England (unlike some others who had joined Charles in exile), they could, technically, be considered "Rebels." Francis Newport, made Viscount in 1675, had served as privy councillor but was dropped in 1679, evidently because of his opposition to the government.[25] Arthur Capel, made Earl of Essex in 1661, had served as Lord Lieutenant of Ireland, but had joined the Whig opposition not long before Dryden wrote.[26] These two peers could fit Dryden's description with some stretching, but it is pre-eminently Anthony Ashley Cooper, Earl of Shaftesbury, who is got at. As we shall see in the next chapter, he served Cromwell during the Civil War and the Commonwealth, was forgiven by Charles, was raised to the highest office by him and created Earl, "cousin" to the King. With these three, but especially with Shaftesbury, the magnanimity of Charles should have bound them to the throne, but they were instead factious and by nature rebels, certainly not to be trusted.

In a later, more extended passage, Dryden details the kinds of rebels and their motives. The "Best" of these "Malecontents" were men who genuinely "thought the power of Monarchy too much" (line 496).

---

[23] Charles Harding Firth, "Hyde, Laurence," DNB, X, 375-78.
[24] Burke's Peerage (1961), pp. 187-88.
[25] James McMullen Rigg, "Newport, Francis," DNB, XIV, 357.
[26] Osmund Airy, "Capel, Arthur," DNB, III, 921-26.

They were of course mistaken: "Not Wicked, but Seduc'd by Impious Arts." Their error arose from placing too great a stress on property: though important to the national economy, it did not, to Dryden's mind, confer the right of governing on its possessors, as it did in Whig theory.[27] By placing too great a stress on property, these Whigs threatened to upset the balance of interests which is essential to good government, just as a person winding the spring of a watch can break it and make it flail out, doing damage to the other works:

> By these the Springs of Property were bent,
> And wound so high, they Crack'd the Government.   [500]

These Whigs were simply in error: another group sought to "embroil the State," so as to advance their own personal interests, "Pretending publick Good, to serve their own" (line 504). These paid lip service to the national interest, though actually putting themselves, factiously, ahead of it. A third group identified the nation's interest with their own, and both with money:

> Others thought Kings an useless heavy Load,   [505]
> Who Cost too much, and did too little Good,

All three of these groups have seen the nation as a whole, however little heed they may have paid to it in their factiousness; but others took a narrower view. Some played demagogue to the mob so as to achieve personal advancement; that mob of London ("The *Solymaean* Rout") presented a still graver danger, "Not only hating *David*, but the King" (line 512). These were led by "Hot *Levites*," Dissenting clergy, whose inadequacy as spiritual leaders, in Dryden's eyes, can be seen in his choice of the word "Levites" for them, for Levites in Israel were merely assistants to priests, not proper priests themselves (see Numbers 18:1-7). These Levites were so factious, and so oblivious to true order, that they sought to reestablish "their old belov'd Theocracy" (line 522), in which, during the Commonwealth, not God but the clergy were rulers. Associated with these Levites were the Levellers:

> 'Gainst Form and Order they their Power employ;   [531]
> Nothing to Build and all things to Destroy.

And lastly, beyond even these who sought to bring disorder, were those who were chaos themselves, the herd "Who think too little, and who talk too much" (line 534), who are driven by unreasoning instinct and blind fate, and who are, in Calvinistic fashion, the Elect:

> Born to be sav'd, even in their own despight;
> Because they could not help believing right.   [540]

---

[27] See the convenient discussion in *Works*, II, 273-74.

What a potentially bewildering array of variety, of hotheads dashing off in all directions at once, and yet Dryden has presented them coherently. The modern reader need only compare his description of the Whigs with that provided in the first chapter of this study, or with Samuel Butler's description of the heterogeneity of Hudibras (the one-person embodiment of Dissenting Whiggery), to appreciate that Dryden has imposed order on disorder, without in any way nullifying that disorder. He has done so by relating, explicitly or implicitly, every facet of the variety to that constant which he has seen within it: the factiousness of the Whigs. This it is that all of the Whig groups have in common, and this it is that makes them such a serious threat to the stability of government in England. As a polemicist Dryden has scored two major points: because he has at least appeared to be so remarkably perceptive and perspicacious, he has not only presented a telling counter-argument against the Whig attack, but he has also established himself as a most discerning man, whose analysis of other aspects of the political situation warrants at least a very serious examination.

This impression he strengthens in his overt handling of the Popish Plot. Whatever his private view of it may have been, he publicly adopts a middle position. The Plot, coming from a few Catholics, was "Bad in itself, but represented worse" by the Whigs (line 109). Both sides, Whigs and Tories, had erred in their handling of it, for it had been "Rais'd in extremes, and in extremes decry'd" (line 110). Not only is Dryden moderate and middle-of-the-road, but he is also humane, for immediately follows the line examined in the first chapter, that is so full of human drama and tragedy: "With Oaths affirm'd, with dying Vows deny'd." The mob, of course, was totally wrong, and to show the wrongness of its attitude, Dryden turns to a metaphor of grain. Usually grain is lifted up in the air so that the chaff may be blown away ("weigh'd" and "winnow'd" respectively with Dryden): it is then cooked for human beings, chewed carefully, and swallowed. But the mob behave like animals: the Plot was

> Not weigh'd, or winnow'd by the Multitude;   [112]
> But swallow'd in the Mass, unchew'd and Crude.

"Crude" has at least three meanings here: generally it reflects the nature of the mob as well as its food; specifically, in referring to food in the stomach, it means "not digested" or, as then expressed, "not concocted"; and connotatively it glances at another meaning, very appropriately, for when diseases or morbid growths were still in an early stage, they, too, were said to be "crude" and hard to be "concocted." From grain as food Dryden then proceeds to grain as the source of liquor:

> Some Truth there was, but dash'd and brew'd with Lyes;
> To please the Fools, and puzzle all the Wise.   [115]

"Dash'd" means "diluted with an inferior admixture," and "brew'd," like "Crude," has a number of meanings operating: "made by fermentation," "diluted"—again with something inferior, and "concocted" or "contrived" with the purpose of producing evil or mischief. The result of this potion is to "please" the fools of the multitude, who liked to be made drunk, and to "puzzle" the wise, i.e., to put them into a state of confusion. The wise moderates, then, were not to be blamed for being confused about the Popish Plot, for to the genuine truth in it the Whigs had added lies: in effect they had slipped a mickey into the drinks of the moderates.

I say the Whigs had, for, while overtly Dryden takes a middle-of-the-road position with regard to the Popish Plot, he at the same time covertly associates the Plot much more with the Whigs than the Catholics. Ostensibly he introduces the discussion we have just examined by saying that the Plot originated with the Catholics, but his actual words are "From hence began that Plot" (line 108), and "hence" refers grammatically, not to the Jebusitic Catholics at all, but to their "Enemies," the "Jewish Rabbins" of line 104. And the first mention at all of the Plot is very much within the context of Whiggery. "*David's* mildness manag'd" the government so well, Dryden says at the end of the first analysis of the Whigs,

> The Bad found no occasion to Rebell.
> But, when to Sin our byast Nature leans,
> The carefull Devil is still at hand with means;   [80]
> And providently Pimps for ill desires:

"The Good old Cause"—a by-word for the Puritan rebellion of the 1640's—"reviv'd,"

> a Plot requires,
> Plots, true or false, are necessary things,
> To raise up Common-wealths, and ruin Kings.

Dryden's covert manoeuvres with regard to the Whigs do not stop here. He has chosen to ignore two sets of their major arguments. They often pointed with scorn to all the pensions and bribes which Charles and his ministers had used to try to control former Parliaments. Perhaps the fact that they were indeed *former* Parliaments would be justification enough for Dryden's ignoring of the arguments: they simply were no longer relevant. Certainly the moderate reader would be more concerned with more immediate and more pressing problems. The other set of arguments ignored had to do with what Queen Mary had done as the prototypical Roman Catholic ruler returning England to Popery. Perhaps Dryden again was justified in not mentioning these, inasmuch as Charles had offered to see to it, by means of a regency if necessary, that when James came to the throne, the effective government of England would be in Protestant hands. However justified or unjustified this omission may have been on Dryden's part (from the point of view of fairness), he was nonetheless astute, from the point of view of polemics, in focusing instead on where the Whigs hurt—in the illegitimacy of their alternative to James and in the fact that some of their members promoted a form of government that looked dangerously similar to that of the Commonwealth. In fact Dryden may have been somewhat unfair in his repeated reminders of the possible return to the Commonwealth, but of course it is not the function of either the polemicist or the satirist (and Dryden in this poem is being both) to be fair: it is his function, rather, to argue for one side and against the other as effectively as he can, and leave the decision—perforce—to his reader.

The Stretch of Grace

Much of Dryden's effectiveness in achieving his satiric and polemical purpose derives from certain artistic means he employs to help him. One we have already noticed is his fictional construct of a never-never land which draws many of its elements, selectively, from the Old Testament and applies them, with equal selectivity, to his contemporary England. He began by siting his land in a time "e'r Priestcraft did begin," but now, a few lines later, in talking about the Jews, he indicates that they have for some time had Priests and Rabbis (lines 50 and 104), while the Hebrews likewise have had their Priests (line 128). Evidently his construct is a changing and malleable thing, very convenient indeed. Actually at one stroke he admits to this convenient changeability and, by making a joke about it, secures its acceptance and greater usefulness. About people implicated in the Popish Plot he says:

> Some thought they God's Anointed meant to Slay [130]
> By Guns, invented since full many a day:

That's quite a Utopia he has constructed, what with polygamy and guns at the same time. The sympathetic reader of course will chuckle appreciatively and read on, to see what further shape-shiftings the construct will undergo in the process of this fluid allegory.

His Biblical construct provided him with at least two sets of images. One has to do with idolators. Early in his description of the Whiggish Jews, Dryden refers to some of their members as "Godsmiths," producing the "Gods" the rest of them "had tri'd of every shape and size" (lines 49-50). Immediately, through this reference to the recurring idolatry of the Israelites and by tying it to the Whigs, he associates with them faction, rebellion against both temporal leader and divine, and the worship of false ideals. This concept he elaborates on by ascribing to the Whiggish Jews the belief that the monarch is an "Idoll" they have made and that he can, at their bidding, be reduced "to that Golden Calf, a State" (line 66)—again an image compact of sacrilege, impiety, and demagoguery. The other set of images derives from the multiplicity of names available for the different inhabitants of Israel. The alien-connoting Jebusites can be identified with the Roman Catholics, the honorific name of Hebrews can be conferred on the Anglicans, and on the Whig Dissenters can be imposed the name of Jews—those very Jews—with whatever opprobrium the individual reader wishes to associate with it. Dryden in his opening lines appealed to the anticlericalism he must have thought to be at least latent in his readers: presumably he was not above using to his advantage whatever antiJewish feeling persisted in England from earlier days.

Not unnaturally linked with idolatry, especially in the time of Moses and later, is the concept of sickness in the body politic, a sickness that can be presented as a form of insanity. Dryden is quick to make use of this complex of images, for they sort well with his idea of the need for maintaining order in government. In a passage we have already examined on the consequences of the Popish Plot (lines 136-41), he presents the Whiggish factions in their growing strength as raging fevers that boil the blood and as hostile humours that, bubbling over and working up to foam, threaten the very existence of what has hitherto contained them. In an age when fevers of one kind or another were a frequent cause of death, this image would have had special force. So too, at a time when visits to Bedlam were entertaining, would the comparisons to lunacy: the Whigs are "giddy *Jews*" who, "govern'd by the *Moon*, . . . once in twenty Years . . . change their Lord" (lines 216-19), and again, when they find David's rule displeasing, their strange behaviour is explained by saying, "The *Dog-star* heats their Brains to this Disease" (line 334). It could be only a disordered state of mind that would seek to disorder the government of England.

People afflicted with this kind of sickness are less than fully human. They are like the fools of the multitude, who in turn are like a herd of cattle that swallow their grain in the mass, without distinguishing (lines 112-13). Samuel Butler had of course made considerable use of animal imagery to demean and diminish his representative Whig Dissenter. Hudibras and his kind were compared with the "long-ear'd rout," with rats and pigs, with blackbirds and widgeons, with "Dog distract" and "Monkey sick."[28] All of these comparisons are effectively reductive, the dogs and the monkeys doubly so, since they are sick as

[28] Samuel Butler, *Hudibras*, ed. John Wilders (Oxford: Clarendon, 1967), First Part, Canto I, lines 10, 27, 52, 54, 230, 210.

well; and they no doubt showed Dryden what he could do in a similar situation. But he still made an important addition to his own animal images. Where all of Butler's are merely demeaning and none of them is really threatening, with Dryden they are usually both. His "herd" of line 533, picking up the "Multitude" of line 112 and completing the group of factions who make up the Whigs, are themselves chaotic, showing the complete disintegration of order that would follow on giving way to the Whigs. His implied dogs, the Levites who "led the Pack" of theocrats (lines 527-28), are not merely deep-mouthed: they are "deepest-mouth'd against the Government." And he concludes his list of Whigs by saying

> a whole Hydra more   [541]
> Remains, of sprouting heads too long, to score.

Not only are they monsters who proliferate, but also, by the implication of the myth, their blood is so virulent that wounds with which it comes in contact become incurable.

As with animal imagery, so with the use of the couplet: Dryden could have learned from Samuel Butler both how to do what he did and how to improve on it. Certainly in at least one couplet Dryden appears to make a grateful bow in the direction of his fellow artist. Two of Butler's couplets ending in double rhyme are particularly telling: about the Civil War he said that the Presbyterians

> Call Fire and Sword and Desolation,
> A godly-thorough-Reformation
>
> (l.l.199-200)

And about Hudibras and his pretensions to logic he twitted,

> He'd run in Debt by Disputation,
> And pay with Ratiocination.
>
> (1.1.77-78)

With a larger sweep (thanks to the extra syllables) Dryden echoed his colleague in lines 523-24, where he described the theocracy of the Commonwealth:

> Where Sanhedrin and Priest inslav'd the Nation,
> And justifi'd their Spoils by Inspiration;

Obvious already in Butler's lines are the pause and balance. They are joined by an effective use of puns in these two couplets, in which he speaks

> Of Errant Saints, whom all men grant
> To be the true Church Militant:
>
> (1.1.91-92)

> [Who] prove their Doctrine Orthodox
> By Apostolick *Blows* and *Knocks*;

(1.1.197-98)

In each tetrameter couplet there is one important pause and hence one important balancing, perched on the pause and coming down with a triumphant snap on the double meaning at the end of the couplet.

By moving to the pentameter couplet, Dryden was able to introduce a variety of interior pauses, which could be put to a number of satiric uses:

> The *Jews*, a Headstrong, Moody, Murmuring race,   [45]
> As ever try'd th'extent and stretch of grace;
> God's pamper'd people whom, debauch'd with ease,
> No King could govern, nor no God could please;

Line 45, with its three internal pauses, provides increasing emphasis as the series of epithets proceeds until, appropriately, the most damning is the most stressed—"Murmuring." After so many pauses in line 45, the absence of any at all in the next line reinforces "th'extent and stretch" both of the line and of the grace, and how, in fact, both are "try'd." Line 47, with its medial pause (whether one puts it after "whom" or both before and after), provides an antithetic balance in which "pamper'd" and "debauch'd" contend with each other as to which is cause and which is effect. Line 48 carries this process to its ultimate. The balance of "King" and "God" suggests an equivalence, and if the God who is omnipotent could not please, the King must indeed be forgiven who could not govern this pampered people. In fact the balance does more, for there is a double antithesis present. As soon as one remembers that it is really not the business of God to please his people, but rather vice versa, then, thanks to the balance, one is reminded that it is not so much the business of a king to govern as it is the business of a people to obey.

Further improvement over Butler can be seen in the ways in which the puns of line 46 are integrated with the couplet. Each of the two meanings of "try'd"—tested and subjected to suffering—is illustrated in the length of the line itself, seemingly longer than usual because of the absence of pause, an absence accentuated by the multiplicity of pauses immediately before. That multiplicity, involving both the pauses and the items following them, also wittily illustrates the "stretch" of grace, which is made to extend itself over not only the headstrong nature but also, what is worse, the moody nature, and as if that were not all, also and further over what is still worse, the murmuring, grumbling nature. Nor does the punning stop there, for the "grace" itself, in the context, refers to kingly grace as well as divine, and that kingly grace is tried in the same way. What a people, these Whigs! And how well Dryden, with his own grace-notes, has caught the essence of their characteristics in the rhyming words of his two couplets: race/grace; ease/please.

Of these Whigs, these grace-proud, factious Whigs, these pampered, ease-debauched Whigs, whom no King could govern, nor no God could please, the chief was false Achitophel.

4

RESOLVED TO RUIN OR TO RULE

A Patriot's Name

Shaftesbury, who was born Anthony Ashley Cooper, cut a peculiar figure in London.[1] He was a small man in spite of his three names (an unusual number for the time) and may have been somewhat squint-eyed in appearance. From 1668, as a result of an operation for a cyst on the liver (thought by many to have been caused by an injury sustained when his coach upset in 1660), he bore with him, fastened in his side, a pipe (first silver, then gold) designed to draw off liquid from the abscess. By 1681, at the age of 60, he was, as a result of constant ill-health, bent over almost double, hobbling and limping, clinging on to life by sheer will power.

His parents had been of the first rank in the gentry and well related to nobility. Shaftesbury himself took care to choose his wives from immediate members of noble families. His first wife (1639-49) was the daughter of the lord keeper Thomas Coventry, his second (1650-54) was the sister of the Earl of Exeter, and his third (wed in 1655) was the daughter of Lord Spencer of Wormleighton and sister of the Earl of Sunderland. It was said, perhaps wrongly, that in between wives two and three he tried to marry Cromwell's daughter, Mary, and that his refusal was what led him to break with Cromwell. To each of his three wives, however, he appears to have been a good and loving husband. His only son, born of his second wife, gave him great concern. At the age of 15 he received wrong medication for a disorder, and as a result, over the next few years, he declined in intellectual and physical ability to the point where Shaftesbury persuaded him to assign the guardian-

[1] Biographical details are drawn from the following studies: W. D. Christie, *A Life of Anthony Ashley Cooper, First Earl of Shaftesbury*, 2 vols. (London: Macmillan, 1871); H. D. Trail, *Shaftesbury* (London: Longmans, Greene, 1886); Osmund Airy, "Cooper, Anthony Ashley," *DNB*; IV, 1035-55; Louise Fargo Brown, *The First Earl of Shaftesbury* (New York: Appleton-Century, 1933); K. H. D. Haley, *The First Earl of Shaftesbury* (Oxford: Clarendon, 1968).

ship of his children (who included the philosopher to be) to Shaftesbury or his nominee in the event of Shaftesbury's death. In worldly
wealth, however, Shaftesbury was more blessed. He owned extensive
estates in England and plantations in Barbados; he had financial interests in Carolina and in a ship engaged in the Guinea trade; he was, in
other words, independently wealthy.

Shaftesbury obviously had more than the average share of political
ambition. He was also a particularly vain man. Bishop Burnet reports
that "he turned the discourse almost always to the magnifying of himself, which he did in so gross and coarse a manner that it shewed his
great want of judgement; he told so many incredible things of himself
that it put me often out of patience; he was mightily overcome with flattery; and that and his private interests were the only things that could
hold or turn him."[2]

Apart from these qualities, however, Shaftesbury's character appears to have been exemplary. The usual charges of whoring were
made against him, but appear to have been unfounded and may even
have originated in an episode which can be interpreted another way altogether. One morning when Shaftesbury, as Lord Chancellor, approached Charles in his presence chamber, the King turned to those
about him and said, "Here comes the greatest whoremaster in England." Instantly Shaftesbury, bowing low, replied, "Of a subject, Sire."[3]
Charles may well have been merely exercising his wit—in view of the
distinctive figure Shaftesbury cut, or referring to the whore which
Shaftesbury, it was reported, provided for Charles's own delight, or
referring—and this I should like to think was the point—to
Shaftesbury's control of the House of Commons.[4]

As Chancellor, part of Shaftesbury's duty was to serve as a judge,
and in doing so he appears to have been scrupulously honest and fair.
Recent critics have wondered whether Dryden was being ironic in his
praise of Shaftesbury's honesty as a judge, but a biographer who published her work in 1933 took the trouble to examine the register books
that record the cases Shaftesbury tried as Chancellor and found every-
where abundant evidence of honesty, efficiency, and a great concern
that justice be done to the individual. He frequently went beyond his
duty on the bench and through personal interviews outside the court
saw to it that appropriate settlements were made. "He was notably in-

---

[2] *A Supplement to Burnet's History of My Own Time*, ed. H. C. Foxcroft (Oxford:
Clarendon, 1902), p. 59.

[3] Brown, *Shaftesbury*, p. 214.

[4] Such a witticism concerning the House of Commons would not be too surprising:
Edward Soxby in 1657 had called the Members of Parliament "pimps of tyranny" who
prostituted people's liberty; Pope was to call the Houses of Parliament the equivalent of
Caesar's fool; and both Gay and Fielding were to make it plain that Walpole used the
House of Commons as if it were his kept woman.

terested in all cases having to do with the property of minors, and very strict about absolute integrity of statement. One case where a daughter's portion was involved he dismissed with costs, 'but the Mother must have no costs for she has varied and Trifled in her Answers.' "[5]

Shaftesbury's relation to the Popish Plot has been much discussed, but no evidence has been presented to show that he instigated it or that Oates was in his pay. Instead he merely seized the opportunity which Oates presented to the nation and used the fears aroused by the Plot to further the aims of the Whigs. Shaftesbury himself is reported to have said of the Plot: "I will not say who started the game, but I am sure I had the full hunting of it."[6]

His political career itself gave the greatest handle to his detractors: it is full of changing sides, back and forth and back again—and almost always to his political advantage. In 1643, when he was 21, he declared himself a supporter of the King against his Parliamentary enemies in arms. Within a year Shaftesbury switched to the Parliamentary side, perhaps because he had been slighted in the matter of command of certain military forces or perhaps because he had had a change of heart about Parliament and the King. While in command of 1500 Parliamentary soldiers in 1644, he besieged and stormed a countryhouse held by a Royalist garrison. In the process he displayed considerable bravery and also, by his own admission, a desire to deny quarter to the Royalists when, the house in flames, they offered to surrender. In 1653, as member of the Barebones Parliament, Shaftesbury emerged as a leader, heading a deputation that invited Cromwell to serve in the Parliament and becoming a member of the council of state. Within 18 months he had broken with Cromwell, perhaps because he had been denied the hand of Cromwell's daughter or perhaps because he genuinely preferred Parliamentary rule to the one-man rule Cromwell wished to follow. In 1659 under the protectorate of Cromwell's son, Shaftesbury took the oath of fidelity to the Commonwealth and in January of 1660 again became a member of the council of state. Along with many others, Shaftesbury then, in February, March, and April, carried out negotiations for the return of Charles, and Shaftesbury was one of twelve deputed to go to Breda in the Netherlands to invite Charles home again. (Ironically, it was near Breda that Shaftesbury's coach overturned, causing the injury which many thought led to the cyst on his liver.)

In May, 1660, he was appointed to Charles's privy council, and at Charles's coronation in 1661 the man we have been calling Shaftesbury but who was known then as Cooper was raised to the peerage as Baron

---

[5] Brown, *Shaftesbury*, p. 217.

[6] James Ferguson, *Robert Ferguson the Plotter* (Edinburgh: Douglas, 1887), p. 42.

Ashley of Wimborne St. Giles. For several years Shaftesbury served the King in various posts, performing well as an administrator and taking part in the infighting that went on within the government. For a short period, while still loosely within the government, he opposed the policies of the pre-eminent minister, Clarendon, and then, when Clarendon fell from the King's favour, Shaftesbury (as Baron Ashley) became one of the five predominant ministers who made up what came to be called the CABAL because of their initials—Clifford, Arlington, Buckingham, Ashley, and Lauderdale. As a minister he argued privately against one of the King's proposals—to "stop the exchequer"—to cease paying their bills and debts for a period of time, but when Charles put the policy into practice, Shaftesbury dutifully defended it in Parliament. In 1672 the man born Cooper and known then as Baron Ashley was made Earl of Shaftesbury (and Baron Cooper of Pawlet as well), and in a few months became Lord Chancellor, filling the highest office open to him. He did not stay long: perhaps because of James's influence on the King, Charles dismissed Shaftesbury in just about a year's time. Within a few days, however, Charles sent an offer to Shaftesbury in an effort to bring him back: Louis of France would give him 10,000 guineas and Charles would give him a dukedom and any office he wished. But Shaftesbury refused, preferring instead to ally himself firmly with the Parliamentary opposition.

As one of the principal leaders of the opposition, Shaftesbury returned to Court to become one of the King's counsellors when Charles in 1679 appointed him president of the newly re-constituted privy council, which had been organized as part of a ploy to conciliate the opposition and which was supposed to come to agreements on matters before they reached Parliament. That was in April: in October Charles had got more money from Louis and dismissed Shaftesbury again. In June of 1680 Shaftesbury pressed the attack in the law courts, attempting to indict the Duke of York and the Duchess of Portsmouth (Charles's reigning mistress) as popish recusants, but the government saw to it that the grand jury before whom the attempt was made was discharged before it could come to a decision. He tried again with the Duke in the same month and failed, but succeeded in having him indicted in February of 1681—only to be thwarted again when the government refused to prosecute. Shaftesbury worked the streets as well, forming the "boys of Wapping" (the porters, seamen, bargemen, and other workmen of the slums) into an aggressive mob which often exerted pressure on those whom the Whigs wished to influence away from supporting the King.[7] In Parliament, throughout the Exclusion Crisis, Shaftesbury was a prime mover in the cause to eliminate James

---

[7] *Bishop Parker's History of His Own Time*, tr. Thomas Newlin (London: Rivington, 1727), pp. 403-04.

from the succession. When his Parliamentary efforts failed and when Charles, again with money from Louis, dissolved the Oxford Parliament and was evidently prepared to rule without a Parliament, Shaftesbury's most effective base of power was gone.

On 2 July 1681 he was arrested on a charge of high treason. The grand jury on 24 November refused to allow the case to proceed further, and Shaftesbury was released. But his power was slipping away. And when the government, with great exertion and pressure, secured the election of Tory sheriffs in London to replace the Whig sheriffs who had packed the grand jury in Shaftesbury's favour, Shaftesbury fled to Holland. There he suffered an attack of gout and died on 21 January 1683.

As one looks at his political career with as much impartiality as possible, one can see that, in his changes of sides, others left him at least as often as he left others. And I for one am quite prepared to believe that a strong motive within him was the desire to strengthen the power of Parliament, in the belief that such strengthening would be good for the country. At the same time, however, it is of course obvious that his many changes of sides (some voluntary and some enforced) and his almost steady rise in power and social rank gave a handle to those of his enemies who wished to charge him with time-serving and overweening personal ambition—the desire for power, for the good, not of the country, but of Anthony Ashley Cooper, Earl of Shaftesbury. It is even conceivable that, at times at least, he aspired, by making Monmouth a bastard king, to become Lord Protector.

Tapski

Not surprisingly Shaftesbury was subjected to a great multiplicity of attacks from the Tory press, and, also not surprisingly, within that multiplicity there was a wide range of tone as well as topic. A few were measured and gentlemanly. Many others called him Tony or "Shiftesbury"—because of his frequent changes of sides; they made easy puns on his name of Cooper and made of the pipe in his side a tap in a barrel of treasonable liquor; some combined the image of tap with the Tory joke that he had applied for the kingship of Poland (which was elective and which he therefore admired) and gave him the sobriquet of "Tapski." As can be imagined, still other attacks were vituperative and scurrilous, nasty and obscene. Dryden had before him ample evidence of what effect certain topics and approaches, certain devices and tones, would likely have on his moderate and uncommitted readers.

Certain topics were evidently too risky for him to touch. It was charged in *Poor Robins Dream*, for instance, that Shaftesbury had manipulated the elections through his traitorous influence on Dissenting preachers.[8] But mention of these elections on Dryden's part would have reminded his readers of the large electoral support the Whigs had received, and this support was to be kept as much out of sight as possible. The same pamphlet charged that Shaftesbury had first corrupted some of the King's courtiers so that he could then attack them,[9] but again Dryden evidently chose to soft-pedal the matter of court corruption, whoever was responsible for it. Another pamphlet charged that it was Shaftesbury who was to blame for stopping the exchequer (refusing for a time to pay the government's bills) and for illegally by-passing Parliament in issuing writs for bye-elections.[10] Both these actions, however, had been done by Charles's government and the degree to which Shaftesbury had been responsible was a matter of public dispute: again, the wiser tactic for Dryden would be to say nothing—at least he would avoid giving the appearance to his moderate readers of trying to dredge up everything possible against Shaftesbury. Likewise the joke of Shaftesbury's having put in for the kingship of Poland probably bore its Tory origin too much in evidence for Dryden to be able to make use of it.

Dryden would of course wish to appear moderate to his moderate readers (a kindred spirit—as we have seen in his handling of the Popish Plot). For this reason he would avoid repeating charges that Shaftesbury indulged in whoring and suffered from syphilis[11]—charges, incidentally, that could also remind his readers of the reputation both Charles and James had as well. He would in addition avoid charging lack of religion[12]—to the moderate reader, no doubt, England had had too much of religion as it was (like Northern Ireland today), and Dryden had begun his poem by appealing to the latent anti-clericalism in his reader. All mention of Shaftesbury's "tap" he likewise avoids —perhaps its inclusion would have detracted from the seriousness of the danger that the figure of Achitophel implies, but also he undoubtedly scored points with his moderate readers for his gentlemanliness in not mentioning a personal handicap that so many other attackers had mentioned. Perhaps, in view of this gentlemanly omission, it is especially surprising that Dryden chose to include mention of Shaftesbury's largely incompetent son,

[8] *Poor Robins Dream, or the Vision of Hell: with a Dialogue between the Two Ghosts of Dr. Tonge and Capt. Bedlow* (London, 1681), p. 3. (Luttrell dated his copy 30 April.)

[9] *Poor Robins Dream*, p. 5.

[10] *A Civil Correction of a Sawcy Impudent Pamphlet, lately published, entituled, A Brief Account of the Designs which the Papists have against the Earl of Shaftesbury, &.* (London, 1681), p. 2.

[11] As made, for instance, in *The Deliquium: or, The Grievances of the Nation Discovered in a Dream* (London: dated by Luttrell 8 April 1681), p. 2, and *The Last Will and Testament of Anthony King of Poland* (London, 1682), p. 2.

[12] As was made in "Let Oliver now be forgotten" (1681) in *A Choice Collection of 180 Loyal Songs . . .* , 3rd ed. (London: N. T., 1685), p. 3.

Got, while his Soul did hudled Notions try;
And born a shapeless Lump, like Anarchy.

(ll. 171-72)

It should be noted, however, that Dryden was not pointlessly abusive, as was the pamphleteer who had Shaftesbury say, in his will, "I leave my *Soul* unto my *Son*,/For *he*, as Wise men think, as yet has *none*."[13] Instead Dryden was evidently taking advantage of the lingering belief in correlatives: that the outward appearance of offspring paralleled the inner nature of their progenitors. Just as the well-ordered completeness of Charles was made manifest in the manly beauty of his son Monmouth, so one could tell the inner factiousness of Shaftesbury by the anarchic nature of his hapless son.

Dryden's moderation in his handling of the Popish Plot, or, more accurately, his kind of moderation, can be better appreciated when compared with what the author of *Poor Robins Dream* did. He said that Shaftesbury had been the sole author of the Plot—"none but he contriv'd it," and he did so because of his bloodlust—"Tho' *Tony's* sides have several teer of holes,/He lusts after bodies, as the Devil after souls." He was the one who caused the death of Sir Edmund Berry Godfrey (the magistrate before whom Oates had first revealed the Plot and who was soon after murdered); he hired and trained the witnesses, and he would in time hang those who had helped him.[14] Dryden's authorial pose of moderation prevented him from even touching most of these charges, but he still was able to make use of the last two —delicately and somewhat indirectly. Concerning Shaftesbury, he said

The wish'd occasion of the Plot he takes,
Some Circumstances finds, but more he makes.
By buzzing Emissaries, fills the ears   [210]
Of listning Crowds, with Jealosies and Fears

Merely a suggestion, but to his informed reader quite enough to imply suborning of witnesses. And what will happen to those witnesses? Since by the time his poem appeared, they had already begun to turn on one another,[15] it was sufficient for Dryden to allude to this state of affairs, as he did at the end of his description of Corah, and, with the earlier reference to Shaftesbury's "emissaries," the informed and alert reader would take the hint:

What others in his Evidence did Joyn,
(The best that could be had for love or coyn,)

[13] *Last Will and Testament*, p. 1.
[14] *Poor Robins Dream*, pp. 3-5.
[15] At the trial of Stephen College, two witnesses, Dugdale and Turberville, who had formerly testified on the Whig side in trials, now testified for the Tories against College and against the testimony of Oates. See Ogg, *England in the Reign of Charles II*, pp. 604, 627.

In *Corah's* own predicament will fall?
For *witness* is a Common Name to all.

(ll. 678-81)

The overt use to which Dryden has Shaftesbury put his emissaries should be noted. Through them he fills ears

with Jealosies and Fears
Of Arbitrary Counsels brought to light
And proves the King himself a *Jebusite*:
Weak Arguments! which yet he knew ful well,
Were strong with People easie to Rebell.   [215]

Shaftesbury's motive is evidently political ambition. The author of *Poor Robins Dream* saw it as bloodlust, and even dragged in the story of Shaftesbury's trying to burn alive the Royalist garrison in the country-house he besieged during the Civil War, but Dryden, seeing a graver danger to the nation as a whole—and not simply the few who might be hanged by the Plot—ignores such charges and fastens instead on political ambition working towards rebellion. The same observation holds for the use he makes of the image of Achitophel, the evil counsellor of the Old Testament, whose character he fixes on Shaftesbury. Another pamphleteer, who likewise had an Achitophel, described him as "a little Crooked, Hucked-back *Devil*" and elaborated thus: "He hath the Eyes of a *Basilisk*, Kills all he looks on: He hath Hands imbrued in the Blood of the Innocent: He hath the Heart of a *Panther*: He feeds on nothing but Revenge; He thirsts after nothing but Human Blood, and the Eternal Ruin of Innocent Souls."[16] Dryden, on the other hand, eschews such bloodthirstiness and fashions his Achitophel as the evil counsellor who seeks rather to further his own personal political ambition through rebellion. In comparison, Dryden appears moderate.

In the same way Dryden can be seen as, in effect, picking and choosing from other images he found used for Shaftesbury. Besides Achitophel, he accepted the related images of Machiavelli and Satan; both represented serious evil and threats to the stability of the state. But badgers, monkeys, and lesser hag-like spirits (which are sprinkled throughout many of the other pamphlets) he avoided, presumably as being contemptible, not dangerous. When he found less than satanic figures who still represented a danger to the state, he used them. Such are the images of pigmy and reckless pilot which appear in a pamphlet, *Sejanus: or the Popular Favourite*, written no later than his own and possibly a little before:[17] the pigmy size emphasized not only (by con-

---

[16] *A Seasonable Invitation for Monmouth to Return to Court* (London: W. B., 1681), p. 2.

[17] [George Seigniour], *Sejanus: or the Popular Favourite, Now in his Solitude, and Sufferings* (London: Smith, Curtiss, Janeway, & Baldwin, [1681]), pp. 2 and 3.

trast) Shaftesbury's overweening ambition, but also his unsuitableness for rule; and the reckless pilot emphasized how dangerous it would be for the state if Shaftesbury were to seize the helm.

False Achitophel

This double emphasis on Shaftesbury's ambition and on his factiousness—both of which make for a grave danger to the state—is at the core of Dryden's presentation of him in *Absalom and Achitophel*. Dryden gets at him in two principal parts of the poem—in the character portrait in which he analyzes what makes him tick, and in the dramatic role of seducer to Monmouth; and in both of these parts the images and the various artistic devices are all used to reinforce the danger of this double threat.

The image of Achitophel from 2 Samuel brought with it certain qualities. Achitophel's counsel was greatly esteemed; in fact inquiring of him was "as if a man had enquired at the oracle of God" (2 Sam. 16:23). But still, when invited by the rebellious Absalom, David's son, to leave David and serve him instead, Achitophel did so, transferring his counsel to the service of filial and national treason—nor that alone, for it was he who advised Absalom to go in unto his father's concubines (2 Sam. 16:21). Certainly in tradition ever afterwards Achitophel has been the archetype of the evil counsellor. To this archetype Dryden has added the figure of Machiavelli, the courtier who, for himself and for the person he advises, gives counsel aimed, in however devious and underhanded a way, at promoting the advancement of personal political ambition.

It is this double figure that Dryden first introduces. He takes the Biblical Achitophel,

> Of these the false *Achitophel* was first: [150]
> A Name to all succeeding Ages Curst.

fastens on his "Counsell" in the next line, but makes it "crooked" in the manner of Machiavelli and equates it with something else Machiavellian, saying that he is "For close Designs, and crooked Counsell fit." Another element of his Achitophel comes directly from the Biblical figure: "unfixt in Principle and Place" (line 154), which refers to the treason of the Biblical figure and also, with regard at least to the change in "Place," to the fact that Shaftesbury had twice been high in Charles's privy council and twice had parted from it. But it is more from Machiavelli that Dryden draws, than from the Bible, when he elaborates further on his Achitophel (lines 173-74):

> In Friendship False, Implacable in Hate:
> Resolv'd to Ruine or to Rule the State.

And it is to Machiavelli that he looks when he makes his Achitophel, in a reversal of the Biblical situation, invite his Absalom to join him in rebellion against David. Throughout, in this fictitious construct, Dryden has added, to his Biblical and traitorous Achitophel, the ambitious and scheming Machiavelli.

Behind both Machiavelli and Achitophel is, of course, the earlier and larger archetype, Satan, whose name means "the adversary." Two aspects of his adversariness Dryden adds to his figure of Achitophel. Just as Satan, especially in Milton's version of the story, rebelled against his lawful lord and pretended to defend the rights of his subordinates against that lord, so Dryden's Achitophel

> . . . stood at bold Defiance with his Prince   [205]
> Held up the Buckler of the Peoples Cause,
> Against the Crown; and sculk'd behind the Laws.

In a more insidious manner, Satan sought to further his rebellion against his lord by assuming the form of a serpent and seducing Adam and Eve to join him in rebellion: so, too, as Achitophel approaches Absalom to win him to his traitorous cause,

> Him he attempts, with studied Arts to please,
> And sheds his Venome, in such words as these.
> (ll. 228-29)

Inherent in Satan's rebellion against the Almighty was a certain element of recklessness—after all, he didn't stand a chance of winning. It is this satanic recklessness that allows Dryden to transform an otherwise hackneyed image and make it particularly applicable to Shaftesbury. The author of *Sejanus* called Shaftesbury "treacherous Pilot, and false Mariner" for having tacked about with the changing wind and tide and for wishing to steer the floating bark, scarcely mended, into the purple waves again.[18] Dryden makes Shaftesbury's piloting an expression of his restless, fiery soul, so basically factious, rebellious, and perverse that, rather than tolerate a calm, he will steer his craft too near the dangerous sands (such, no doubt, as the Goodwin Sands, for centuries the notorious graveyard of ships):

> A daring Pilot in extremity;
> Pleas'd with the Danger, when the Waves went high   [160]
> He sought the Storms; but for a Calm unfit,
> Would Steer too nigh the Sands, to boast his Wit.

Those few degrading images Dryden uses for Shaftesbury all share a peculiar quality. He took Shaftesbury's small size and used the image of pigmy for him, but, whereas in *Sejanus* Shaftesbury was pictured as

---

[18] *Sejanus*, p. 2.

a "Pigmy Lord . . . that's only fit to fight with Crane,"[19] Dryden uses his diminutive body to emphasize, directly and by contrast with his soul, how unfit he is to rule:

> A fiery Soul, which working out its way,
> Fretted the Pigmy Body to decay:
> And o'r inform'd the Tenement of Clay.
>
> (ll. 156-58)

What sensible reader would choose to support a politician whose fiery soul is so insatiable that it destroys the body that contains it and that, by implication, would destroy—or try to destroy—anything else that tried to contain it? In a somewhat similar way Dryden points, in lines 194-95, to the "Cockle," the weed among the promising grain in the soil of Shaftesbury's character: although contemptible in itself, this particular "Cockle" had an important and destructive effect, in that it "opprest the Noble seed." Actions, too, can be degrading, and the "pleasing Rape" which Achitophel urges Absalom to commit (line 474) is certainly such, but, at the same time, since it is "a pleasing Rape upon the Crown," it is an action that threatens the whole nation. The same with another manifestation external to Shaftesbury—his son: even though that unfortunate person was "born a shapeless Lump" (line 172), that "Lump," being "like Anarchy," further demonstrates the danger to the state that rages inside the factious soul of Shaftesbury. "Pigmy body," "Cockle," "pleasing Rape," and "shapeless Lump"—all are degrading, but all are also fraught with danger.

The degree of deliberateness with which Dryden crafted his description of Shaftesbury can be better appreciated if we make a brief comparison of the images he used for his description in *Absalom and Achitophel* with those he used in *The Medall*. This latter poem he wrote after the grand jury had acquitted Shaftesbury of the charge of treason and after the Whigs, in celebration, had issued a medal that not only commemorated the event but also depicted Shaftesbury's bust on one side as if he were a monarch. Appropriately, Dryden fastened on the image of "Idol" for Shaftesbury (line 7), an idol whom his priests preached up "for God" (lines 268-69).[20] He also made use of the closely associated images of "*Lucifer*" (line 22), "*Fiend*" (line 81), and "*Jehu*" rushing headlong into anarchy (lines 119-22). All these continue the theme of danger that Dryden used in *Absalom and Achitophel*. But in continuing to use the image of "Pigmee" (line 27), he dropped all explicit mention of danger to the state, and as he extended his degrading imagery into other objects, he often departed from any import at all of serious danger: although in one line Shaftesbury is said to have been

---

[19] *Sejanus*, p. 3.
[20] The text referred to for *The Medall* is that provided in *Works*, II, 43-52.

"A Vermin, wriggling in th'Usurper's Ear" (line 51) and so is associated, in a belittling way, with danger, in other lines he has "an
Eunuch face" (line 23), he behaved like a "white Witch" (line 62), and,
among the Whiggamore saints, he was "The lowdest Bagpipe of the
squeaking Train" (line 35). All these latter images (and especially the
last, for an Englishman) degrade the quality of Shaftesbury, but also
lower his stature, something Dryden was careful not to do in *Absalom
and Achitophel*.

But Dryden in *The Medall* sank below even this level of attack and
indulged in the kind of street-fighting, with no holds barred, that some
of his fellow Tory pamphleteers had engaged in. He glanced at
Shaftesbury's tap in referring to the Earl's "Stumm" which his
"Priests" used to "ferment their fainting Cause" (lines 268-70). And he
depicted Shaftesbury in a series of sexual images of increasing vile-
ness. The Whig leader is "the Pander of the Peoples hearts," "Whose
blandishments a Loyal Land have whor'd" (lines 256-58). His name is
"blasted" (by syphilis, presumably), "For all must curse the Woes that
must descend on all" from "Age to Age" (lines 260-62). That he is
syphilitic is confirmed by the depiction of his "*Mercury*," which "Has
pass'd through every Sect" (lines 263-64). But that is not all, for from
being first a pander, then a syphilitic, and then the treatment for
syphilis, he now becomes the syphilis itself, for "what thou giv'st, that
Venom still remains;/And the pox'd Nation feels Thee in their Brains"
(lines 265-66). Since it is the nation which suffers, the imagery continues the concept of grave danger that appeared in *Absalom and
Achitophel*, but certainly the sense of moderation in its depiction has
been lost.

That sense of moderation which we feel in *Absalom and
Achitophel* all the more acutely because of the contrast with the
method used in *The Medall* must have appeared impressive enough to
the readers of 1681, before the later poem was written, especially since,
into the midst of the many images, grand and degrading, that convey
most graphically (as we have seen) the immense danger to England that
Shaftesbury represented, Dryden in his third edition inserted lines of
high praise for Shaftesbury's performance as a judge. It has been conjectured, rather persuasively, that Dryden had in fact included these
lines in his manuscript but that, for some reason—possibly objection
from the King—he removed them.[21] I for one would like to think that
Dryden had intended including them from the beginning, for they constitute an admirable polemical ploy. After he has pointed out how
dangerous Shaftesbury is as a politician, what better way would there
be to impress the moderate reader with how fair (and discerning) the

[21] See *Works*, II, 250-51, 411-12. The text for this inserted passage is that presented in
Works, II, 11.

author is than by graciously granting the praiseworthy performance as a judge?

> Yet, Fame deserv'd, no Enemy can grudge;
> The Statesman we abhor, but praise the Judge.
> In *Israels* Courts ne'r sat an *Abbethdin*
> With more discerning Eyes, or Hands more clean:
> Unbrib'd, unsought, the Wretched to redress; [190]
> Swift of Dispatch, and easie of Access.

High praise, indeed, and such as should win the confidence of the moderate and uncommitted reader. (How different from lines 57-58 of *The Medall*: "Ev'n in the most sincere advice he gave / He had a grudging still to be a Knave.") But note then what follows. Dryden manages to have it both ways, for, having demonstrated how fair he is, he turns his gracious concession to further advantage. First he expresses a pious wish that the good qualities represented by Shaftesbury's judgeship had not been oppressed by the evil, as, of course, they had:

> Oh, had he been content to serve the Crown,
> With vertues only proper to the Gown;
> Or, had the rankness of the Soyl been freed
> From Cockle, that opprest the Noble seed: [195]
> *David*, for him his tunefull Harp had strung,
> And Heaven had wanted one Immortal song.

It has been suggested that the "one Immortal song," which Heaven would have lacked because it would have been addressed to Achitophel (in a different vein) rather than to Heaven, is Psalm 109, in which King David complains of his slanderous enemies.[22] Again I should like to think that this is what Dryden intended by his allusion, for then his informed reader would have had these verses in mind from the opening of the Psalm:

> For the mouth of the wicked and the mouth of the deceitful are opened against me: they have spoken against me with a lying tongue.
> They compassed me about also with words of hatred; and fought against me without a cause.
> For my love they are my adversaries: but I give myself unto prayer.
> And they have rewarded me evil for good, and hatred for my love.

Having thus proceeded from a display of generous praise, through a mingling of ostensible charity and implied denunciation, to this point, Dryden then sums up the whole character portrait by reiterating the double charge of rebellious perversity and personal ambition:

> But wilde Ambition loves to slide, not stand;
> And Fortunes Ice prefers to Vertues Land: (ll. 198-99)

---

[22] H. Hammond, " 'One Immortal Song,' " *RES*, 5 (1954), 60-62.

Incidentally, if the modern reader wonders how readily Dryden's contemporary reader would have picked up the allusion to Psalm 109 and have been aware of its opening verses, there is this consideration to be borne in mind. When speaking in the House of Lords on 23 December 1680, Shaftesbury mentioned "the chargeable ladies at court" and commented, perhaps spontaneously, by quoting words Samuel used to Saul in 1 Sam. 15:14: "What means the bleating of this kind of cattle?" He proceeded to express the hope that the King would answer as Saul did, "That he reserved them for sacrifice, and means to deliver them up to please his people."[23] An opponent who replied to him in a pamphlet used the same source against him: "His lordship may read in the same place, that obedience is better than sacrifice; but if a sacrifice must be made, it is not to the people, but to God and justice."[24] The matter of sacrificing to God refers to 1 Sam. 15:15, and the matter of obedience refers to 1 Sam. 15:22. If the pamphlet had been written a few months later, no doubt the author would also have quoted verse 23: "For rebellion is as the sin of witchcraft, and stubbornness is as iniquity and idolatry." Concerning Psalm 109 itself, there is the further consideration that the original collaborator with Titus Oates in communicating the Popish Plot to the authorities was Isreal Tonge. How tempting for a person seeking to discredit Tonge and his testimony to have quoted David: "they have spoken against me with a lying tongue."

Throughout the character portrait of Achitophel, Dryden uses a handful of rhetorical devices to reinforce the factiousness that is communicated, less indirectly, through the images of denigration. The reinforcement occurs once the content is known: I do not in any way suggest that sound creates meaning, but once the meaning of the content is known, such things as sound and movement can reinforce the emotional effect of the content.

For instance, in the opening line of the portrait, as soon as the Biblical image of Achitophel establishes the content, rhetoric is able to make a contribution. Dryden has just sketched in what sort of people made up the rebels; then he says, "Of these the false *Achitophel* was first" (l. 150). Normally it would be ironic for someone false to be first, but in this group it is only appropriate. Hence there is double irony, and this double irony of *false* and *first* is reinforced by the positioning of the words, by their being balanced one against the other, and by the alliteration. Dryden proceeds:

[23] Quoted in Haley, p. 613.

[24] *A Letter from Scotland: written occasionally upon the Speech made by a Noble Peer of this Realm* (London, [1681]), in *Somers' Tracts*, VIII, 209. (Scott dates it as 1679 (?), but he was evidently right to put the question mark.)

> A Name to all succeeding Ages Curst.
> For close Designs, and crooked Counsell fit;
>
> (ll. 151-52)

The close pattern of k sounds does two things. It suggests that for Dryden the name Achitophel was pronounced a-KIT-o-fel and not in the alternative way, a-HIT-o-fel. It also slyly associates with Achitophel such opprobrious things as being curst and practising close designs and crooked counsel.

To the balancing of his lines Dryden often adds antithesis, as in the couplet in which he asks why Achitophel (who is really a sick old man) should

> Punish a Body which he coud not please;
> Bankrupt of Life, yet Prodigal of Ease?
>
> (ll. 167-68)

Normally Shaftesbury's sickness would elicit sympathy. But the perversity he displays in his sickness radically modifies that feeling, and rhetoric helps to modify it further, by highlighting how opposite Achitophel's conduct is to what would be normal. In the first line, instead of trying at least to protect a body which he could not please, Achitophel chooses to punish it. This antithetic substitution of opposite elements for similar ones Dryden then inverts ironically in the second line. Where a normal person, realizing that he was bankrupt of life, would seek to preserve his ease, Achitophel, being thoroughly perverse, extends the bankruptcy (instead of confining it) and is prodigal of ease.

Even tighter antithesis can be achieved through chiasmus, the device of balancing four elements in the inverted order *a, b, b, a*. Such a device invites a comparison of what is balanced, and in line 155, "In Power unpleas'd, impatient of Disgrace," the comparison is particularly rewarding. Since "unpleas'd" and "impatient" (the *b*'s) are virtually the same, it is suggested that to Achitophel "Power" and "Disgrace" (the *a*'s) are also virtually the same. To him it makes no difference which he is in, power or disgrace: the restlessness of his turbulent wit (the subject of the preceding lines) makes him fret, makes him quintessentially factious.

All these rhetorical devices come together in the couplet which serves as the climactic summing up of Achitophel's character:

> In Friendship False, Implacable in Hate:
> Resolv'd to Ruine or to Rule the State.
>
> (ll. 173-74)

The chiasmus emphasizes the perversity in each element, false in friendship and implacable in hate (when the qualities of firmness and flexibility should be reversed), and this perversity is further reinforced by the sound linking within each element, in *friendship false, implacable in hate.*[25] In the next line the antithetic balancing, reinforced by alliteration, accomplishes much of the destruction. Flanked by resolved and state, appears "to Ruine or to Rule." What should be diametrically opposite is, as suggested by the context of meaning and reinforced by the balance, all the same to Achitophel and his embodiment, Shaftesbury; what matters to the ambitious politician is power and the exercise of power. Nor does the rhetorical patterning stop here, for there are vertical relations as well as horizontal. The rhyming words of the couplet, hate/state, further imply the danger to the nation in Shaftesbury's ambition. And the remaining vertically parallel positions of the two lines in the couplet also contribute: ironically, whereas he is false in friendship, he is resolved (firm) to ruin; but in the comparison of hating and ruling, he is the same: implacable. Let England beware.

Hell's Agent

The figure of Achitophel, here built up and here fortified with Machiavelli and Satan himself, Dryden then puts into action as a dramatic character. Naturally he makes him do all sorts of evil things. Such arbitrariness was early complained about:

> to tell
> How *Absalom* and wise *Achitophel*
> Were *wicked* (once) two thousand years ago,
> And therefore (*whom they hate*) must still be so.[26]

But that is only part of what Dryden does. As mentioned earlier, he reverses the roles of Absalom and Achitophel: whereas in the Bible it is Absalom who seduces Achitophel to join the cause, with Dryden it is the other way round. There is another reversal as well: the Biblical Achitophel gave Absalom such wise counsel that, in order to avoid having David captured and slain as a result of it, the Lord himself had to intervene: he prompted another counsellor, Hushai (who had joined Absalom as an undercover agent for the King), to give counsel which ran counter to Achitophel's wise advice but which Absalom accepted (2 Sam. 17:1-14). With Dryden, however, the "counsel" which Achitophel gives Absalom is a speech of political seduction.

Obviously, Dryden's fictitious construct differs again from his principal Biblical source. Not only that, but it differs in such a way that

---

[25] Dryden almost certainly pronounced the first *a* in impla*c*able as *ay*, the same as in *hate*. Such a pronunciation is the first one listed in modern dictionaries and was the only one listed in William Johnston's *A Pronouncing and Spelling Dictionary* of 1764.

[26] *The Mushroom: or, a Satyr against Libelling Tories and Prelatical Tantivies* (London, 1682), p. 15.

at least one of his contemporary readers was led to protest against the arbitrariness. All of which prompts the question: just what kind of reader did Dryden have in mind? Evidently one familiar enough with the Bible to pick up the reference to Psalm 109 and yet one sophisticated and literary enough not to be bothered by the differences between the Bible and his construct—and hopefully even to enjoy those differences and to look for more. The basic question of the nature of Dryden's reader will be discussed at greater length later on: right now we can look at those further differences as they relate to Achitophel, for they reveal still further depths in his character.

To begin with, Dryden's Achitophel trafficks in the Jebusitic Plot, having found it as a wished occasion and having then elaborated on it to the end of furthering rebellion against David (lines 208-15). He aims at "a Democracy" (lines 224-28), which, in those days, was as low as one could aim and of course entailed the destruction of the monarchy. He admits to having been the one responsible for blackening the reputation of the King's brother (lines 401-04). He commits blasphemy, first in hailing Absalom as a type of Christ—"second *Moses*" (line 234) and the one

> Whose dawning Day, in every distant age,
> Has exercis'd the Sacred Prophets rage:
>
> (ll. 236-37)—

and then in addressing Absalom/Monmouth as the "*Saviour*" himself (line 240). Perhaps worst of all, he prompts Absalom to filial treason with the most revolting arguments. Now is the time to rebel, he says, now that his father is without strength, "Naked of Friends, and round beset with Foes" (line 280). And pay no attention to your father's love, he says:

> Our fond Begetters, who woud never dye,
> Love but themselves in their Posterity.
>
> (ll. 425-26)

To what depths can factiousness, rebellion, and political ambition descend? No wonder Dryden calls his Achitophel "Hells dire Agent" (line 373). But a still more disturbing question is "What sort of son would listen?"

5

DEBAUCHED WITH PRAISE

James, Duke of Monmouth, had three things going for him. He was Charles's eldest son and so could carry on his line direct. He had been commander of British forces on the continent and in Scotland, and so could lead an army that would protect the people's liberties from any papist attack. He was immensely popular, and so his succession to the throne would please a great many of the populace. These three advantages Dryden had to try to undercut.

The People's Darling

Of those Whigs who supported Monmouth in his bid to replace the Duke of York as successor to the throne, some insisted that his mother had really been secretly married to Charles, and others simply ignored his illegitimacy, as if it did not matter. One pamphleteer in particular put his case in the most favourable way. After playing with the allegory of place names (Shaftesbury, York and Monmouth), he wrote, concerning Monmouth and with an eye to the threat from France, "And we may remember for its Glory, and as a good Omen, that [the town of Monmouth] gave Title and Birth to one of the most Victorious of our *English* Kings, who brought *France* under the subjection of his Sword, and at this time yields a Title to the most hopeful Prince, the Eldest Son of our Great *Monarch* . . . . "[1] The obvious counter was, of course, to emphasize Monmouth's illegitimacy, for primogeniture, after all, applied only to sons who were legitimate. Many Tory pamphleteers did this, but none so wittily as Dryden in the opening lines of the poem. There he was at his most satirically effective, and all he had to do, on this topic, in the rest of the poem was to throw in an odd reminder now and then.

[1] *Advice to the Men of Monmouth Concerning the Present Times* (London: T. Ben skins, 1681), p. 1.

Monmouth had gained both reputation and experience as commander of the English forces on the continent. To this he added his command of the loyal forces in Scotland in 1679 when a small rebellion broke out after the murder of Archbishop Sharp. Both Monmouth's easy victory at Bothwell Bridge and his magnanimous treatment of prisoners afterwards added greatly to his reputation.[2] It was only to be expected, then, that a Whig writer should try to capitalize on that reputation and on his Protestantism. Addressing the city of London, the writer said: ". . . the greatest danger accruing to your Persons, as well as to the whole Kingdom, upon the King's untimely death, will proceed from a confusion and want of some eminent and interessed person, whom you may trust to Lead you up against a *French* and *Popish* Army: for which purpose no person is fitter than his Grace the Duke of *Monmouth*, as well for quality, courage and conduct, as for that his Life and Fortune depends upon the same bottom with yours: he will stand by you, therefore ought you to stand by him."[3]

Dryden chose to undercut this advantage of Monmouth in two ways. One was to suggest that his military reputation was simply that: reputation, a name, without much substance behind it. This he did in the early lines of the poem, as we have seen, by moving from supposedly acknowledged bravery (line 18) to an equation of it with "Renown" (line 23), and then by suggesting that it was secondary (at best) to another quality:

> In Peace the thoughts of War he coud remove   [25]
> And seem'd as he were only born for love.

The other method was to point to the danger inherent in Monmouth's military actions. Accordingly when Dryden reintroduces him, at line 221, it is as "Warlike *Absolon*," and he concludes his description of Monmouth's illicit progress through the West of England by saying, having shown Shaftesbury's scheme behind it:

> Thus, in a Pageant Show, a Plot is made;
> And Peace it self is War in Masquerade.
>
> (ll. 751-52)

What there was of military prowess about Monmouth could be used to start another civil war, and of that kind of political disturbance Dryden's moderate readers had had more than enough.

Monmouth had been popular with the populace before his exploit in Scotland, and that increased the adulation. When in November of 1679 he returned to London against his father's command, he was received enthusiastically by the crowds in the street. The aristocratic Charles Hatton, writing in a private letter, described his reception thus:

[2] See, for example, *DNB*, XVII, 968.
[3] [Charles Blount], *An Appeal from the Country to the City*, p. 25.

... yᵉ bells in all churches rung all yᵉ morning incessantly, and bonnefires presently kindled in severall places, and great acclamations in all streets: 'Joyful news to England, yᵉ Duke of Monmouth return'd!' I say not this by hearsay from others, for I heard those expressions and saw yᵉ bonnefires. The truth is, it is very difficult to expresse fully yᵉ prodigious acclamations of yᵉ people, nor can any one credit them who wase not an eye and eare witness. Last night ther wase more bonnefires, I am confident, then ever wase on any occasion since those for yᵉ restoration of his Maᵗʸ. I seriously protest I am most confident yᵗ there wase above 60 betwixt Temple Bar and Charing Cross. The rabble being very numerous stopp'd all coaches, even my Lᵈ Chancelor's, and wou'd not let him pass till he cry'd: 'God bless yᵉ Duke of Monmouth!' They made most other personns come out of their coaches and cry: 'God bless yᵉ Duke of Monmouth!' And to severall personns they offer'd kennel-water, and told them they must drinke the Duke's health in yᵗ, or pay for better liquor. I mention what fires I saw, and I am very credibly inform'd yᵗ in most other streets ther wase as many.[4]

Some Tory pamphleteers tried to dismiss the enthusiasm and the bonfires as belonging merely to "the shouting Rabble," "the wild herd," "the Giddy-headed *Mobile*."[5] Dryden modified that approach: he ignored the bonfires, as he did Monmouth's conduct in Scotland, but still emphasized that the basis of Monmouth's popularity was in fact, as the root meaning of the word indicated, the populace, the plebeians, the mob. Shaftesbury "Would keep him still depending on the Crowd" (line 225). Monmouth himself asks why should he "Turn Rebell, and run Popularly Mad" (line 336), and, when he does, he sets out to "Popularly prosecute the Plot" (line 490).

But Monmouth's popularity was still very real and very dangerous if taken seriously; so Dryden used another approach as well. The most obvious manifestation of that popularity was, of course, the praise showered on Monmouth. Could the validity of that praise and therefore the popularity it expressed be called into question? Yes, through exaggeration: if Dryden could exaggerate the praise to a ludicrous extreme, his moderate readers might see that the actual praise heaped on Monmouth was itself extreme and unwarranted. So Dryden has his Achitophel address the man who was a bastard by-blow, admittedly of the King, but also of a Welsh whore little better than an orange wench, in these terms:

> Auspicious Prince! at whose Nativity   [230]
> Some Royal Planet rul'd the Southern sky;
> Thy longing Countries Darling and Desire;

---

[4] *Correspondence of the Family of Hatton*, ed. E. M. Thompson, Camden Soc., n. s., v. 22 (London, 1878), I, 203-04. (Charles Hatton to Lord Hatton, 29 Nov. 1679).

[5] [Thomas D'Urfey], *The Progress of Honesty; Or, a View of a Court and City* (London: Hindmarsh, 1681), p. 12, and *A Seasonable Invitation for Monmouth to Return to Court*, p. 2.

> Their cloudy Pillar, and their guardian Fire:
> Their second *Moses*, whose extended Wand
> Shuts up the Seas, and shews the promis'd Land: [235]
> Whose dawning Day, in every distant age,
> Has exercis'd the Sacred Prophets rage:
> The Peoples Prayer, the glad Deviners Theam,
> The Young-mens Vision, and the Old mens Dream!
> Thee, *Saviour*, Thee, the Nations Vows confess;   [240]
> And, never satisfi'd with seeing, bless:
> Swift, unbespoken Pomps, thy steps proclaim,
> And stammering Babes are taught to lisp thy Name.

After that, who could take any fulsome praise of Monmouth seriously? Let the rabble rave: we know better.

But still Monmouth did more than receive praise from the London mob. He collected most alarming support from all sorts of people during his progress through the West of England. A Whig pamphlet provides a description which, though probably it should be somewhat discounted on the grounds of exaggeration, is full of graphic detail. Monmouth proceeded from one country-house to another, enjoying the hospitality of the wealthy gentry and nobility, and being welcomed by large crowds of commoners along the way. He was

caressed with the joyful Welcomes and Acclamations of the people, who came from all parts, 20 miles about, filling and lining the Hedges with Men, Women and Children, some going before, some following after for some miles in the High-ways, all the way, and incessantly with hearty and great shouts crying, God bless our King *Charles*, and God bless the Protestant Duke. Some Towns and Parishes expressed also their Country-respects in strewing their streets and ways thorough which he passed, with herbs and flowers, as was seen at *Ilchester*, and *Pithyton*, &c. In some places where no other better present could be expected or made, the honest kind Good-women with rustick sincerity presented to him bottles of Wine, which he courteously accepted and tasted. Some of these good Dames could not restrain their joys, but in their homely phrase call'd out to him thus, *Master, we are glad to see you, and you are welcome into our Country*. And then some caught hold of his Feet, some took him by the Hand, some by the Coat, but all cried, Welcome, welcome, no *Popery*, no *Popery*, &c. When he drew near to Esq; *Speaks* by 10 miles, he was met by 2000 persons on Horseback, who were so increast before they arrived at Mr. *Speaks*, that some conjectured they were in number near 20000, others said, they were many more.[6]

More alarming still to those who valued peace was the appearance, just outside Exeter,

of a company of brave stout young men, all clothed in linnen Wastcoats and Drawers, white and harmless, having not so much as a stick in their hand, but

---

[6] *A True Narrative of the Duke of Monmouth's Late Journey into the West* ... (London: Janeway, 1680), p. 2. The next quotation is from p. 3.

joining hands, their number was reputed to be 10 or 1200 (the least conjecture of them was 800) these met the Duke within 3 miles of the City, being put into order on a small round hill, and divided into two parts, and so attended the coming of the Duke, who when arrived rode up between them, and after rode round each company, who then united, and went hand in hand in their order, before the Duke into the City.

Certainly Dryden's moderate readers would be aware of the reception given Monmouth in the West, and probably also of the presence of those regimented youth. So Dryden was able again to use a double approach. Once more he exaggerated the popular praise which the plebeians had heaped on Monmouth in the West:

> The Croud, (that still believes their Kings oppress)
> With lifted hands their young *Messiah* bless:
> Who now begins his Progress to ordain;
> With Chariots, Horsemen, and a numerous train: [730]
> From East to West his Glories he displaies:
> And, like the Sun, the promis'd land survays.
> Fame runs before him, as the morning Star;
> And shouts of Joy salute him from afar:
> Each house receives him as a Guardian God;   [735]
> And Consecrates, the Place of his aboad:

Rather undiscerning about his merit, weren't they? But Dryden does something more in this particular passage than merely point to the lack of popular discernment.

One thing he does may answer a question that may well have been forming in the mind of twentieth-century readers: how does Dryden's mock-heroic treatment of Monmouth, through this kind of exaggerated praise for Monmouth as a second Moses and a new Messiah, differ from his earlier mock-heroic treatment of Charles, through the exaggerated description of the King's god-like power in procreating multitudinously? Can Monmouth really come off appreciably worse than his father, for would it not appear the Moses' robes fit Monmouth not much worse than God's fit Charles? With regard to the initial impression, I would have to agree that Charles and Monmouth appear pretty much on a par, and this parity of course points to the danger inherent in the rhetorical gambit Dryden is attempting. As the poem proceeds, Dryden will seek to rehabilitate Charles by reminding the reader that, after all, the King had been anointed with holy oil, he had been consecrated as God's vice-regent within the realm. As a private person Charles might well sin, but as God's appointed and anointed he remained a sacred officer in the exercise of his divine office. Dryden's contemporaries would remember Charles's counterpart, David himself, who, though sinning egregiously with Bathsheba (as we are reminded in line 710), remained the Lord's vice-regent in Israel. Monmouth, on the other hand, has in no way been anointed. His elevation to a dukedom was entirely secular, and his conduct has been both factious and subversive, threatening treason both national and filial. Moreover, the exaggerated praise of him, attributed to the populace in the passages we have been concerned with, rises in outrageousness and then descends abruptly into belittlement, even into bathos. After being hailed as a second Moses, Monmouth proceeds to receive the blasphemous titles of *Saviour* and *Messiah* (titles properly reserved, of course, for Christ) and approaches as glorious as the sun surveying the whole world. But then, among the country people, who ironically think they are doing him an honour, he is suddenly reduced, in "Each house," to "a Guardian God" (line 735), simply one of the many little Roman lares and penates who were said to protect individual houses. At bottom, in other words, Dryden reminds his readers that the praise of Monmouth, and the people's regard for him, is based on ignorance of character, political hysteria, and pagan superstition.

That ignorance extends to the true purpose of the progress Monmouth was making through the West, and the pointing out of the true purpose is Dryden's remaining method of dealing with his popularity:

> This moving Court, that caught the peoples Eyes,
> And seem'd but Pomp, did other ends disguise:
> *Achitophel* had form'd it, with intent
> To sound the depth, and fathom where it went:
> The Peoples hearts, distinguish Friends from Foes;
> And try their strength, before they came to blows:
> . . . .
> Thus, in a Pageant Show, a Plot is made;
> And Peace it self is War in Masquerade.
>
> (ll. 739-44, 751-52)

One incident in particular that occurred during the progress was calculated to persuade the English people of Monmouth's right to rule. *The Protestant (Domestick) Intelligence* for 7 January 1681 printed, as its first item, a report from Crookhorn in Somerset which was attested to by the minister of the parish, two captains, and six other worthies. It concerned a poor woman, twenty years old and named Elizabeth Parcet, who for many years had suffered from the King's Evil (scrofula), having four running sores in her right hand, two more on the arm, a "bunch" in her breast, and another sore in her left eye. Her mother would have liked to send her to London to be touched by the King (for the touch of the sovereign would cure the King's Evil), but she was simply too poor. She tried physicians in vain, and a visit to a seventh son—another source of cure—but likewise in vain.

But now, in this the Girls great extreamity, God the Great Physitian Dictates unto her, thus Languishing in her miserable, hopeless condition; what course to take, and what to do for a Cure, which was to go and touch the Duke of Monmouth. . . .

This she did when, during his progress through the country, he passed nearby.

. . . she prest in among a Croud of People, and caught him by the hand, his Glove being on, and she had a Glove likewise to cover her wounds, she not being herewith satisfied with this first attempt of touching his Glove only, but her mind was, she must touch some part of his bare skin; she waiting his coming forth, intended a second attempt: The poor Girl, thus betwixt hope and fear waited his motion, on a suddain was news of the Dukes coming, which she to be prepared, rent off her Glove that was clung to the sores in such haste, that broke her Glove, and brought away not only the Sores, but the Skin: The Dukes Glove, as providence would have it, the upper part hung down, so that his hand-wrest was bare: she prest on and caught him by the bare hand-wrest with her running hand: (saying, God bless your Greatness, and the Duke said God bless you) the Girl was not a little transported with her good success. . . .

As one might expect,

Her six running wounds in her hand and arm, in four or five days were dryed up, the bunch in her breast was dissolved in eight or ten days of which now is no sign: her eye that was given for lost, is now perfectly well, and the Girl in good health. . . .

The conclusion did not have to be stated: it was clear enough. The Duke of Monmouth had the true blood royal and was obviously not only legitimate but also the divinely chosen successor to the throne, whose right of succession had thus been made manifest by Providence. An unknown Tory pamphleteer replied in the best way possible—by parody. He began: "The Extraordinary Cure of the Kings-Evil, lately perform'd by his Grace the Duke of Monmouth, in his Western Progress, has no doubt alarm'd many people, and open'd the eyes of the most unbelieving, to see Heaven by this Miracle proclaim his Legitimacy, and God Almighty himself declare for The Black Box."[7] (This Black Box was reputedly the receptacle for the certificate of marriage between Charles and Monmouth's mother.) The pamphleteer then detailed a parallel cure for the King's Evil worked on one Jonathan Trott by Mrs. Fanshaw, who, being the uterine sister of the Duke of Monmouth, must have similar power. The writer went on to add a further touch: since it was well known that a lion would not harm a legitimate prince of the royal blood, the Duke of Monmouth was going to be shut up with one of the greatest lions in the Tower of London, so as to prove to all the world that he was not a bastard. After that kind of riposte, Dryden had no real need to deal with Monmouth's touching during his progress. But still he does, for the

[7] A True and wonderful Account of a Cure of the Kings-Evil, by Mrs. Fanshaw, Sister to his Grace the Duke of Monmouth ([London, 1681]), p. 1.

benefit of the more discerning of his readers. When in between the two speeches of Achitophel, Dryden elaborates on Absalom's ambition, he says, with tongue in cheek, that "Desire of Power"

> is of Cælestial Seed:
> In God 'tis Glory: And when men Aspire,
> 'Tis but a Spark too much of Heavenly Fire.
>
> (ll. 305-08)

He then refers to Absalom as

> Th' Ambitious Youth, too Covetous of Fame,
> Too full of Angells Metal in his Frame;
>
> (ll. 309-10)

Of course there is a pun on metal/mettle and there is also a use of mocking exaggeration in comparing Monmouth to an angel because of his ambition. But there is also a brilliant reference to the angel (or angel-noble), a gold coin minted from Edward IV to Charles I. A month after Dryden's poem appeared, a Whig writer likewise made a witty allusion through the word "angel." Referring to an incident in Numbers 22, in which the sight of the angel of the Lord made a donkey speak, he asked,

> If but one angel could make Balaam's ass
> Speak, then what may not many bring to pass?,

the "many" being the several angel coins paid to witnesses for swearing falsely against the Earl of Shaftesbury.[8] Dryden's allusion is even more penetrating, for, according to the *OED*, the angel "was the coin always presented to a patient 'touched' for the King's Evil. When it ceased to be coined, small medals having the same device were substituted for it, and were hence called *touch-pieces*." Being "too Covetous of Fame," Monmouth had exposed to Elizabeth Parcet that part of his frame found in his wrist, and so had proved, to moderate eyes, much too full of angel's medal. That Dryden should thus refer both to the original gold coin and to the lesser medal which was substituted for it, and apply both to Monmouth, was only appropriate, for, as well as being anxious to undercut the Duke's three political advantages, he was particularly concerned with showing what kind of man existed behind and within the ducal display.

So False Within

His pamphleteering colleagues who had attacked Monmouth, in one way or another, had been divided about what kind of man they had to deal with. One group presented him as a good man seduced into evil

---

[8] "Advice to the Painter: The Witnesses against Shaftesbury," ll. 39-40, in *Poems on Affairs of State*, II, 496.

ways. Thomas D'Urfey praised him liberally and then lamented,

> None Favour'd more, nor none more Great than he,
> Till Hells curst Agents caus'd his Sense to stray,
> Out of his once lov'd Path, his Loyal way . . . .[9]

Lord Halifax agreed and urged Monmouth to repent and "to throw himself at the king's feet."[10] And the author of another pamphlet went even farther: not only was Monmouth a good man seduced, not only should he repent and beg his father for forgiveness, but also he should tell his father "of any Trayterous Conspiracies against Him" and should "pour into His Ears all the Secrets of [the rebels'] *Cabals*."[11] Dryden took the middle road, stopping short of suggesting that Monmouth should inform against his colleagues. Instead, Dryden shows, dramatically, how his Absalom fell to the temptation of "Hells dire Agent" and then has his David express the wish that Absalom

> woud repent and live!
> How easie 'tis for Parents to forgive!
> With how few Tears a Pardon might be won
> From Nature, pleading for a Darling Son!
>
> (ll. 957-60)[12]

Some other pamphleteers looked only to the end product—the use made of Monmouth by Shaftesbury and others—and called the royal bastard such opprobrious terms as cully, tool, catspaw, and stalking horse. Dryden, through his narrator, made it plain that Monmouth was in fact all those things, but did not himself use the terms. Achitophel chose to manipulate the "Warlike *Absolon*" so that, when he was a king dependent on the crowd, kingly power might be "Drawn to the dregs of a Democracy" (lines 220-28). Accordingly the "Deluded *Absalom*" was then "made the Lure to draw the People down" into treason (lines 683 and 928). But Dryden, characteristically, also had it both ways, for, although he was careful not to present any opprobrious terms through his narrator, he did put them in the mouth of "God-like *David*." When the King makes his pronouncement at the end of the poem (lines 965-68), Absalom/Monmouth is there dismissed not only as a gull, a "Politician's Tool," and an outright fool, but also—and perhaps the most damning of all—as "the People's Brave"—"brave" being a variant of "bravo," which meant then a bully and a hired assassin: and notice who hires him—the "People," the populace, the mob.

[9] *Progress of Honesty*, p. 11.

[10] Halifax, *A Seasonable Address*, p. 232.

[11] *A Seasonable Invitation for Monmouth to Return to Court*, p. 2.

[12] These lines, given here in the form presented in *Works*, II, 34, were not in the first edition. Professor Dearing argues that they were probably in the manuscript and the first proof: see *Works*, II, 411-12.

At least one pamphleteer took an even harsher view of Monmouth. To him the royal duke was "A Fool by Nature, and a Knave by Custom grown, / A Gay *Fop-Monarch*."[13] This actually, for all the indirection of allegory and frequent elevation of diction, is the evaluation of the man that Dryden, too, presents. The quality of being *Fop-Monarch* he displayed in the opening lines of the poem. The other qualities, of Fool and Knave, he lets Monmouth appear to reveal for himself through the dramatic character of Absalom.

Various admissions which Absalom makes in his speeches prepare the reader for passing judgement. David, he admits, rules well:

> Good, Gracious, Just, observant of the Laws;
> . . . .
> Mild, Easy, Humble, Studious of our Good;
> Enclin'd to Mercy, and averse from Blood.
> (ll. 319, 325-26)

The lawful successor, Absalom admits further,

> Of every Royal Vertue stands possest;
> . . . .
> His Mercy even the'Offending Crowd will find,
> For sure he comes of a Forgiving Kind.
> (ll. 355, 359-60)

Similarly Absalom listens to Achitophel admit that he himself has been the cause of David's troubles and will be the cause of more: he is the one who has made the lawful successor disliked (lines 401-04), and he will "ply [David] with new Plots" or "plunge him deep in some Expensive War" so that he must give "the Remains of Kingship" in return for money from the Sanhedrin (lines 389-96). Absalom personally has no right or reason to rebel. The King's

> Favour leaves me nothing to require;
> Prevents my Wishes, and outruns Desire.
> What more can I expect while *David* lives,   [345]
> All but his Kingly Diadem he gives;
> And that: But there he Paus'd; then Sighing, said,
> Is Justly Destin'd for a Worthier Head.

Then why does he rebel?

One reason is that he is a born fool. What other quality would allow him to accept Achitophel's argument that he should join the rebel cause? Achitophel says that the rebels abhor kings (line 290) and cry for a commonwealth (line 292); for this reason Absalom as a prince of royal blood should join them and become a king with "limited

---

[13] "The Loyal Scot" (dated by Luttrell 5 Apr. 1682), in *A Choice Collection of 180 Loyal Songs*, p. 191.

Command" (lines 293-99)—though how one could be the king at all of a commonwealth ruled by people who abhor kings is a question obviously raised but just as obviously not answered. Nor is this the only piece of illogic which the foolishness of Absalom accepts. To the people freely thronging to see him on his Western tour he says, "Now all your Liberties a spoil are made" (line 704), and asks them, as they look at him moving freely before them, "Behold a Banisht man" (line 700).

Little wonder that the images used for him are full of temptation, falsity, and degeneracy. Achitophel begins his tempting argument, after his egregious parallel of Absalom with Christ, in a way that reminds one of Satan tempting Christ. Milton's Satan urged the Son of God not to

> deprive
> All Earth her wonder at thy acts, thyself
> The fame and glory . . .
>> (*Paradise Regained*, III, 23-25),

but instead to seize the rule of Rome (and with it all the world)—from, incidentally, a king who was "Old, and lascivious, and from *Rome* retired . . . His horrid lusts in private to enjoy" (IV, 90-108). Correspondingly, Dryden's satanic character asks Absalom,

> How long wilt thou the general Joy detain,
> Starve, and defraud the People of thy Reign?   [245]
> Content ingloriously to pass thy days
> Like one of Vertues Fools that feeds on Praise;
> Till thy fresh Glories, which now shine so bright,
> Grow Stale and Tarnish with our daily sight.

and then urges him to seize

> Not barren Praise alone, that Gaudy Flower,
> Fair only to the sight, but solid Power:
>> (ll. 297-98)

Milton's Satan urges Christ to emulate David:

> . . . thy Kingdom though foretold
> By Prophet or by Angel, unless thou
> Endeavour, as thy Father *David* did,
> Thou never shalt obtain . . . .
>> (III, 351-54)

Not surprisingly, Dryden's Achitophel remarks to Absalom:

> Had thus Old *David*, from whose Loyns you spring,
> Not dar'd, when Fortune call'd him, to be King,
> At *Gath* an Exile he might still remain,
> And heavens Anointing Oyle had been in vain.   [265]
> Let his successfull Youth your hopes engage,

In Milton's earlier epic, Satan's temptation of Eve worked round a tree which, with its fruit, served as a symbol of obedience, temptation, and fall. Similarly Achitophel urges upon Absalom the argument,

> Believe me, Royal Youth, thy Fruit must be   [250]
> Or gather'd Ripe, or rot upon the Tree.

In the same speech of Achitophel there reverberates a famous passage from a speech of another rebel against royal authority. When, four years earlier, Dryden had rewritten Shakespeare's *Antony and Cleopatra* for the Restoration stage and called it *All for Love*, he on various occasions chose to parallel certain Shakespearean passages quite closely. When he did so, he usually followed the same line of thought as Shakespeare's and used a few of his key words (sometimes slightly altered in the context), but provided alternative imagery, of the same general category but a different example, and often elaborated to greater length than Shakespeare's.[14] Consequently an alert reader of Dryden's polemical poem, who had attended a performance of *All for*

---

[14] Consider, for example, the speech of Ventidius in Act I that begins "Does the mute sacrifice upbraid the priest?" (ll. 168-79 in John Dryden, *All for Love*, ed. N. J. Andrew [London: Benn, 1975], pp. 28-29). It continues, referring to Antony and then, in the "she," to Cleopatra:

> He knows him not his executioner.
> Oh, she has decked his ruin with her love,
> Led him in golden bands to gaudy slaughter. . . .

These lines pick up 3.10.18-21 of *Antony and Cleopatra*, repeating the word "ruin" and replacing the image of a mallard with that of an unspecified animal being led to slaughter:

> She once being loofed,
> The noble ruin of her magic, Antony,
> Claps on his sea-wing, and (like a doting mallard)
> Leaving the fight in heighth, flies after her.

(The "golden bands" could also parallel Antony's image, "My heart was to thy rudder tied by th' strings, / And thou shouldst tow me after"—3.11.57-58.) Ventidius pursues his slaughter image by saying "And made perdition pleasing," which echoes Enobarbus' comment about Cleopatra:

> For vilest things
> Become themselves in her, that the holy priests
> Bless her when she is riggish.
>
> (2.2.239-41)

Ventidius continues:

> . . . she has left him
> The blank of what he was.
> I tell thee, eunuch, she has quite unmanned him.

These lines continue to reflect Shakespeare's description of Antony's flight, picking up the ideas of manhood and violation in particular:

> I never saw an action of such shame;
> Experience, manhood, honor, ne'er before
> Did violate so itself.
>
> (3.10.22-24)

Love (or read the play) in the intervening years, would have been able to recognize that Dryden was doing the same sort of thing with the famous speech of Brutus:

> There is a tide in the affairs of men,
> Which, taken at the flood, leads on to fortune;
> Omitted, all the voyage of their life
> Is bound in shallows and in miseries.
>
> *(Julius Caesar,* 4.3.218-21)

Dryden has Achitophel pick up the word "fortune" twice, the first time modifying it to "Some lucky Revolution of their Fate," pick up "taken" and "Omitted" and modify them to "if we watch and guide with Skill," and, in the place of the tidal image, offer the alternative motion of Fortune rolling (presumably on a ball) down "a smooth Descent," the whole being elaborated thus:

> Heav'n, has to all allotted, soon or late,
> Some lucky Revolution of their Fate:
> Whose Motions, if we watch and guide with Skill,

In the rest of his speech, Ventidius parallels the opening speech of Shakespeare's play, mixing images from its two parts. Shakespeare had written:

> Take but good note, and you shall see in him
> The triple pillar of the world transformed
> Into a strumpet's fool.
>
> (1.1.11-13)

Dryden has Ventidius pick up the concepts of "transformed," the joint ruler of the world, and the woman's dupe, and rephrase them thus:

> Can any Roman see and know him now,
> Thus altered from the lord of half mankind,
> Unbent, unsinewed, made a woman's toy....

The words "unbent" and "unsinewed" derive from the earlier part of Shakespeare's opening speech, as do the rest of Ventidius' lines. Here are Ventidius':

> Shrunk from the vast extent of all his honours,
> And cramped within a corner of the world?

These are the key phrases from Shakespeare:

> ... those his goodly eyes
> That o'er the files and musters of the war
> Have glowed like plated Mars, now bend, now turn
> The office and devotion of their view
> Upon a tawny front. His captain's heart,
> Which in the scuffles of great fights hath burst
> The buckles on his breast, reneges all temper....
>
> (1.1.2-8)

Similar methods of paraphrase can be found on comparing the dying speeches of Dryden's Antony in Act V (ll. 387-97, 401-02), beginning "But grieve not, while thou stay'st," with these lines from *Antony and Cleopatra:* 4.15.51-55; 4.15.19-21; 4.14.50-54; 4.15.20-21. Looser parallels are found on comparing (a) Cleopatra's speech in Act II (ll. 327-40). "How shall I plead my cause," with *Ant.* 1.3.32-39; (b) Cleopatra's speech in Act II (ll. 408-18), "No; you shall go," with *Ant.* 1.3.88-91; 1.5.50-61; (c) Cleopatra's speech in Act V (ll. 458-63), "Dull that thou art!" with *Ant.* 5.2.227-29; 5.2.282-87.

> (For humane Good depends on humane Will,)   [255]
> Our Fortune rolls, as from a smooth Descent,
> And, from the first Impression, takes the Bent:
> But, if unseiz'd, she glides away like wind;
> And leaves repenting Folly far behind.

On recognizing the paraphrastic allusion, Dryden's reader would have remembered that Shakespeare's speaker was a regicide and, moreover, that Brutus not only presented his argument in the midst of civil war but also used his speech, unwittingly, to lead his forces on to disaster at Philippi. The potential parallel would not have been lost on Dryden's readers. Nor would the parallels with Milton's Satan, especially since *Paradise Lost* had appeared only fourteen years before and *Paradise Regained* only ten. Actually these parallels to the great tempters and tempted of literature serve to show how doubly duped Absalom really is: not only does he fall to temptation, but he also eagerly accepts the form and phrasing of temptation suitable to persons much greater than he—Brutus (who tempted himself), Eve, and Christ.

Having thus fallen to temptation, Absalom is then "made the Lure to draw the People down" (line 928), and the image of an object insidiously attractive on the outside but falsely dangerous within fits well with the other images of falsity used for Absalom. He is the false Messiah (lines 230-40), the false sun, morning star, and guardian god (lines 732-35); he is the false prodigal son (because unrepentant) and the false Samson (because destructive in the wrong cause—line 955). He is altogether like the medal of Dryden's next poem: "so golden to the sight, / So base within" (lines 8-9). To this falsity is added a still-farther-going degeneracy. Absalom's ambition, though sprung "of Cælestial Seed," is still "on Earth"—where Absalom is, after all—"a Vitious Weed" (lines 305-06). When in fact he turns rebel and runs popularly mad, he is similar to those he leads, about whom he has said, "The *Dog-star* heats their Brains to this Disease" (lines 333-36). And about his birth he himself asks, recoiling from his "Mothers Mold," "Why am I Scanted by a Niggard Birth?" (lines 360-69).

All imagistic themes of falsity, temptation, and degeneracy coalesce in a literary allusion that would have particularly appealed to those of Dryden's readers who remembered their schoolday Vergil. When Absalom himself turns seducer and prepares to address his traitorous speech to the people in the West of England, he is described in these words:

> Thus, form'd by Nature, furnish'd out with Arts,
> He glides unfelt into their secret hearts:
> Then with a kind compassionating look,
> And sighs, bespeaking pity ere he spoak: [695]

Few words he said; but easy those and fit:
More slow than Hybla drops, and far more sweet.

"Hybla" is of course a classical allusion, referring generally to a hill in
Sicily, often mentioned by poets for its thyme, bees, and sweet honey.
But one classical line in particular, if it is recognized as being referred
to, adds greatly to the satiric effect of Dryden's line and explains why it
is used as the climax to the introduction of Absalom's seductive
speech. In Vergil's *Eclogue VII*, Corydon, taking part in a singing con-
test, says (line 37), "Nerine Galatea, thymo mihi dulcior
Hyblae"—Nerean Galatea, to me more sweet (*dulcior*) than Hybla's
thyme. The verbal parallel is close, and in itself innocuous, but the
satiric point is in the speaker, Corydon. He it is who sings the whole of
the second Eclogue, which Byron was later to refer to as "that horrid
one" (rhyming nicely with "Corydon"),[15] an eclogue of pederastic passion that was directed at a young shepherd boy and that was undoubtedly notorious among English schoolboys.[16] There is even a further
connection between the line of Vergil Dryden has alluded to and the
infamous second Eclogue: the line addresses Galatea, and the second
Eclogue was modelled on two idylls of Theocritus, one being concerned with the cruelty of Galatea.[17] The point is of course that Absalom, in all his manly beauty and in all his sweet-appearing discourse,
is really like Corydon, handsome without and blessed with arts of
speech, but inside the vilest kind of seducing wretch.

Evil, in fact, sits at the heart of Absalom. This is made plain in his
dramatic situations. He accepts blasphemous flattery, he accepts
treasonable arguments presented in an obviously satanic way, and he
himself, as part of his filial treason, uses those arguments on others. In
doing this last, in going about the West of England professing to be the
defender of the people's liberties against assaults on them sanctioned
by his father, Dryden's Absalom is doing what the Biblical Absalom did
when he stationed himself by the gate of the city and proclaimed, "Oh
that I were made judge in the land, that every man which hath any suit
or cause might come unto me, and I would do him justice!" In this way
"Absalom stole the hearts of the men of Israel" from David (2 Sam.
15:1-6). It comes as no surprise when we see Dryden's Absalom acting
in this way against his father, for we have seen him, as mentioned in
the last chapter, listening without objection to Achitophel's urging that
he take advantage of his father's current weakness and that he pay no
heed to his father's love for him, since that love is only

---

[15] *Don Juan*, 1.42.7-8.
  [16] It is evident that English schoolboys were frequently required to learn the *Eclogues*
by heart (Foster Watson, *The English Grammar Schools* [London: Cass, 1968], p. 372).
  [17] *Virgil*, tr. H. R. Fairclough, Loeb Classical Library (London: Heinemann, 1965), I,
11n.

> Nature's trick to Propagate her Kind,
> Our fond Begetters, who woud never dye,   [425]
> Love but themselves in their Posterity.

Having accepted this argument, Absalom then has the audacity to accept the advice "Urge now your Piety, your Filial Name" (line 419) and
to say to the people in the West:

> My Father, whom with reverence yet I name,
> . . . .
> He gives, and let him give my right away:
> But why should he his own, and yours betray?
> . . . .
> Take then my tears (with that he wip'd his Eyes)
> 'Tis all the Aid my present power supplies:
> No Court Informer can these Arms accuse,
> These Arms may Sons against their Fathers use,
> (ll. 707, 713-14, 717-20)

The way Absalom sees himself is of particular interest. He evidently looks upon himself as the equivalent of one of the heroes in
Dryden's own heroic tragedies: a man with a soul born to empire and
sway, regardless of whatever other circumstances may appear to stand
in his way. But when he comes to express this view, we see him doubly
undercut, for, not only have we come to realize that he really does not
have the soul for the position, but also he chooses to repine about his
birth instead of vaulting over it as an Almanzor would:

> Yet oh that Fate Propitiously Enclind,
> Had rais'd my Birth, or had debas'd my Mind;
> To my large Soul, not all her Treasure lent,   [365]
> And then Betray'd it to a mean Descent.
> I find, I find my mounting Spirits Bold,
> And *David*'s Part disdains my Mothers Mold.
> Why am I Scanted by a Niggard Birth,
> My Soul Disclaims the Kindred of her Earth: [370]
> And made for Empire, Whispers me within;
> Desire of Greatness is a Godlike Sin.

Yet, of course, sin it is. And he is rather ungentlemanly in disdaining
his "Mothers Mold." But the choice line is of course "Had rais'd my
Birth, or had debas'd my Mind": he evidently has no idea, as we do, of
just how debased that mind is already. Actually, as with many other
aspects of the poem, King David at the end puts the whole matter of
Absalom's character and ambition in the right perspective:

> Had God ordain'd his fate for Empire born.
> He woud have given his Soul another turn:
> (ll. 963-64)

In Achitophel Dryden has shown Shaftesbury as ambitious and cunning; in Absalom he has shown Monmouth as ambitious and stupid. Outwardly Shaftesbury is insignificant, but inwardly astoundingly satanic; outwardly Monmouth is most prepossessing, but inwardly, though evil, he is mean. These two men Dryden has presented as the chief leaders of the Whigs: what about the other leaders? What kind of men are they? Will the moderate reader be likely to support them or the King?

6

ROGUES' GALLERY

From the numerous leaders of the Whigs, Dryden chose eight more to depict for the benefit of his moderate and uncommitted readers. Three of these he chose to present at full satiric length and the others in brief sketches just as satiric. His reasons for selecting these eight and for emphasizing the three were of course in themselves polemical and satiric, as will be seen as we proceed. But what Dryden says about each is of primary concern (and provides the reason for selection); so we can do no better than follow his example in observing that "In the first Rank of these did Zimri stand."

Zimri: So Full of Mercury

George Villiers, the second Duke of Buckingham, became a legend in his own lifetime.

He was a man blessed with considerable intelligence. Perhaps in part because he had been raised within the royal family of Charles I, he had not only a lively wit and perspicacity, but also the ability to express pithily what he had observed. He summed up Charles II and James in a way which a contemporary, who knew the brothers well, said was "severe" but "true": "The king could see things if he would, and the duke would see things if he could."[1] He often turned this ability to a variety of entertainments. In 1671 he wrote and produced *The Rehearsal*, a play that mocked heroic tragedies in general and Dryden's in particular—as no doubt Dryden remembered when he wrote his poem. To amuse the pretty but somewhat childish Miss Stuart (the current object of Charles's affection), Buckingham built card-castles with her, related gossip, composed comic ditties, and mimicked the absurdities of other people.[2] He could play the buffoon

[1] *Burnet's History of My Own Time*, ed. Osmund Airy, I (Oxford: Clarendon, 1897), 295.

[2] Anthony Hamilton, *Memoirs of the Comte de Gramont*, tr. Peter Quennell, ed. C. H. Hartmann (New York: Dutton, 1930), p. 138.

extremely well. When one of the court ladies, Lady Muskerry, became pregnant, she had the misfortune to protrude somewhat lopsidedly. In order to appear before the court and go dancing, she on one occasion inserted into her dress a small cushion to round out her figure. As she danced, "the pillow, becoming detached without her noticing it, fell out plump in the middle of the first dance; whereat, the Duke of Buckingham, who was following on her traces, tenderly picked it up, wrapped it in the skirts of his coat and, imitating the puling cries of a new-born babe, went among the Maids of Honour, asking after a wet-nurse for poor little Muskerry."[3]

This same man could and on occasion did apply his intelligence to the affairs of state. In a pamphlet he wrote, anonymously, to answer a book by Slingsby Bethel, Buckingham argued cogently and with at least a modicum of grace on matters political and economic.[4] And the following passage from a speech he made in the House of Lords, presumably on the Test Act, will speak for itself: "It is certainly a very uneasie kind of Life to any man, that has either Christian Charity, Good Nature, or Humanity, to see his Fellow-subjects daily abused, devested of their Liberties and Birthrights, and miserably thrown out of their Possessions and Freeholds, only because they cannot agree with some others in Opinions and Niceties of Religion, to which their Consciences will not give them leave to assent, and which, even by the consent of those who would impose them, are no way necessary to Salvation."[5]

Unfortunately this man of great ability proved most unstable. Not only was he a blab who had to tell all, but he could never, according to contemporary testimony, "fix his thoughts" or "govern his estate."[6] Even Sir John Reresby, to whom Buckingham had been a patron and who declared that Buckingham was the "finest gentleman of person and wit" he ever saw, had to admit that he "could not be long serious or mind business."[7]

He indulged in many diversions. "He was the most accomplished man of the age in riding, dancing, and fencing."[8] He pursued, at times frantically, "pleasure, frolic, and extravagant diversions."[9] Not surprisingly these last included "a monstrous course of studied immoralities

---

[3] Hamilton, p. 275.

[4] *A Letter to Sir Thomas Osborn . . . upon the reading of a book, called, The Present Interest of England Stated* (London, 1672).

[5] Quoted in John Toland, *The Art of Governing by Partys* (London: Lintott, 1701), p. 16.

[6] Burnet, I, 478, 182.

[7] *Memoirs of Sir John Reresby*, ed. Andrew Browning (Glasgow: Jackson, 1936), p. 24.

[8] Joseph Spence, *Anecdotes*, ed. James M. Osborn (Oxford: Clarendon, 1966), No. 666.

[9] Burnet, I, 182.

of the worst kind."[10] He was accused by private citizens of sodomy, but turned the tables on them and led to their conviction for conspiracy and perjury.[11] But he went a-whoring (heterosexually) so assiduously that he frequently required the standard treatment for syphilis —mercury, a fact which allowed Burnet to sum up his immorality and his instability in one witty sentence: "He was so full of mercury that he could not fix long on any friendship or to any design."[12] Or, indeed, to any hostility, for twice he accepted a challenge to a duel and failed to show up, but each time he did report his challenger to the authorities so that he might be punished.

Curiously, he was able to stick with two things for a fair length of time. He indulged in chemistry—or more properly alchemy, spending a great deal on his laboratory, equipment, and supplies, and thinking for some years that he was very near to finding the philosopher's stone—the way to change base metals into gold.[13] The other lasting attachment was to the Countess of Shrewsbury, his paramour, whose husband he mortally wounded in a duel while, legend had it, the Countess (disguised as a page) stood by, holding Buckingham's horse and watching him run her husband through. So constant was he in living with her illicitly, in fact, that the House of Lords required each of them to give bonds of £10,000 that they would not cohabit again. Admittedly, the Lords may have been somewhat exercised by the fact that the illicit couple had had the temerity to bury a bastard son of theirs, with full solemnity, within the sacred confines of Westminster Abbey and under the title of the Earl of Coventry.

Strangest of all his instabilities was his behaviour towards Louise de Keroualle. He found her in France and made her his protégée with the intent of establishing her as the reigning mistress of Charles, in the place of the then paramour-in-chief, the Duchess of Cleveland. (In time she became mistress regnant and received the title of Duchess of Portsmouth.) Making arrangements to send her to England, Buckingham "sent her with a part of his equipage to Dieppe, and said he would presently follow. But he, who was the most inconstant and forgetful of all men, never thought of her more, but went to England by the way of Calais. So Montague, then ambassador at Paris, hearing of this, sent over for a yaught for her, and sent some of his servants to wait on her, and to defray her charge till she was brought to Whitehall: and then Lord Arlington [the political rival of Buckingham] took care of her. So the Duke of Buckingham lost the merit he might have pretended to, and

[10] Burnet, I, 477.
[11] Luttrell, I, 45.
[12] Burnet, I, 477.
[13] Burnet, I, 182.

brought over a mistress [for the King] whom his own strange conduct threw into the hands of his enemies."[14]

He was just as unstable in the more formal kind of politics. In fact his career contained even more fluctuations than Shaftesbury's and what follows is the merest summary. At the age of 15 he served under Prince Rupert in a military engagement against the Parliamentarians and for a few years accompanied and fought for Charles II. When Charles denied him supreme command of the royalist army (at the age of 23), he sulked and withdrew. Then he tried to marry the widowed Princess of Orange, and this attempt to bull his way into the royal family produced a complete estrangement from the King. In 1657 he left the continent (where he had been in voluntary exile with Charles) and went to Cromwellian England, where he married the only daughter of Fairfax, one of the highest officials in the Commonwealth government. Cromwell was not particularly pleased and Buckingham came close to being executed.

When Charles was restored, Buckingham was again received into his councils and got back his extensive estates which the Commonwealth had confiscated—so extensive were they that they produced an income of £26,000 a year and he was said to be the richest man in England. While loosely a member of the government, Buckingham conspired against the current Lord Chancellor, Clarendon, and for a while Charles had Buckingham placed under arrest and confined to the Tower. When Clarendon fell, Buckingham became the predominant adviser to Charles, though he held no high office—except the mastership of the horse, which he had purchased from the Duke of Albemarle. While in power Buckingham intrigued and feuded and slowly slipped from eminence. When the House of Commons attacked him in 1674 and in his defence he revealed governmental secrets which it was ungentlemanly of him to reveal, Charles dismissed him.

Thereupon Buckingham made the most startling change of his life. "He reformed his way of living, was seen in church with his wife, kept regular hours, and began to pay his debts."[15] At the same time he joined the opposition to the government and was received by the country group as one of their leaders. Not that he got along well with the other leaders of the opposition: he avoided supporting Monmouth, possibly because as a descendant of the Plantagenets (he said) he considered himself a more suitable pretender than the Protestant Duke. Yet at the same time this proud aristocrat attempted to have himself chosen a member of the common council of London, so as to expand his power base.[16] He failed in this attempt, as in almost all others, and by 1681 he had separated himself from the rest of the opposition.

[14] Burnet, I, 599.

[15] Charles Harding Firth, "Villiers, George," *DNB*, XX, 342.

[16] "The Life of James the Second, Written by Himself," in James Macpherson,

To complete the legend of this astonishing man, it must be recorded that in a play he wrote in 1683 he sneered at Shaftesbury, that shortly after James succeeded to the throne in 1685 he retired to his country house ("worn to a thread with whoring"), and that when he died in 1687—not in a country inn as rumour (and later Pope) had it, but in the house of one of his tenants, nothing at all was left of the estates that had once made him the richest man in England.

Even without this completion of the legend, it is obvious that Buckingham was England's own whirling dervish. As such he presented two particular problems to Dryden: how, as an artist, could he capture and hold the essence of this constantly shifting man, and how, as a satiric polemicist, could he apply whatever he captured to the purpose of denigrating the Whigs?

What Dryden in the end did succeed in achieving can be best appreciated if we first look at what two other authors attempted when dealing with Buckingham. The first, anonymous and writing in 1679, used the popular litany form of attack: "From such-and-such, dear Lord, deliver us." What follows is about half of the poem: the rest is of the same kind but filled so full of obscure topical references that it would be meaningless without extensive annotation.[17]

The Litany of the D. of B.

From a Sensual, Proud, Atheistical Life,
From Arming our Lacqueys with Pistol and Knife,
From Murthering the Husband and Whoring the Wife:
                    Libera nos.

From going Ambassadors only as Panders,
From Re-killing dead Kings with Monstrous Slanders,
From Betraying the Living in *Scotland* and *Flanders*:
                    Libera nos.

From a Wild Rambling no-where Abode,
Without Day or Night, nor at Home nor Abroad,
From a Prince to Unhorse us on *Dover* Road:
                    Libera nos.

From Crowning the Herse of our Babe of Adultery,
Interred among Kings by a Lord of the Prelacy,
Whom we got Cashier'd for Carnal Arsery:
                    Libera nos.

From Selling Land twice, ten thousand a year
All Spent, no Mortal can tell how, or where,
And then Reform Kingdoms as a Sanctifi'd Peer:
                    Libera nos.

Original Papers (London: Strahan, 1776), I, 112.

[17] The full text (a little different from the one offered here) and full annotation are available in *Poems on Affairs of State*, II, 192-99.

From Monstrous Sucking, till both Tongues have Blisters,
From making our Boasts of giving three Glisters,
By giving our Claps to three cheated Sisters:

Libera nos.

. . . .

From Wretched Pasquills against *Shadwel* and *Dryden*,
From Casting Nativities with Learned *Heyden*,
And Casting of Dollars at *Antwerp* and *Leyden*:

Libera nos.

. . . .

From being still Cheated by the same Undertakers,
By Levellers, Bawds, Saints, Chymists and Quakers,
Who make us Gold-Finders, and themselves Gold Makers:

Libera nos.

. . . .

From Mortally Hating all those that Love us,
From Mimical Acting all those Above us,
Till our Master at last is forc'd to Remove us;

Libera nos.

From Cringing to those we Scorn to Condemn,
In hopes to be made the Citizens Gem,
Who now Scorn us more than e're we did them:

Libera nos.

. . . .

This is not the actual ending, but that is just as sudden and illustrates the major artistic failing of the poem, for while the *Litany* does reflect a considerable amount of the whirligig variety of Buckingham, it fails to impose (or elicit) any artistic pattern—the author simply turns a tap, lets it run for some time, and then shuts it off.

The other author, Samuel Butler, chose as his vehicle the character sketch, which, being analytical by nature, offered some kind of artistic pattern to begin with. Butler opens by pointing to the disproportionate and unnatural qualities of his subject and illustrates these by the Duke's practice of turning night into day:

A Duke of Bucks

Is one that has studied the whole Body of Vice. His Parts are disproportionate to the whole, and like a Monster he has more of some, and less of others than he should have. He has pulled down all that Fabric that *Nature* raised in him, and built himself up again after a Model of his own. He has dam'd up all those Lights, that Nature made into the noblest Prospects of the World, and opened other little blind Loopholes backward, by turning Day into Night, and Night into Day.[18]

[18] Text from Samuel Butler, *Characters and Passages from Notebooks*, ed. A. R. Waller (Cambridge: Cambridge University Press, 1908), pp. 32-33. This character sketch was

Butler shifts to the related qualities of disease, extravagance, and excess, and illustrates again by the turning of night into day:

His Appetite to his Pleasures is diseased and crazy, like the Pica in a Woman, that longs to eat that, which was never made for Food, or a Girl in the Greensickness, that eats Chalk and Mortar. Perpetual Surfeits of Pleasure have filled his Mind with bad and vicious Humours (as well as his Body with a Nursery of Diseases) which makes him affect new and extravagant Ways, as being sick and tired with the Old. Continual Wine, Women, and Music put false Values upon Things, which by Custom become habitual, and debauch his Understanding so, that he retains no right Notion nor Sense of Things. And as the same Dose of the same Physic has no Operation on those, that are much used to it; so his Pleasures require a larger Proportion of Excess and Variety, to render him sensible of them. He rises, eats, and goes to Bed by the *Julian* Account, long after all others that go by the *new Stile*; and keeps the same Hours with Owls and the *Antipodes*.

Having repeated the motif of night into day, Butler elaborates on it:

He is a great Observer of the *Tartars* Customs, and never eats, till the great *Cham* having dined makes Proclamation, that all the World may go to Dinner. He does not dwell in his House, but haunts it, like an evil Spirit, that walks all Night to disturb the Family, and never appears by Day. He lives perpetually benighted, runs out of his Life, and loses his Time, as Men do their Ways in the Dark; and as blind Men are led by their Dogs, so is he governed by some mean Servant or other, that relates to his Pleasures. He is as inconstant as the Moon, which he lives under; and altho' he does nothing but advise with his Pillow all Day, he is as great a Stranger to himself, as he is to the rest of the World.

Having introduced the related quality of inconstancy, Butler elaborates on this, again illustrates by the turning of night into day, and for some unknown reason adds an ending that is really not an ending:

His Mind entertains all Things very freely, that come and go; but, like Guests and Strangers they are not welcome, if they stay long—This lays him open to all Cheats, Quacks, and Impostors, who apply to every particular Humour while it lasts, and afterwards vanish. Thus with St. *Paul*, tho' in a different Sense, he *dies daily*, and only lives in the Night. He deforms Nature, while he intends to adorn her, like *Indians*, that hang Jewels in their Lips and Noses. His Ears are perpetually drilled with a Fiddlestick. He endures Pleasures with less Patience, than other Men do their Pains.

This character sketch contains less of Buckingham's variety than does the *Litany*, but it does provide an analysis, an attempt to find something, some attribute, around which an artistic whole can be built. Unfortunately, the turning of night into day seems much too insignificant a phenomenon to serve that role. And as far as Dryden's purposes were concerned, neither previous work gave any indication

probably written between 1667 and 1669. It stayed in MS until 1759, but was probably circulated, especially among Tory readers such as Dryden.

of how to use the character of Buckingham against the Whigs: he seems far too singular a sport to be identified with anybody else.

In the light of these two only partially successful attempts to come to grips with the essence of the constantly shifting Buckingham, Dryden's achievement in handling his character sketch can be better appreciated. He begins, after calling his subject Zimri, by fastening on the immense variety within the man:

> A man so various, that he seem'd to be   [545]
> Not one, but all Mankinds Epitome.

Potentially admirable, that; so immediately we are shown the perversity and then the inconstancy of that variety:

> Stiff in Opinions, always in the wrong;
> Was every thing by starts, and nothing long:
> But, in the course of one revolving Moon,
> Was Chymist, Fidler, States-Man, and Buffoon: [550]
> Then all for Women, Painting, Rhiming, Drinking;
> Besides ten thousand freaks that dy'd in thinking.
> Blest Madman, who coud every hour employ,
> With something New to wish, or to enjoy!

Here is represented the magnificent clutter of Buckingham's variety—a clutter which the *Litany* was able to reflect in part, but it is here also presented in such a way that belittling judgement is quietly passed upon it. The serious chemist is immediately reduced to the fiddler, the statesman to the buffoon. Zimri's literary activity ("Rhiming") is no more important, to him, than his women, his drinking, and his painting—whether of canvas or his face. And the images complete the diminution. From mere association with the moon (and hence lunacy), Zimri is moved through the giddiness of "ten thousand freaks" (causeless changes of mind) to the overt but still light-handed tag "Blest Madman."

Within all his variety, within all his constant changing, however, there was one thing lacking—the middle ground (so dear to moderates):

> Rayling and praising were his usual Theams;   [555]
> And both (to show his Judgment) in Extreams:
> So over Violent, or over Civil,
> That every man, with him, was God or Devil.

In his personal affairs he was spendthrift, but not only that—he was constantly taken:

> In squandring Wealth was his peculiar Art:
> Nothing went unrewarded, but Desert.   [560]
> Begger'd by Fools, whom still he found too late:
> He had his Jest, and they had his Estate.

In each couplet, the last part of the second line acts like a delayed action bomb, exploding back in the direction we have just come; and its percussion goes on reverberating in the rhyming words, especially "too late" and "Estate." In his political activity Zimri was just as ludicrously ineffectual:

> He laught himself from Court, then sought Releif
> By forming Parties, but coud ne're be Chief:
> For, spight of him, the weight of Business fell   [565]
> On *Absalom* and wise *Achitophel*:
> Thus, wicked but in will, of means bereft,
> He left not Faction, but of that was left.

In speaking of this character sketch, Dryden himself said, "I avoided the mention of great crimes, and applied myself to the representing of blindsides, and little extravagancies...."[19] Actually, while the blindsides are certainly represented, one wonders how "little" are the extravagancies of Zimri, and there really is mention made of great crimes—through the Biblical name Zimri. In the Old Testament there are two Zimris: the one mentioned in Numbers 25:6-15 is a prototype of an adulterer, and so for many of Dryden's readers Buckingham's affair with the Countess of Shrewsbury would be brought to mind; the other Zimri, of 1 Kings 16:9, was captain of half of Israel's chariots (roughly parallel to Buckingham's being Master of the Horse) and committed treason against his king. If any of Dryden's readers were willing to extrapolate wittily (as men of the Restoration often did), they could then proceed from the captain of the chariots to the Master of the Horse and from there homonymically (as Falstaff did[20]) to Master of the Whores, thereby achieving an allusion to Buckingham's notorious sexual licence.

Without actually using Burnet's witty image, "so full of mercury," Dryden has shown in Buckingham the essence of mercurial inconstancy. At the same time he has kept his description of that inconstancy from flying apart by threading through it a progressive development from wealth to poverty. Zimri begins as a man so crowded with variety that he seems "all Mankinds Epitome." Soon, however, leaks appear: "ten thousand freaks ... dy'd," after all, "in thinking"; all the middles between the various extremes are found to be missing: he squanders wealth until he has lost his estate; and all that remains to him, his political support, likewise evaporates, and he is left "wicked but in will, of means bereft."

There is another device Dryden uses to provide order within disorder, a device which is even more pervasive and which deserves an

---

[19] *A Discourse concerning the Original and Progress of Satire* (1693) in *Essays of John Dryden*, ed. W. P. Ker (New York: Russell, 1961), II, 93.

[20] When in *1 Henry IV* Prince Hal says, "I have procured thee, Jack, a charge of foot," Falstaff replies, "I would it had been of horse" (3.3.178-79).

even closer look, both because of its use here and because its use here
will reflect on an even more important matter to be discussed in a later
chapter. When in lines 557-58 Dryden says that Zimri was, in speech,
"So over Violent, or over Civil, / That every man, with him, was God or
Devil," the use of chiasmus is fairly obvious. First appear the elements
of extreme disparagement ("over Violent") and extreme praise ("over
Civil"); these elements are then repeated, but in reverse order: extreme
praise ("every man ... was God") and extreme disparagement ("or
Devil"). The preceding couplet is likewise based on chiasmus: first
disparity ("Rayling and praising") and unity (in the sense that these
were his *usual*, recurring "Theams"); then unity ("both," each showing
his "Judgment") and disparity ("in Extreams"—plural). The effect of
this chiastic structure in the two couplets can probably be appreciated
better if we visualize the pattern that is implied in the word chiasmus
(derived from *khiasmos*, meaning "cross arrangement") and that is
illustrated in the standard example given in the Concise *OED*:

This pattern can be reduced to elements thus:

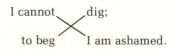

and to terms or letters thus:

In both couplets just examined, the polar opposition of the elements
that could be called *a* and *b* has been emphasized— in fact they appear
to be flying apart; yet at the same time the use of chiasmus has, as it
were, fixed the poles in place for the moment, while further emphasizing their antithetic nature and the absence of any middle ground.

   The box of four corners formed by a chiasmus is basically an inversion of a directly parallel structure that can likewise be presented as a
box, thus:

$$a\text{———}b$$
$$|\qquad|$$
$$a\text{———}b$$

Consequently it is not surprising to find that the direct parallel is sometimes used to accompany instances of chiasmus. In the Zimri passage,

however, Dryden goes beyond simple accompaniment: he often combines the two in the same line or couplet. Lines 559-60 will illustrate:

> In squandring Wealth was his peculiar Art:
> Nothing went unrewarded, but Desert.

On being alerted, by either the sentence structure or the typographical
arrangement of a passage, that it probably contains either a direct parallel or an inverted one (chiasmus), the first step in playing the word
game is to reduce the four elements present to two, each one of which is
repeated. Here, of course, is where another reason for employing the
word game becomes evident, for, on accepting the invitation to regard
two elements as essentially variations of the same thing, the reader can
come to recognize a similarity between the two which he had previously glossed over. In the couplet before us, the word "peculiar" in the
phrase "his peculiar Art" indicates that this element can be called
"idiosyncracy." It then becomes evident that the exclusion of "Desert"
from reward can likewise be regarded as "idiosyncracy." The elements
of squandering wealth and rewarding everything then need a name for
the category into which they both fit, and "distributing largesse" will
do as well as any. A direct parallelling can now be seen, thus:

distributing largesse	—	idiosyncracy
("squandring Wealth")		("peculiar Art")
distributing largesse	—	idiosyncracy
(everything was		(except desert, which others
rewarded)		would have rewarded)

At the same time, if we look to see whether a chiastic arrangement is
also present, we come to a much more satiric reading. Dryden's actual
phrase "Nothing went unrewarded" so words the thought of rewarding
everything that it emphasizes the idiosyncracy of the activity. Making
this phrase the repeated b element produces a chiasmus and forces us
to look upon the last phrase in the couplet in a slightly different way:

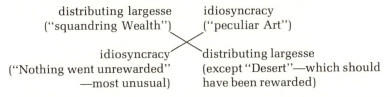

In the final element ("but Desert"), both grammar (the "but") and Zimri
have abstracted the proper object of reward from the process, and in so
doing they have negated the fit distribution of largesse. In the directly
parallel reading Zimri is damned enough, for being foolishly idiosyn-
cratic; in the chiastic reading he is damned even more, for perversely
failing to do what he should have done and what he was eminently able
to do.

Presumably Dryden's readers, at least the well educated ones, would make both readings, being well trained in rhetoric. Presumably, too, they would, from habit, visualize the box form of a chiasmus even when that device appeared in a single line. In this way the apparently disparate elements of line 550 (in which it is said that Zimri "Was Chymist, Fidler, States-Man and Buffoon") would be fixed, however temporarily, in a double pattern. The four elements (in their two categories) can be read as being in direct parallel: serious ("Chymist"), non-serious ("Fidler," being both a player on the fiddle and a trifler); serious ("States-Man"), non-serious ("Buffoon")—with each non-serious element serving to deflate the importance of the preceding serious one. At the same time, however, the line can be read chiastically: self-fooled ("Chymist" as alchemist seeking the philosopher's stone), fooler of others ("Fidler," which meant, in addition to the preceding meanings, a cheater and a swindler); fooler of others ("States-Man," amounting to the same thing as "Fidler," especially with those Whigs who favoured republics—"States"); self-fooler ("Buffoon," who doesn't recognize his own buffoonery). The next line likewise invites double reading. "Then all for Women, Painting, Rhiming, Drinking" poses the usual problem of reducing four elements to two categories. Drinking and painting are both concerned with liquids, and since rhyming is concerned with form, we can try placing women in that category too, thus producing a direct parallel: form ("Women"), liquid ("Painting"); form ("Rhiming"), liquid ("Drinking"). At the same time, seeing whether chiasmus might be present leads to even sharper satire, for categories something like these would emerge: consuming ("Women"), applying to exterior ("Painting"); applying to exterior ("Rhiming"), consuming ("Drinking"). Again, simply by placing elements in a certain order, Dryden has invited us to see Buckingham's attitudes towards each of those elements reflected in the order in which Dryden has arranged them. More generally, with regard to the actual disorder in Zimri's activities, the use of parallel and chiasmus in the two couplets examined has served to fix that swirling chaos for a moment, with double patterns of lightning boxing the compass and etching the convolutions of cumulonimbus.

That lightning on occasion overlaps. Consider the couplet, "Blest Madman, who coud every hour employ, / With something New to wish, or to enjoy!" (lines 553-54). Chiasmus works in the first line itself, proceeding from what is desirable ("Blest") to flightiness ("Madman," who has just been characterized as having "ten thousand freaks"—causeless changes of mind) and then from flightiness ("every hour," which is to have something new) to what is usually desirable ("employ"—but to what end?). Chiasmus also operates over the whole couplet, making use of slightly larger elements: from happiness ("Blest Madman") to flightiness ("every hour employ"—differently); from flightiness ("something New") to ostensible happiness ("to wish, or to enjoy!"). By pinpointing the four corners and by criss-crossing from one to the other and by doing so again, Dryden further illuminates the unending swirl within.

Just as he extends the terms of the chiasmus in this couplet, so in others he modifies them further. "A man," he writes in lines 545-46, specifying oneness, then proceeds to variousness ("so various"), repeats the variousness in a phrase that is elaborated ("Not one, but all Mankinds"), and returns to the concept of oneness ("Epitome"). In lines 563-64, he uses three clauses and appears to be talking about three different activities, but still he sets the lines up chiastically: "He laught himself from Court" points to losing of place; "then sought Releif" indicates salving of ego; "By forming Parties" further indicates salving of ego; and "but coud ne're be Chief" returns to losing of place. Zimri just can't win, whatever he tries, and whatever he tries politically has to do with bolstering his ego. In the following couplet there appear again to be three elements, instead of two repeated, but again chiasmus works so as to expose the truth. After an introductory "For, spight of him," we are told that "the weight of Business fell / On *Absalom* and wise *Achitophel.*" The attribution of being "wise" to only one of the two and the root meaning of "Business" point to the chiasmus, for in "weight" we encounter seriousness, in "Business" we have busy-ness; and, appropriately, in "*Absalom*," the pretender dashing about the countryside, we again have busy-ness, and in "wise *Achitophel*" we again encounter seriousness, the really serious threat to the peace of the realm. Although Dryden abandons the specifics of chiastic terms, he continues to apply the structural principle of the device.

Many of the variations Dryden has worked on chiasmus in the character of Zimri come together, as one might expect, in the couplet which concludes the description (lines 567-68):

> Thus, wicked but in will, of means bereft,
> He left not Faction, but of that was left.

The first of these lines sets up a standard chiasmus—from desire ("wicked") to agency ("will") and from agency ("means") to desire ("bereft"), with the last element, as indicated, being negated: Zimri used to have the combination of desire and means, but now, with the removal of the one, the other is made inoperative. Conversely, the last line begins with an element negated: it has to do with parting ("He left"), and shows that "He" was not allowed to do the parting. The second element appears in "Faction" and immediately reappears as the repeated b element ("of that"), and is followed by a parting ("was left") that this time is actual. In addition the two lines can be read together, both in direct parallel and chiastically. Will ("wicked but in will") leads to deprivation ("of means bereft"), and again will (as reflected in his wish concerning the relation between him and faction) leads to deprivation, for he "was left." At the same time Zimri's wickedness ("wicked but in will") reflects his ineffectuality ("of means bereft"), and that ineffectuality ("He left not"—he was not able to do the leaving) is associated with wickedness (the "Faction" that "left" him, the "Faction" that had both the will and the means to dump their leader).

Two further functions of chiasmus in the Zimri character should be noted. As might be expected from the pervasive presence of the device in the lines we have examined, chiasmus can be found operating in all the lines of the character. Supporting analysis of the remaining lines will be found in the footnote, and all that I would do here is to point to the comprehensiveness of the device.[21] That comprehensiveness extends, in fact, not simply to every line, but also to the structure of the character as a whole, and this is the second function referred to.

[21] Those lines in the character of Zimri not already analyzed in the text reveal the following use of chiasmus, often in combination with direct parallel. In line 547 the last phrase, "always in the wrong," provides the elements of time and quality, which can be seen parallelled in the first half of the line, "Stiff in Opinions"—constant as long as they lasted and of poor quality in view of the stiffness, which would make for opinionatedness. Also one proceeds from the undesirable ("Stiff") to the opinionated ("Opinions"), and from the stubbornly opinionated ("always") to the undesirable ("wrong"). Line 548—"Was everything by starts and nothing long"—has an obvious parallelism, proceeding from quantity ("every thing") to time ("starts") and again from quantity ("nothing") to time ("long"), but it also reads chiastically, from the encompassing ("every thing") to the small ("by starts") and from the small ("nothing") to the encompassing ("long"). Line 549—"But, in the course of one revolving Moon"—employs two elements, process and oneness, and arranges them in two patterns. In parallel they are contained in "course," "one," "revolving," and, as one unique object, "Moon." In chiastic order they are contained in "course," "one," that single object which revolves so as to return to the former state and so remains the same, and "Moon" as that which moves through phases. Line 552 is similar to 547 in that the last phrase, "that dy'd in thinking," provides the elements that can be seen parallelled in the first half: "ten thousand," indicating, from their sheer number, a short life for each, and "freaks" being a form of mental activity —notions, vagaries, changes of mind. At the same time chiasmus operates, proceeding from flightiness of thought (inherent in the "ten thousand") to a short life (characteristic of "freaks") and from a short life ("dy'd") to flightiness of thought (Zimri's form of "thinking"). The couplet comprising lines 561-62 contains an overlap. The first line presents a chiasmus, proceeding from deception (behind the "Begger'd") to superior fool (represented by those "Fools" who had beggared him) and from superior fool (he did find them out) to deception ("too late"—the deception lasted too long for its exposure to do any good). The next line builds on an obvious grammatical parallel—"He had his Jest, and they had his Estate"—but also adds chiasmus, inasmuch as we proceed from Zimri ("He") to the fools (on whom he "had his Jest"), and from the fools ("they") to Zimri (on whom the fools had *their* jest by relieving him of "his Estate"). At the same time the couplet as a whole can be read chiastically: from being taken ("Begger'd by Fools") to ineffectual activity ("he found too late"), and from ineffectual activity ("He had his Jest") to being taken ("they had his Estate"). The usual effect of the chiasmus, in addition to providing order within disorder, is to suggest a basic similarity beneath ostensible differences: e.g., not only is Zimri as much of a fool as those who beggared him, but also they undoubtedly enjoyed their jest on him as much as he on them.

Lines 545-54 can be seen as an elaborated first element, being concerned with factiousness (the variousness of Zimri's pursuits and the constantly changing nature of his interests), lines 555-58 depict extremes (his railing and his praising); similar extremes (this time in rewarding and in being taken) appear in lines 559-62, and prepare for the return in lines 563-68 to factiousness (the forming of parties)—and, typically, to the negation of even this activity. Although the form of the terms or elements has been elaborated beyond immediate recognition, Dryden has used the structural principle of the device to organize, not only the parts, but also the whole, of his character.

In his chiastic return to factiousness at the end of the character, it should be noted, Dryden has achieved the second purpose behind including Buckingham in his poem. Not only has he succeeded in showing the whirling ineffectuality of Buckingham, but he also succeeds in tying this mercurial whirligig to the Whigs in two destructive ways. Buckingham, in his factiousness, is made to appear the epitome, not just generally of all mankind, but very specifically of the Whigs themselves. And since this particular leader, because of his factiousness, is so inept, "the weight of Business fell / On Absalom and wise Achitophel." They, the effective leaders of the Whigs, lead "Faction" and, unlike Buckingham, are "wicked" both in "will" and in "Means." Doubly damned are the Whigs to have such a fool for a leader and to be so wicked (and so factious) in their factiousness.

Shimei: Chaste Were His Cellars

The next full-length satiric portrait is of a man who was really not a leader of the Whigs but who was certainly prominent among them. Slingsby Bethel was born and bred a gentleman, being the son of Sir Walter Bethel and his wife Mary, whose father was Sir Henry Slingsby.[22] But being the third son, he was placed in business to earn his living and was in fact sent to Hamburg in Germany, where he stayed from 1637 to 1649. Returning to the England of the Commonwealth era, he became a Member of Parliament in 1659 and in early 1660 was appointed to the council of state. With the Restoration, he retired into private life, living in London on income from the considerable property he had acquired in Yorkshire and amusing himself with writing books and tracts about how superior republics were for business. On 24 June 1680 he was propelled into the thick of the political crisis by being elected one of the two sheriffs of London and Middlesex (a man named Henry Cornish being the other). As sheriff he would be responsible for choosing members of juries, and at this time juries had

[22] Biographical details are drawn from William Prideaux Courtney, "Bethel, Slingsby," DNB, II, 425-26.

of course become one of the battlegrounds between Whigs and Tories. As part of the reaction from the Popish Plot there were charges of Whig plots against the government and when the Tory government put London Whigs on trial for treason, the Whigs tried to pack the juries with Whig supporters so that the accused would be acquitted and released.

Certain aspects of Bethel's character and opinions showed up starkly in the light of the publicity trained on him as a result of his being sheriff. His republicanism was evident in his book entitled *The Interest of Princes and States* (London, 1680)—"state" often, as noted before, being a synonym for "republic." He pointed to the great advantage of having banks, "but of these, I confess there are no thriving and flourishing examples, save under Republicks."[23] He praised the United Netherlands and several other republics for the greater civil liberties and freedom of trade they enjoyed, and in writing about the United Netherlands he used the phrase "laying aside the Prince."[24] Then Bethel became involved in the execution of Lord Stafford.

One of the Roman Catholics unjustly accused by Titus Oates of complicity in the Popish Plot, Lord Stafford had been tried and found guilty in the House of Lords, sitting as the highest court of the land. He was sentenced thus:

You must go to the place from whence you came; from thence you must be drawn upon a hurdle to the place of execution: When you come there, you must be hanged up by the neck, but not till you are dead; for you must be cut down alive, your privy-members must be cut off, and your bowels ript up before your face, and thrown into the fire. Then your head must be severed from your body, and your body divided into four quarters; and these must be at the disposal of the king. And God Almighty be merciful to your soul.[25]

Exercising his royal prerogative of showing mercy, King Charles ordered writs issued under the great seal of England saying that the man who used to be known as Lord Stafford (for his title had been removed from him on his conviction) was to be executed merely by having his head cut off. Bethel and Cornish, who as sheriffs were responsible for the arrangements for the execution, objected. On 21 December 1680 they petitioned the House of Lords as if the King did not exist, saying that they had received a writ "under the great seal of England" (no mention of the King) which commanded a form of executing different from that required by the House of Lords at the time of sentencing, and asked the House of Lords for directions concerning the execution. That House abruptly declared "that the king's writ ought to be obeyed."[26]

[23] Slingsby Bethel, *The Interest of Princes and States* (London: [By S. Bethel], 1680), p. 13.

[24] *Interest of Princes and States*, pp. 111-12, 121.

[25] T. B. Howell, *A Complete Collection of State Trials* (London: Bagshaw, 1816), VII, 1558.

[26] Howell, VII, 1562-63.

Thereupon the inveterate republicans turned to the House of Commons and asked for answers to these questions:

1. Whether the king, being neither judge nor party, can order the execution?

2. Whether the lords can award the execution?

3. Whether the king can dispense with any part of the execution?

4. If the king can dispense with some part of the execution, why not with all?[27]

In reply the House of Commons resolved that it was content to have Stafford executed "by severing his head from his body only." The House of Commons, being dominated by Whigs, had likewise ignored the King and his role as dispenser of mercy.

This instance of republicanism was not the only one Bethel was charged with. As he remarked in his *Vindication of Slingsby Bethel Esquire* (1681), it was charged that when he was in Hamburg and learned of the impending execution of Charles I, he said "That rather than he should want [i.e., lack] an Executioner, I would come thence to perform the Office."[28] When the charge was made, Bethel instituted a law suit for slander, incidentally assuring that the charge would be widely known among the public.

Not only was Bethel a notorious republican; he was also a Dissenter of decidedly pronounced views. In his *Interest of Princes and States* he objected to the order issued requiring that the congregation sit bare-headed throughout the sermon: "As it is without authority, so it is against the practice of all Christian Churches, in antient as well as modern times, and never known in *England* until of late . . . : and this unwarrantable Ceremony keeps (upon several accounts) many out of the Church, as some from weakness of Constitution, no Caps being so good a fence against Cold in a wide empty Church, as a broad-brim'd Hat, others upon an account of Conscience, as thinking the Ceremony superstitious, and a third sort upon a political account, as not daring to trust the Church with an Arbitrary Power of imposing what Ceremonies they please. . . ."[29]

On being elected sheriffs, he and Cornish first refused to take the oath required of sheriffs, to the effect that they would not endeavour any alteration of government either in church or in state. But then, so as to be able to take up their office (and thereby serve the Whigs), they changed their minds and took the oath. In order to dispel any thought that they as Dissenters were hypocritical in taking the oath, Bethel (presumably) issued a pamphlet, *An Account of the New Sheriffs, Holding their Office* (1680), in which he showed how they had been

[27] Quoted in Cobbett, vol. IV, cols. 1260-61.
[28] *The Vindication of Slingsby Bethel Esquire* (London: F. Smith, 1681), p. 3.
[29] *Interest of Princes and States*, p. 27.

able to square the taking of the oath with their conscience. They had looked for the meaning of the oath in what "the *major* part of both Houses that passed the Act" requiring the oath must have meant by it, and so they interpreted the key clause as meaning alteration in the government of the church or state in a manner not warranted by the constitution of the land or by an act of Parliament.[30] However valid such reasoning may have been, it of course provided the Tories with evidence of typical Dissenting casuistry. They also found ample evidence of another puritanical attitude. Not only did Bethel say in his *Interest of Princes and States* that trade is "the true and chief intrinsick Interest of *England*," but he also praised the adherents to the "Reformed Religion" because "the greater their zeal, the greater is their inclination to Trade and Industry, as holding Idleness unlawful."[31] And in his *Vindication* he prayed God "that Pride, fullness of Bread, and Idleness, which was charged upon *Sodom* and *Jerusalem*, as the Cause of God's Judgements, may not grow to that height of Excess in this City, as to become the Ruine and Destruction of it."[32]

Bethel also had another marked trait—a consuming interest in saving money, but details of that later. It is already clear that Bethel in his own person happened, most fortunately for the Tories, to provide a living embodiment of a literary archetype that was already in existence. In Hudibras Samuel Butler had written at length of the true-blue Presbyterian who had caused civil wars and would gladly do so again, and Sir John Denham in 1661 had published a poetic character sketch of the typical "Presbyter" which ran to about the same length as Dryden's was to. In 1680 Denham's poem was reprinted as a broadside, not surprisingly, for, not only was it still most topical in a general way, but also very specifically it had come to fit Slingsby Bethel.

Denham's Presbyter showed zeal, of course: he consecrated a secret room where small groups of the faithful met in conspiracy, and,

> *Shimei*-like, to all the men he meets,
> He spews his frantick Venome in the streets:
> And though he says the Spirit moves him to it,
> The Devil is that Spirit made him do it.[33]

[30] *An Account of the New Sheriffs, Holding their Office* (London: Snowden, 1680), pp. 1-2.

[31] *Interest of Princes and States*, pp. 10, 47.

[32] *Vindication*, p. 9.

[33] Sir John Denham, *The True Presbyterian without Disguise: or, a Character of a Presbyterians Ways and Actions* (London, 1680), p. 1. T. H. Banks, in his edition of *The Poetical Works of Sir John Denham*, 2nd ed. ([Hamden, Conn.]: Archon, 1969), p. 326, rejects this poem as Denham's. Curiously, he overlooks the quarto edition of 1661, cited in Wing (a copy of which is in the Huntington Library), and so his reasons for rejecting it are not as strong as he indicates. Nonetheless, in view of his opinion, I would invite the reader to understand quotation marks around the name "Sir John Denham" in the text of my argument.

But it was principally in his opposition to the King that he shone:

> A *Presbyter* is he, whose heart is bent
> To cross the Kings designes in Parliament,
> Where whilst the place of Burgess he doth bear,
> He thinks he ows but small Allegiance there;
> But stands at distance, as some higher thing,
> Like a *Licurgus*, or a kind of King.
> Then as an Errant, times bold Knights were wont
> To seek out Monsters, and adventures hunt,
> So with his wit, and valour, he doth try
> How the Prerogative he may defie;

By happenstance the Presbyter and Bethel as sheriff had come together; by greater happenstance the actions and writings of Slingsby Bethel had come to parallel the lines following:

> Thus he attempts, and first he fain would know
> If that the Soveraign Power, be new, or no:
> Or if it were not fitter, Kings should be
> Confin'd unto a limited degree;
> And for his part likes a Plebean State,
> Where the poor Mechanicks may still debate
> All matters at their pleasure, not confin'd
> To this, or that, but as they cause do find;
> When though that every voice against him go,
> He'l slay the Giant, with his single (no.)

With the literary archetype and the real live embodiment in front of him, Dryden was able, in effect, to tighten Denham's phrasing and to reinforce the literary depiction with concrete allusions to the doings and sayings of Slingsby Bethel.

Dryden retained the name *Shimei*, for it was particularly appropriate. When King David was fleeing from the rebellion of his traitorous son, Absalom, Shimei, for one stretch of the way, proceeded beside David, cursing him and throwing stones and dirt at him (2 Sam. 16:5-14). To this Biblical association of the name Dryden added a concrete illustration, alluding (it would appear evident) to Bethel's alleged willingness, as a zealous Dissenter, to behead Charles I:

> The wretch, who Heavens Annointed dar'd to Curse,
> *Shimei*, whose early Youth did Promise bring   [585]
> Of Zeal to God, and Hatred to his King;

To these antithetic qualities, balanced so quintessentially, Dryden adds the qualities of concern for money and sabbatarianism, the puritan work ethic and distaste for sin, and the peculiar dilemmas in which the conflicts between these concerns can place Dissenters—dilemmas which are exceptionally well expressed through the heroic couplet with its antithetical balancings and sudden reversal of direction:

> Did wisely from Expensive Sins refrain,
> And never broke the Sabbath, but for Gain:

The religious hypocrisy reflected here had its counterpart in politics, and in this regard Bethel's public casuistry about his oath of office was a godsend:

> Nor ever was he known an Oath to vent,
> Or Curse unless against the Government.   [590]

Thus is the typical Presbyter introduced, with his qualities illustrated in Slingsby Bethel and applied by implication to all other Whigs who side with him.

The peculiar form that one of these qualities in particular took among the Whigs is what Dryden chooses to elaborate on in the second section of Shimei's character sketch. What could be more hypocritical than a magistrate sworn to serve a king but actually, as a republican at heart, working against him?

> Thus, heaping Wealth, by the most ready way
> Among the Jews, which was to Cheat and Pray;
> The City, to reward his pious Hate
> Against his Master, chose him Magistrate:
> His Hand a Vare of Justice did uphold;   [595]
> His Neck was loaded with a Chain of Gold.
> During his Office, Treason was no Crime,
> The Sons of *Belial* had a glorious Time:

The phrase "Sons of *Belial*" has many barbs to it. In general the Dissenters are compared to those debauched, vicious, and traitorous men called "sons of Belial" in various passages in the Old Testament.[34] More specifically, as Professor Swedenberg has pointed out and especially since these "Sons" are attached to "Treason," the phrase alludes to a passage in the Book of Common Prayer referring to the cruel men, sons of Belial, who imbrued their hands in the blood of God's Anointed, King Charles I:[35] presumably among the Whigs were similar cruel men, sons of Belial, all too willing to imbrue their hands in the blood of King Charles II. In addition, since Bethel in one of his books had gone out of his way to protest against Presbyterians' being called "Sons of *Belial*,"[36] Dryden could well be pointing another barb at Bethel specifically. From the sins of Belial Dryden shifts to the hypocritical justification of such a magistrate as Shimei for his working against his King. Like most Dissenters, and like Denham's Presbyter, Shimei was able to find Biblical texts which, with a peculiar twist, could be made to support his un-Biblical behaviour:

[34] Deuteronomy 13:13; Judges 19:22; 1 Samuel 2:13, 10:27; 2 Chronicles 13:7.
[35] *Works*, II, 263.
[36] *Interest of Princes and States*, p. 38.

> For *Shimei*, though not prodigal of pelf,
> Yet lov'd his wicked Neighbour as himself: [600]
> When two or three were gather'd to declaim
> Against the Monarch of *Jerusalem*,
> *Shimei* was always in the midst of them.
> And, if they Curst the King when he was by,
> Woud rather Curse, than break good Company.   [605]

A specific application of Bethel's republicanism had to do with his office of sheriff, in which he was responsible for selecting jurymen:

> If any durst his Factious Friends accuse,
> He pact a Jury of dissenting Jews:
> Whose fellow-feeling, in the godly Cause,
> Would free the suffring Saint from Humane Laws.
> For Laws are only made to Punish those,   [610]
> Who serve the King, and to protect his Foes.

So completely dedicated to his republicanism is this magistrate of the King that he even spends his leisure time in trying to forward it:

> If any leisure time he had from Power,
> (Because 'tis Sin to misimploy an hour;)
> His business was, by Writing, to Persuade,
> That Kings were Useless, and a Clog to Trade: [615]

Thus the complete republican: money-grabbing and Bible-quoting, totally dedicated and utterly hypocritical. Bethel must, of course, have been a considerable embarrassment to the Whigs in his outspoken republicanism, and Dryden has sought to increase that embarrassment.

But Bethel's republicanism was not the only source of embarrassment, or even the chief source. That was his parsimony—or at least what looked like parsimony. In his *Interest of Princes and States* he complained of the customs whereby men proceeding through public offices in towns and cities—such as that of sheriff in London—had to make large expenditures for feasts.[37] In a pamphlet which is anonymous (as most were) but for which there is presumptive evidence for believing that Bethel wrote it, he reprinted an act passed by the London city council in the reign of Popish Philip and Mary, requiring that city feasts have no more than one meat course—though that one course might contain as many as seven different dishes of meat. This act had fallen into desuetude and, as a result, each sheriff had to pay £300 as his share of the Spittle Feast alone and proportionate amounts for other feasts which custom—contrary to law—required him to offer to the citizens of London each year: "the management of this Expence is in a rude and disagreeable way to any sober person, a great part of it being spent on Popular Feasts, where the Ravenous Attendants and their

---

[37] *Interest of Princes and States*, pp. 15-16.

Rabble Acquaintance, are like so many Beasts of Prey."[38] Accordingly, he proposed that all great feasts be laid aside, except that of the Lord Mayor's Day, and that no part of the expense of that feast be charged to the sheriffs as was then the custom.

In his *Vindication* he took note of the double charge that he lived in a garret and "kept no house"—i.e., did not provide a festive table for citizens to visit whenever they felt like inviting themselves—as was again the custom for sheriffs. In reply he said that he rented, not a garret, but a whole house except for the garrets, the cellars, and one small room on the first floor, and was sure that this was sufficient accommodation for a gentleman of better quality than he.[39] With regard to giving feasts, he pointed out that he had in fact given the first two feasts that custom required of him (before he was aware of the laws about limiting them), but that, on receiving considerable slights from the citizenry of London and because he respected the law—"I think no Laws are more properly called wholesome than those that prohibit the excess of Feasting,"[40] he changed his plans to set up a festive table. In his pamphlet he went on at great length to point out the evil results—the extravagance and ruinous expense—that follow on obeying the wicked custom. But this was not the only custom that he attacked: he also admitted to the charge that, most contrary to custom, he did not make a voluntary contribution to the necessities of the poor prisoners in the city prisons and county jail.[41] His reason was a desire to force the reactivation of those laws requiring the City to look after the prisoners and to encourage a larger number of charitable persons to contribute to their upkeep: in this way, as a result of his withholding action, the prisoners would benefit much more in the long run.[42] Curiously, in fact, Bethel did—in October of 1681—donate several hundred pounds for the relief of the poor prisoners in for debt,[43] but no doubt in this instance and with the aid of Tory propagandists, his words would outspeed his deed.

One may well feel that Bethel had all the reason on his side in protesting against customs which victimized officials so that others could luxuriate at their expense—either by devouring the victims' substance or by withholding their own substance from charitable giving. But custom was against him, and his way of expressing himself gave a very considerable handle to his enemies. Dryden took that handle and carved upon it.

[38] *An Act of Common-Councill of the City of London (Made in the first and second years of the Reign of Philip & Mary) for Retrenching of the Expenses of the Lord Mayor & Sheriffs, etc.* (London: Fr. Smith, 1680), p. 7. The next sentence derives from p. 8.

[39] *Vindication*, p. 5.

[40] *Vindication*, p. 5.

[41] *Vindication*, p. 9.

[42] *Vindication*, pp. 9-10.

[43] Luttrell, I, 140.

First came a characteristically smooth transition from Bethel's writing, coupled with ironically exaggerated praise in comparing Bethel to the Rechabites who proved obedient to the Lord in not touching wine (Jeremiah 35:1-11, 18-19):

> And that his noble Stile he might refine,
> No *Rechabite* more shund the fumes of Wine.

The same mocking exaggeration, adopting Bethel's point of view, continues, as Dryden turns to Bethel's execution of his duties of hospitality as sheriff:

> Chast were his Cellars, and his Shrieval Board
> The Grossness of a City Feast abhor'd:

Rhyme has done its work: now for the reversal of direction:

> His Cooks, with long disuse, their Trade forgot;   [620]
> Cool was his Kitchen, tho his Brains were hot.

Then back to ostensible agreement:

> Such frugal Vertue Malice may accuse,
> But sure 'twas necessary to the Jews:
> For Towns once burnt, such Magistrates require
> As dare not tempt Gods Providence by fire.   [625]

Actually the ambiguity of "frugal Vertue" undermines nicely, and the allusion to the Great Fire of London contains two and possibly three references. Certainly it points to the fire's origin in a bakery shop, and probably to Bethel's comparison (quoted earlier) of London with Sodom and Jerusalem punished by God. Possibly it is also meant to remind Dryden's contemporaries of another curious fact about the Great Fire: that the Whigs controlling the House of Commons had passed a resolution, saying that the Great Fire had been deliberately set by Papists[44]—a rather peculiar form of Divine Providence. Having already done great damage to Bethel, Dryden then ends on the aspect in which the Dissenting magistrate's reputation would have been the most vulnerable: his great palaver about reducing the number of meat courses at City feasts:

> With Spiritual food he fed his Servants well,
> But free from flesh, that made the Jews Rebel:
> And *Moses*'s Laws he held in more account,
> For forty days of Fasting in the Mount.

[44] Resolution passed on 10 Jan. 1680/1: "*Resolved*, That it is the Opinion of this House, That the City of *London* was burnt, in the year 1666, by the Papists; designing thereby to introduce arbitrary Power and Popery into this Kingdom" (Anchitell Grey, *Debates of the House of Commons, from the year 1667 to the year 1694* [London: Becket, 1763], VIII, 289-90).

It should be noted that Dryden has used many of Bethel's own phrases and concepts. Some of these, such as expensive sins and idleness, would be shared with other Dissenting writers; but some were pre-eminently Bethel's: the oath against the government, kings' being useless and a clog to trade, the shrieval board, and the grossness of a city feast. And certainly the phrase "Sons of *Belial*" took very specific aim. In addition, the proposal, in another part of the poem, "for laying Honest *David* by" (line 507) closely parallels Bethel's own phrase "laying aside the Prince,"[45] which must have been especially offensive to the Tories. Such a close parallelling of Bethel's phrases throughout the sketch and in other parts of the poem indicates, of course, a close reading and use of Bethel's pamphlets and further increases the likelihood that Dryden read and used the pamphlets of other writers as well.[46]

When it came to handling Titus Oates, however, Dryden used the writings of others with a difference.

Corah: Thou Monumental Brass

Titus Oates was born the grandson of a ribbon-weaver and the son of a Norfolk man who was an Anglican clergyman until it was to his advantage to become an Anabaptist, and an Anabaptist until it was to his advantage (at the Restoration) to return to the Church of England.[47] Titus was entered at Merchant Taylors' School, expelled within a year, entered at Gonville and Caius College, Cambridge, and was expelled within two years—both expulsions presumably because of sodomy (the practice of male homosexuality). He migrated to St. John's College (Cambridge), where his tutor described him as "a great dunce" and whence he left without taking a degree. In spite of having no degree, however, he somehow got himself admitted into Anglican orders and was instituted in 1674 into a vicarage in Kent, from which, however, he secured a licence to absent himself, so that he could go to serve as curate to his father, who at the time was back in the Church of England, at Hastings.

[45] *Interest of Princes and States*, p. 121.

[46] Before leaving Bethel, note should be made of an additional charge made against him. It had to do with his escorting Lord Stafford to the execution block. The story went that Stafford asked Bethel to hush the crowd gathered round the block so that he could die in peace, but that Bethel replied, "Sir, we have orders to stop nobody's breath but yours." As far as I can determine, however, the source of this story is a violently Tory work not written until 1725 (Bevill Higgons, *Historical and Critical Remarks on Bishop Burnet's History of His Own Time* [London: Meighan, 1725], p. 326). Certainly there is considerable question, not only as to whether Bethel had in fact behaved in this way, but also as to whether even the story was current in 1681.

[47] Biographical details are drawn from Thomas Seccombe, "Oates, Titus," *DNB*, XIV, 741-48; John Pollock, *The Popish Plot* (London: Duckworth, 1903); Jane Lane, *Titus Oates* (London: Dakers, 1949); John Kenyon, *The Popish Plot* (London: Heinemann, 1972).

Within a few months Titus and his father trumped up a charge of sodomy against a local schoolmaster: the charge fell flat, and Titus was arrested in an action for damages and imprisoned, while his father was ejected from the parish. Titus escaped from jail, went to London where he hid for a time, and then obtained a berth as Chaplain to one of the navy's ships and appears to have made a trip with it to Tangier. Before long he was expelled from the navy—for sodomy. As usual, however, he managed to land on his feet and became chaplain to the protestants in the Roman Catholic Duke of Norfolk's household at Arundel.

Within months he was once more out of a job and in London. There he met Israel Tonge, a Church of England clergyman who was intent on writing against the Jesuits, because, he thought, they were plotting an English equivalent to the St. Bartholomew massacre in France. Oates allied himself with Tonge, sought out Jesuits in their favourite coffee houses, and made the acquaintance of the Jesuits who lived at Somerset House, where the Queen had her private chapel. In April of 1677 he professed himself converted to Roman Catholicism and asked to become a Jesuit. In June he was sent to the Jesuit seminary at Vallodolid in Spain, where he stayed five months before being expelled for sodomy. On the basis of his abortive stay in Spain, he claimed to have received the degree of Doctor of Divinity from Salamanca and in fact thereafter styled himself Doctor Oates.

In spite of his expulsion, he talked his English Jesuit friends into sending him to another seminary, this one at St. Omer in France, where he stayed six months before being expelled. On his return he again teamed up with Tonge, and, feeling that he now knew enough about the Jesuits to allow him to fabricate a story about their plotting against the King, he did so. After first failing to alarm the authorities through an intermediary, Oates, in company with Tonge, went on 6 September 1678 before a justice of the peace, Sir Edmund Berry Godfrey, and deposed to the truth of a long written narrative of a popish plot which he submitted to Godfrey. Evidently Godfrey passed it on to the government, for on 28 September Oates was summoned before the privy council, where he repeated his story, now greatly expanded with many more details and more names mentioned. The King disbelieved him, but the others were impressed, and he was immediately sent about London, with a guard, to arrest as many of those he had accused as he could find. Already he was a terrifying power to be reckoned with. In October Sir Edmund Berry Godfrey was found dead and presumed murdered. Immediately most people concluded that the Jesuits had killed him, out of revenge, for having listened to Oates. Both Houses of Parliament passed resolutions declaring their belief in the Plot, and the witch-hunt was on.

To us, the details of the Plot would probably make the whole thing appear incredible. According to Oates, there were plans to kill the King and bring England back to Catholicism through James, who would of course immediately succeed Charles. Pope Innocent VI, so the story went, had ordered the Jesuits to take over England (though in fact Innocent was opposed to the Jesuits). The King, being a Protestant and therefore a heretic, deserved to die and was to be killed, to obtain which end three schemes were laid: Sir George Wakeman, the Queen's physician, was to poison him, four Irish ruffians were to stab him, and two Jesuits were to shoot him with silver bullets especially consecrated to the task. The King's councillors were then to be assassinated, the French army was to invade Ireland, there was to be a general massacre of the Protestants (as there had been in France), and James was to be offered the crown as long as he agreed to the establishment of a Jesuit government.

Why did people believe Oates? To begin with, many were willing to believe anything bad about the Jesuits: Oates capitalized on this willingness. He spoke with most impressive assurance and with such a mass of circumstantial (though often irrelevant) detail that many thought no one could possibly invent so much detail. (Dr. Goebbels with his Big Lie had his predecessors.) A few of his details were proved right, for he had had enough acquaintance with the Jesuits to be able to get minor things right now and then: for instance, when in the early days of the Plot Father Dupuis was brought before Oates, the Saviour of the Nation (for so Oates styled himself) said, "This is Father Dupuis, who was to write the King's life after they killed him." When searched, Dupuis's pockets gave up an almanac in which he had in fact been keeping a record of what the King had said and done. Furthermore, the discovery of incriminating letters which Edward Coleman, secretary to the Duchess of York, had written to France in hopes of promoting a change in religion in England greatly enhanced the credibility of Oates's charges. Then of course there was Godfrey's death, which could not have been better timed (a fact which led some to think that Oates had had him murdered), and a chap named William Bedloe, deciding to cut himself into the caper, came forward as an informer to corroborate what Oates had said. Underlying these adventitious aids was the fact, of course, that the Whigs saw Oates's story as a godsend to them in their attempt to have James excluded from the succession to the throne. And finally, for a while whenever, at the trials of those Oates accused, evidence was presented proving that he had lied, that evidence came always from Roman Catholics, and the London juries refused to believe Roman Catholics, a refusal in which they were aided and abetted by the presiding judge, Lord Chief Justice Scroggs.

Then a few things gradually began to go against Oates. In 1679 it was proved, by independent evidence, that he could not have done the things he claimed to have done in Spain. In July of 1679, when he gave evidence at the trial of Wakeman, the Queen's physician, Wakeman pressed him so hard in interrogation that Oates had to feign illness and retire. Scroggs, who was again the presiding judge, this time (perhaps out of enlightenment or because he knew that the Queen would be implicated if her physician were found guilty) chose to discredit Oates's testimony and hinted to the jury that they should believe Wakeman and his supporters—which they did. In January of 1680, when Oates sought revenge on Scroggs by accusing him of certain misbehaviour, Scroggs defended himself well and routed Oates. In the summer of that year Oates and Tonge, presumably being too much in liquor at a dinner given them by the city of London, revealed too much of what had gone on and further discredited themselves. These were merely the early stages of waning, however, for Oates still retained a great deal of power, and he did so because it served the Whig interests that he continue to be believed and credited. So much power did he retain throughout 1680, in fact, that in December of that year, an eye-witness reported, when Oates, while dining in company with the Bishop of Ely, reflected very coarsely on the Duke of York, the Queen Mother (a Papist), and the Queen, nobody dared to "contradict him (for fear of being made a party to the Plott)," until finally Sir John Reresby plucked up courage and did so, whereupon Oates left in a heat.[48] By August of 1681, however, the waning had progressed much farther, and Oates, through his behaviour and through the gradual exposure of his lies, was discredited to the point where he could be attacked without the attacker having to fear that he would be convicted in a court of law on a charge of treason brought against him by the Doctor.

It was safe, accordingly, for Dryden to attack Oates, and at the same time it was both necessary for him to disabuse those moderate readers who still believed Oates's testimony and advantageous to remind those others, who had already been disabused, that Oates was a major figure among the Whigs. Consequently Dryden fastens on Oates's credibility as a witness:

> To speak the rest, who better are forgot,   [630]
> Would tyre a well breath'd Witness of the Plot:
> Yet, *Corah*, thou shalt from Oblivion pass;

The name Corah itself would do considerable damage. Corah was very specially a Levite, being descended of Levi: he rebelled against Moses and, with his followers, was rebuked by Moses with the words, "Ye take too much upon you, ye sons of Levi." Not only that, but as punishment for his rebellion, God caused the earth to open up and swallow him and all his followers (Numbers 16:1-35). Henry Dove in 1680 had publicly used the Biblical Corah as a representative of a rebel

---

[48] *Memoirs of Sir John Reresby*, p. 209.

against the Lord and his governors: Dove did so in a sermon which he preached on Guy Fawkes day before the House of Commons and which must have made quite a stir, for to that House controlled by Whigs he had said, "Beware of the way of *Corah*, lest ye perish in the gainsaying of *Corah*: God hates the dispositions, which are the cause of Rebellion, and will never let the practices go unpunished."[49] Dryden had good reason to appropriate the name and to apply it to another plotter, Titus Oates. In the process Dryden committed a technical inaccuracy, inasmuch as he uses the name Levite consistently for Dissenting ministers and Oates was an ordained clergyman in the Church of England. But Dryden evidently felt that Oates's close association with the Dissenters made him, to all (satiric) intents and purposes, one of them, and so did not hesitate to make him a Levite. The oblivion from which Corah was to be made to pass was presumably, since Oates himself was still very far from oblivion, the extinction which the Biblical Corah had suffered on being swallowed up: he was now, in effect, reincarnated in the person of Titus Oates.

Immediately Dryden establishes the overweening presumption of the man:

> Erect thy self thou Monumental Brass:
> High as the Serpent of thy metall made,
> While Nations stand secure beneath thy shade.   [635]

Several meanings are operating in these three lines. The primary allusion has of course to do with the plague of fiery serpents that beset the Israelites (Numbers 21:4-9), in the course of which Moses, being instructed by the Lord, erected high on a pole a serpent of brass, so that all those Israelites who had been bitten by the fiery serpents might look upon the brazen serpent and live. Oates had the effrontery to style himself the Saviour of the Nation: Dryden seizes on both the claim and its impudence and portrays them both in terms of Moses's elevated and saving serpent of brass, especially appropriate since (as the OED notes) "brass" then, as now, had the meaning of effrontery or impudence, and "monumental" had the meaning of vast or stupendous. In fact there was a double appropriateness, for Christ had compared himself to the serpent of Moses in a passage (John 3:14-15) in which he had identified himself as the Saviour. How monumental could the brass of Titus be? There are also two allusions in the phrase "Monumental Brass." For those of his readers who remembered their Horace, Dryden provides an allusion to the opening of Horace's Ode XXX in Book III: Exegi monumentum aere perennius—I have finished a monument more lasting than brass. As Horace through his lyric words achieved a monument of glory that would outlast one of brass, Oates through his words

---

[49] Henry Dove, *A Sermon Preached before the Honourable House of Commons . . . November 5, 1680* (London: 1680), p. 22.

of brazen testimony has erected a monument to his infamy. The other allusion, likewise concerned with infamy, relates to the Biblical Corah himself, for in Numbers 16:38-40 it is recorded that the Lord ordered the brazen censers which Corah and his followers had used be made into "broad plates for a covering for the altar: To be a memorial unto the children of Israel, that [any] stranger, which is not of the seed of Aaron . . . be not as Korah, and as his company . . . ." In Titus's "Monumental Brass" the Corah of old has once more secured a memorial, which should again remind the children of Israel to shun his ways.

There is still another meaning possible in line 633. Most attacks on Oates made much of his notorious sodomy: the refrain of one song—"And a Buggering we will go"—is typical.[50] Dryden's readers would accordingly be on the look-out for some reference to that activity, and the line "Erect thy self thou Monumental Brass" may provide it. According to the *OED*, "erection" by Dryden's time had its sexual meaning, and presumably "erect" did too; "monumental," as noted, meant stupendous; and "brass", especially since it was used for brass cannon and brass guns, can be read imagistically. It is all too easy, especially in this century, to read sexual meanings into passages where they were not intended, and I for one am usually sceptical, but I must admit to the possibility here, for, not only were the sexual meanings available, but also there was something of a precedent in a particularly virulent broadside attack on Oates. After referring to Oates's two porters "whose *Posteriors* he often taw's," the author continued: "and when he has rais'd his own Beastly Concupiscence, *Tilts* at 'em with his *Nasty Clyster-Pipe*"—clyster meaning enema and the medical clyster-pipe quite likely being of brass.[51] If Dryden in fact meant a reference to Oates's sodomy, we should note two things about it: Dryden has made it briefly and wittily, through verbal ambiguity, and he has kept it very much subordinate to his undermining of Oates's credibility. Dryden's concern is not so much with the man as with the witness.

The presumption of this witness, who took too much upon him, is then further elaborated on, as Dryden mockingly adopts the mob's point of view:

> What tho his Birth were base, yet Comets rise
> From Earthy Vapours ere they shine in Skies.
> Prodigious Actions may as well be done
> By Weavers issue, as by Princes Son.

In the context of the poem and the activities of the Whigs, the chances would appear good that the prodigious action done by the Prince's son was the touching done by Monmouth: the illegitimacy of both his ac-

---

[50] "The Swearers Chorus to the Presbyterian Plot," in *A Choice Collection of 180 Loyal Songs*, p. 33.

[51] *The Character of an Ignoramus Doctor* (London: M. T., 1681), p. 2.

tion and Oates's would make the parallel suitable. Then, with a glance out at Oates's acquiring a coat of arms, which officially made him of noble blood, Dryden continues:

> This Arch-Attestor for the Publick Good,   [640]
> By that one Deed Enobles all his Bloud.
> Who ever ask'd the Witnesses high race,
> Whose Oath with Martyrdom did *Stephen* grace?

The particular point of this reference to the slaying of the first Christian martyr is that it was occasioned by the testimony given by *false* witnesses (Acts 6:11-14).

The same presumption and falsity continue, as Corah/Oates is associated with those other false witnesses (note the stress on "Ours"):

> Ours was a *Levite*, and as times went then,
> His Tribe were Godalmightys Gentlemen.   [645]

Again the texture is complex. There is an allusion to Corah and his fellow Levites and followers who were, as assistants to priests, separated from the congregation and brought "to do the service of the tabernacle of the Lord"—in effect serving as gentlemen in waiting to their Lord and King (Numbers 16:8-9). As Dissenting ministers, the Restoration counterparts to the Levites, the clerical Whigs with whom Oates associated could also be called gentlemen in waiting to the Lord. But in view of the emphasis just before on the baseborn nature of Corah and the Witnesses, and, earlier, on Corah's claim to be the Saviour of the Nation, a further reading is at least possible and perhaps even the primary one. It has to do with the fact that Dryden spelled "Godalmightys" as one word. As such it can mean either or both of two things: used seriously, it means "God's," but used derisively, as Dryden himself was later to use it in line 110 of *The Medall*, it means belonging to one who poses as omnipotent, or is so regarded by others. And there we have Titus again. Oates, for Dryden, was the equivalent of a Dissenting minister, and his gang of fellow informers and witnesses (actually a group of baseborn thugs) were, thanks to the anomalies of the times, regarded as if they were gentlemen in waiting as they clustered about and served that greatest Godalmighty of all, Doctor Titus Oates.

From this climax of Corah's presumption, Dryden turns to his physical appearance. In this too Titus was remarkable. He was short and broad-shouldered, bull-necked and bow-legged. He had an extraordinarily large, purplish face, with a low forehead and a chin so long that the wide slit of his mouth appeared to be at the middle of his face. His eyes were small and set deep. His voice was strident and rasping, often emerging in a nasal drawl as he gave evidence that sent thirty-five innocent men to their deaths. Such an appearance lent itself to caricature. How extreme that could be can be seen in this description of him.

In his *Brazen Forehead* is writ *ABOMINATION*. His *Eyes* are *Murdering* as the *Basilisk's*; tho' *Blindish* too as the *Batt's*. With his *Screech-Owl's Voice*, he bodes Death and Destruction. His *Tongue*, like the *Serpent's*, is *Forked* and *Double*. His *Mouth*, with that of the *Revelation-Beast*, speaks *Lies* and *Blasphemies*, and out of it issues Wildfire, in which (tho' others are consum'd) the *Salamander-Fiend* himself, subsists. His *Throat* is an *open Sepulchre*, and no *Camel* was ever so big as to choak him. Like the *Fabulous Minotaur*, he really *lives* upon *Humane Entrails*, and is fed with the *Quarters of Sacrific'd Men*, and glutted with their Bloud, the Unchristen'd *Canibal* looks *Flush* and *Ruddy*. No Morsel is so *Hard* and *Bloudy*, but his *Ostrick-Stomack* can digest it: but to sweeten the Stench of his Carrion-breath, the *Savage* for *Dessert* chews Tobacco, and that, 'till it runs out of his Chaps again like Juice of *Toad*.[52]

Especially in comparison, Dryden's description is moderate, a fact his moderate readers would appreciate. It is also fairly witty, once more mockingly assuming the mob's point of view:

> Sunk were his Eyes, his Voyce was harsh and loud,
> Sure signs he neither Cholerick was, nor Proud:
> His long Chin prov'd his Wit; his Saintlike Grace
> A Church Vermilion, and a *Moses's* Face;

When Moses descended from Mount Sinai after speaking with the Lord, the skin of his face shone (Exodus 34:29); but when Oates's face shone, especially with a vermilion flush, it was probably from a clerical claret, and the inner light, so much a part of the Dissenters' grace, had a spirituous rather than spiritual origin.

From Oates's appearance Dryden proceeds, by way of Mosaic miracle, to his memory, a memory prodigious in itself but still assisted, when need be, by prophecy and vision:

> His Memory, miraculously great,   [650]
> Could Plots, exceeding mans belief, repeat;
> Which, therefore cannot be accounted Lies,
> For humane Wit could never such devise.
> Some future Truths are mingled in his Book;
> But, where the witness faild, the Prophet Spoke: [655]
> Some things like Visionary flights appear;
> The Spirit caught him up, the Lord knows where:
> And gave him his *Rabinical* degree
> Unknown to Foreign University.

Having thoroughly undermined Oates's credibility, Dryden then offers an explanation of the motive for Oates's actions: he was an opportunist par excellence (and if Senator Joseph McCarthy comes to mind, there is reason):

> His Judgment yet his Memory did excel;   [660]
> Which peic'd his wondrous Evidence so well:

[52] *The Character of an Ignoramus Doctor*, p. 1.

> And suited to the temper of the times;
> Then groaning under Jebusitick Crimes.
> Let *Israels* foes suspect his heav'nly call,
> And rashly judge his writ Apocryphal;   [665]
> Our Laws for such affronts have forfeits made:
> He takes his life, who takes away his trade.
> Were I my self in witness *Corahs* place,
> The wretch who did me such a dire disgrace,
> Should whet my memory, though once forgot,   [670]
> To make him an Appendix of my Plot.

Oates did in fact make a practice of suddenly "remembering" evidence that would damn anyone rash enough to cross him. When Edward Warcup dared to protest against Oates's abuse of the Duke of York, Oates replied: "He is a traitor & in the plot, & you are a Yorkist, & Ile remember you for it."[53] In view of this well-known practice of Oates, the motive which Dryden ascribes to him in these lines would probably appear, to his moderate readers, to be the right one.

By this time Oates had done most of his damage: he had killed his thirty-five innocent people. But there remained one man whom he could still injure (and whom he was actively trying to injure) and through him the whole cause of the King's party. That man was James, Duke of York. In a later chapter I shall offer an argument for reading Agag, in the next section of Dryden's description of Corah, as James. If for now we simply take the identification on temporary faith, we can see Dryden doing with Oates in relation to James what he had done with Shaftesbury in relation to James. He seeks to transfer the odium in which the Duke was held to those who, he claims, were responsible for it; he has already shown Shaftesbury as the cause of part of that odium and has discredited him for his treasonable motives, and now, having discredited Oates for his motives of personal ambition working through political opportunism, he has him attack James, his Prince:

> His Zeal to heav'n, made him his Prince despise,
> And load his person with indignities:
> But Zeal peculiar priviledg affords;
> Indulging latitude to deeds and words.   [675]
> And *Corah* might for *Agag's* murther call,
> In terms as course as Samuel us'd to *Saul*.

Oates, now totally discredited, can be dismissed—doubly so because in fact the various witnesses, already turning on one another (as noted earlier), will destroy one another.

---

[53] Keith Feiling and F. R. D. Needham, "The Journals of Edmund Warcup, 1676-84," *English Historical Review*, 40 (1925), 260. The entry in the Journal is for 19 June 1684 but refers to a previous time unspecified yet presumably associated with the Oxford Parliament of 1681, in view of testimony at the trial of Oates for libel, *State Trials*, X, 139.

What others in his Evidence did Joyn,
(The best that could be had for love or coyn,)
In *Corah*'s own predicament will fall: [680]
For *witness* is a Common Name to all

So much for the Whig Saviour of the Nation.

A Leash of Lords

Dryden did not run together the three full-length character pieces we have just examined. In between Zimri and the other two he inserted thumbnail sketches of three Whig lords:

> And, therefore in the name of Dulness, be
> The well hung *Balaam* and cold *Caleb* free.
> And Canting *Nadab* let Oblivion damn,
> Who made new porridge for the Paschal Lamb.
>
> (ll. 573-76)

Each of the Whig lords referred to by these Biblical names and the accompanying epithets was far more prominent in Whig circles than either of Slingsby Bethel or Titus Oates, to each of whom Dryden will devote a full-length portrait, and yet Dryden turns off the Whig lords with only a name and an epithet. Why? Evidently because we have already had a sufficient variety of lords: an earl who is a most dangerous and evil knave, a duke who is a laughable fool, and a royal duke who is a stupid cat's-paw; we shall soon have extended descriptions of a parsimonious republican businessman and the perjuring issue of a ribbon-weaver—both of whom are presented as important men among the Whigs. So right now all we need is a quiet ticking-off of any other disreputable lords among the Whig leaders who could be made to appear to damn their side. One suspects also that any other attributes that would have proved damaging to these particular Whigs would also have proved repetitious and thereby damaging to Dryden's art.

In the phrase "well hung *Balaam*," as James Kinsley has pointed out,[54] there is double meaning, in both the epithet and the Biblical name. "Well hung" meant fluent and voluble and was often applied to a person's tongue; the Biblical Balaam was summoned by Balak to curse the enemy, "for I wot that he whom thou blessest is blessed, and he whom thou cursest is cursed" (Numbers 22:5-6). At the same time the phrase "well hung" meant well provided with genitalia, and the Biblical Balaam was responsible for teaching the children of Israel to commit fornication (Revelation 2:14). It is this latter meaning which certain of Dryden's contemporaries picked up: the authors of two verse

[54] James Kinsley, "Historical Allusions in *Absalom and Achitophel*," *Review of English Studies*, n.s. 6 (1955), 292-94.

pamphlets that comment on *Absalom and Achitophel* both associate Balaam with Priapus, the Roman god of lechery (whose distinguishing mark was an oversized penis) and identify him as Theophilus Hastings, seventh Earl of Huntington.[55] In addition, Narcissus Luttrell annotated his copy of Dryden's poem thus: "Ld Huntington who hath a swinging P-----, as is said." The name of Balaam is even more appropriate, for, as Balaam repented of his notion of cursing Israel (Numbers 23:8-10), so, about a month before Dryden's poem appeared, Huntington had left Shaftesbury and had been received back into favour with Charles.

But the well hung Balaam is not confined to half a line: he contributes to the whole line and must be considered in conjunction with the "cold *Caleb*" who is balanced on the other side of the caesura. Since Dryden's day there have been two claimants to the designation Caleb. Arthur Capel, Earl of Essex, was proposed in *A Key (With the Whip)* and by both E. S. de Beer and James Kinsley.[56] These last see a play on the name Caleb, being a near anagram for Essex's family name, Capel, and they read "cold" as referring to Essex's character, which led contemporaries to describe him as "stiff and sullen," usually dry, and "a sober, wise, judicious, and pondering person" of "sober and religious deportment." But how politic it would have been for Dryden, in a polemic aimed at persuading the moderates, to sneer at a sober, wise, and judicious person as "cold" is indeed a good question. In fact the character of the Biblical Caleb provides another puzzle, for the outstanding characteristic of Caleb was the fact that he "wholly followed the Lord" (Joshua 14:9), and it is not likely that Dryden would invite his readers to view any of the Whig leaders as wholly following the Lord, unless in some way that act of following were perverted.

If, however, we look not so much to the Biblical character as to the Biblical name, we may find the point of the phrase, for Caleb has two possible meanings: "a dog" or "as a heart." To balance the well hung Balaam with a dog is to set up a sexual parallel, which Dryden then turns into an antithesis by adding the epithet "cold" to Caleb. Alternatively, to balance the well hung Balaam with a "cold heart" likewise sets up an antithesis. Either meaning (or both) can apply to Lord Grey of Wark, who was the Whig lord whom Luttrell saw aimed at in the phrase (though, I think, for the wrong reason—"cold because no children"). There was current in 1681 a rumour to the effect that Monmouth was having an affair with the wife of Lord Grey, who was his close friend and supporter. There is admittedly some dispute as to whether in fact there was such an affair. The Dowager Countess of

---

[55] *Absalom's IX Worthies: or, a Key to a late Book or Poem, Entituled A.B. & A.C.* ([London, 1682]), p. 1; *A Key (With the Whip) To open the Mystery & Iniquity of the Poem Called, Absalom & Achitophel* ([London]: Janeway, 1682), p. 30.

[56] E. S. de Beer, "*Absalom and Achitophel*: Literary and Historical Notes," *Review of English Studies*, 17 (1941), 308, and Kinsley, "Historical Allusions," pp. 293-94.

Sunderland on 30 January 1680 wrote to a friend that Monmouth had been responsible for Lord Grey's abruptly carrying his wife into Northumberland, and she commented: "My Lord Grey was long in believing the Duke of Monmouth an unfaithful friend to him."[57] Shortly after, Grey went with Monmouth to Chichester, a fact that has led the Duke's biographer to comment: "Which is fair evidence that the cause of the dismissal of [Lady Grey] to the north was not of a serious character."[58] I would suggest, however, that the same fact can be seen as evidence of Grey's acceptance of the affair, an acceptance warranting the epithet "cold" and even fitting the Biblical character who "wholly followed the Lord"—the wrong lord. In any event, whether in fact there was or was not an affair, public rumour held that there was, as can be seen abundantly reflected in such a pamphlet as *A True Relation of a Strange Apparition which appear'd to the Lady Grey* (dated by its purchaser 10 February 1681). In other words, there was in the public mind a report which Dryden was able to make use of, to finish off a beautifully antithetic couplet, in which two Whig excesses are balanced on either side of the caesura, the well hung fornicator with the willing cuckold. Such are the leaders of the Whigs.

A similar pattern of proceeding from one extreme to another can be seen in Dryden's next couplet, with the difference that this time both extremes have been present in one and the same Whig lord:

> And Canting *Nadab* let Oblivion damn,
> Who made new porridge for the Paschal Lamb.

In the Old Testament, Nadab was one of the sons of Levi, through Aaron (Exodus 6:23), and was noted for having offered strange fire (of sacrifice) before the Lord (Leviticus 10:1). In lines 519-25 Dryden identified as Levites those Dissenters who "Resum'd their Cant" and thought that their clergymen would make fit governors. It was with multiple appropriateness, then, that Dryden referred to William Howard, third Baron Howard of Escrick, as "Canting *Nadab*." The author of *A Letter to a Friend, Occasioned by my Lord Howard of Escricks Letter to his Friend* (published not long after 3 July 1681) referred to Howard's having passed through "all the Sects of Religions," even into a "sanctified Tub" from which he had gulled men of their souls—a phrasing which indicated that the author believed Howard had been a preacher of a Dissenting sect.[59] Presumably, then, Lord Howard is in fact the Mr. William Howard referred to in a letter to Cromwell as "a greate preacher in the Anabaptist congregation" and as one who still kept up

---

[57] Fea, p. 90.
[58] Fea, p. 93.
[59] *A Letter to a Friend, Occasioned by my Lord Howard of Escricks Letter to his Friend* (London: A. B., 1681), p. 4.

a correspondence outside the country.[60] Certainly Dryden believed he had preached among the Dissenters, in view of the Levite name he gave him.

This same Lord Howard, when in later years he was imprisoned in the Tower, took the sacrament of Holy Communion in lamb's wool, i.e., he put the wine and wafer into a container filled with hot ale mixed with the pulp of roasted apples, and consumed it that way.[61] This profane act is what Dryden refers to in the phrase "made new porridge for the Paschal Lamb." The paschal lamb was the lamb slain and eaten at the Jewish Passover and came by extension to refer to Christ as Agnus Dei (the Lamb of God), who is in some manner present in the elements of Holy Communion. "Porridge," meaning conglomeration or hotchpotch, is the term which the Dissenters applied abusively to the Order of Service in the Church of England: Dryden turns it back on the Dissenters, through the person of Howard, who by adding "lamb's wool" (involving a further play on "lamb") to the elements of Holy Communion did in fact make quite a hotchpotch. Since, furthermore, the elements of Holy Communion represent a sacrifice offered before the Lord, Howard in presenting the elements in lamb's wool did in effect offer "strange fire" (of sacrifice) "before the Lord"—as did Nadab, son of Aaron. While enjoying the allusive richness of his phrasing, however, we should not overlook Dryden's primary meaning: Lord Howard in his own person represented the hypocrisy of the Whig lords, proceeding, in the course of his own life, from one religious extreme to another, from an Anabaptist preacher to a sacrilegious libertine.

Whig lords were not the only victims of Dryden's one-two punch.

A Brace of Gentlemen

Both Thomas Thynne, Esquire, and Sir William Jones received the left hook of an epithet and the right uppercut of a Biblical name.

When Monmouth made his progress in the summer of 1680, he was twice received and entertained at Longleat in Wiltshire by its wealthy master, Thomas Thynne, known as "the Protestant Squire" and "Tom of Ten Thousand." Dryden refers to these visits when, in lines 737-38, he says:

> But hospitable treats did most Commend
> Wise *Issachar*, his wealthy western friend.

How it was that Thynne merited the name of Issachar and the epithet "wise" has been admirably explained by James Kinsley.[62] The Hebrew

---

[60] Thomas Birch, *A Collection of the State Papers of John Thurloe* (London, 1741), V, 393. The author of the *DNB* article on Howard accepts the identification (X, 83).

[61] *Letter . . . Occasioned by . . Howard*, p. 3.

[62] Kinsley, "Historical Allusions," pp. 296-97.

Issachar is described as "a strong ass couching down between two burdens: And he saw that rest was good, and the land that it was pleasant; and bowed his shoulder to bear, and became a servant unto tribute" (Genesis 49:14-15). Early in November of 1681 the news came out of Thynne's marriage to Lady Ogle. She, however, protested that she had been duped and refused to have the marriage consummated. In addition Lady Trevor began suit against Thynne on the grounds that he was already married or at least under contract of marriage to her daughter. Furthermore the marriage with Lady Ogle apparently involved Thynne in vast payments to people who thereby acquired legal claims on him. So we may see the two burdens of Thynne alluded to in his name Issachar as being either Lady Ogle and the Duke of Monmouth, as Mr. Kinsley believes, or, as I think more likely, the two women themselves, Lady Ogle and the daughter of Lady Trevor, between whom Thynne figuratively lay down, unable to enjoy either but compelled to support the burden of both. This latter reading is made all the more likely by the fact that Dryden, as Mr. Kinsley points out, had in March of 1680 written this exchange in his play, *The Spanish Fryar* (III.ii):

> *Dominic.* How dar'st thou reproach the Tribe of Levi?
> *Gomez.* Marry, because you make us Lay-men of the Tribe of *Issachar:* you make Asses of us, to bear your burthens: when we are young, you put Paniers upon us with your Church-discipline; and when we are grown up, you load us with a Wife. . . . a fine phrase you have amongst you to draw us into Marriage, you call it Settling of a Man; just as when a fellow has got a sound Knock upon the head, they say he's settled: Marriage is a settling Blow indeed.

Sir William Jones came under Dryden's attack for a number of reasons. Regarded as England's leading lawyer, he for a time served Charles as attorney-general (prosecuting those accused by Titus Oates), but in 1679 he quit the King's service and a year later entered the House of Commons as a Whig. He may well have drawn up the Exclusion Bill and certainly he spoke warmly for it, encouraging many other M.P.'s to support it.[63] In particular he argued that any decision on sending relief to the English garrison in Tangier must wait on the passage of the Exclusion Bill.[64] This contention, coupled with the rest of his support for the Bill, caused an anonymous Tory pamphleteer to characterize him in this way:

> That *formal Don* that undertook to prove
> The *Ignoramus Bill*, an *Act* of Love,
> From his *Law-Logick* might have drawn
> As well this weighty *Inference*,
> The loss of *Tangier* too, when gone,
> Will be to th' *Merchants* of good *Consequence*.

[63] Cobbett, *Parliamentary History*, IV, 1208-10.
[64] Cobbett, *Parliamentary History*, IV, 1217.

> And since the *Duke* and that must *both* be *Lost*,
> Since *He* the *Jonas* is, that rais'd the *Storm*,
>   Fling Him o're-Board, that some Officious *Whale*,
> May the kind *Office* once again perform,
>   And *Spew* Him out upon the *Affrick-Coast.*[65]

(Luttrell identified the *"formal Don"* as Jones and the *"Ignoramus Bill"* as the Exclusion Bill, and also called the poem a "Tory pamphlet"; consequently, although the grammatical relation of "He" in the fourth last line is ambiguous, there is no doubt that Jones is meant.)

The reference to raising the storm reminds us that Jonah, for whose name *Jonas* was a variant (Matthew 12:39-40), was as notorious for having caused a storm and being cast overboard so as to still it (Jonah 1:7-15) as he was famous for having been swallowed and then disgorged by a large fish (Jonah 1:17, 2:10). Dryden may have seen the earlier poem on Jones or he may have been independently reminded of Jonas through the similarity of sound and the fact that, as Jonah had fled from the service of the Lord, so Jones had recently quit the service of the King. In either case, it is clear that he regarded Sir William Jones as having been responsible for raising the storm over the Exclusion Bill:

> ... Bull-fac'd-*Jonas*, who could Statutes draw
> To mean Rebellion, and make Treason Law.
>
> (ll. 581-82)

The implications in this couplet are confirmed by lines in *A Key (With the Whip)*:

> Why must Sir *William Jones* thy *Jonas* be?
> Is it because th' *Storm Raiser's* only He;
> What is the Storm which makes thee thus to foam?
> Is't: 'cause the Ship will not steer right to Rome:
> . . . .
> Or *Jonas* he's, to be cast over Board,
> Will this in th' *See of Rome* a calm afford?[66]

The epithet "Bull-fac'd" puzzled the author of *A Key (With the Whip)*: at least he realized that, even if perhaps Sir William Jones did look a little like a bull, Dryden would not refer to him as "Bull-fac'd" without having some artistic and polemical purpose. Accordingly the author protested,

> What *bold fac'd Bard* art thou that dares to call,
> This *Sage [Bull fac'd,]* as if God made not all:

One might alternatively wonder whether the minotaur is alluded to, inasmuch as Jones would have been at the heart of the labyrinthine

---

[65] *A Voice for Moderate Counsels* (London, 1681), p. 12.
[66] *A Key (With the Whip)*, p. 32.

maze of legal terminology in his treason bill, but the minotaur and Jonah have little in common. Actually there is a Biblical use of bulls that would fit. In several passages in the Old Testament, but especially in Leviticus 4:13-21, the Israelites are instructed, when as a congregation they have sinned—even unwittingly—to take a bull and sacrifice it as a sin-offering. The crew of the ship on which Jonah took his passage found themselves in a position similar to that of the congregation: they were unwittingly involved in the sin of Jonah's defiance of God. They accordingly acted in much the same manner and threw Jonah overboard as the sin-offering, the only thing that could placate the Lord and allay the storm. It would appear that Dryden is suggesting, through his epithet "Bull-fac'd," that, as Jones was responsible for the storm, he should be made the sacrifice in atonement for the sin that had caused it and in hopes of allaying it.

Thus was Dryden able, through his simple combination of epithet and Biblical name, to continue reminding his moderate and uncommitted reader of just how factious and at least potentially treasonable the various Whig leaders were. Half his polemical and satiric mission was completed.

In his *Discourse concerning the Original and Progress of Satire* Dryden was later to state that, as the author of satire is to caution his reader against one particular vice, so is he also to inculcate the opposite virtue.[67] Accordingly, while in *Absalom and Achitophel*, as we have seen, he argued against the vice of treason (or treason and factiousness) and satirized its proponents and practitioners, he was at the same time bound to argue for the opposite of treason and factiousness: loyalty and support. Loyalty to what and support for whom? The answer appears to be loyalty to what Charles himself was loyal to: the principles of kingship and legitimate succession. The support would follow for those who upheld that loyalty.

[67] *Discourse concerning the Original and Progress of Satire*, II, 104.

7

THE BROTHERS ROYAL

As Dryden turned from the bad guys to the good guys, he was faced with a variety of problems. There was of course the recurring literary problem of how to make good people appear attractive, and this problem for Dryden was accentuated by the fact that, thanks to his satiric power, he had succeeded in making the bad guys most interesting indeed. What does one do for an encore, especially when the material is inherently much less interesting? (The same problem besets the critic who wishes to discuss what the writer has done with the material.) Yet Dryden was of course a consummate artist and can be counted on to capitalize on whatever aspects there might have been among Charles, James, and their supporters that could be made attractive to his reading audience. But actually Dryden was faced with a further problem, for, taken as a whole, the group of "good" people had far more bad points than good; so not only had he few good points to work with, but also he had somehow to cope with the bad points in such a way that his group of "good" people would indeed appear reasonably good. Actually it is in this peculiar difficulty that Dryden solves his critic's problem, for Dryden's skill in overcoming his difficulty provides the critic (and *his* readers) with much that is fascinating to observe.

In Charles and James, those embodiments of kingship and legitimate succession Dryden wished to defend, there was to be found a mixture of literary assets and liabilities, with more of the latter than the former. To this inherent literary problem Dryden added a particularly difficult one of his own making. As we have noted in the second chapter, he chose to laugh off Charles's lechery at the beginning of the poem. In doing so, he had to make of the King a figure of fun, and yet by the end of the poem this same Charles had to appear as a virtual demigod, a sublime figure, "Righteous *David*" who speaks inspired by heaven and with heaven's approval. The sleight of hand whereby Dryden achieves his metamorphosis is well worth examining.

Too Good a King

Once Dryden had disposed of Charles's lechery in the opening lines, the greatest liability remaining was the apparent laxity of Charles's government. In part Dryden had already begun to deal with that problem in the opening lines also, by suggesting that what looked like laxity was but an extension of fatherly indulgence. Then intermittently, while the poem proceeds for another 700 lines and while he is primarily concerned with other subjects, he reminds his moderate readers that the government, after all, is governing and that Charles's government, with whatever laxity it may really have (much less, no doubt, than the Whigs contend), is vastly preferable to civil war and a return to the Commonwealth, which would be the result of the Whig alternative. The Jebusites (Roman Catholics) have been required to submit to "*David's* Government" (line 93)—a rather convincing demonstration that the government was functioning. Pardoned rebels have grown kinsmen to the throne "by their Monarch's fatal mercy" (lines 146-47)—another demonstration that should have impressed even the Whigs. And the "Prince" with whom Achitophel "stood at bold Defiance" (line 205) must have been a power to contend with for the defiance to be considered bold in the first place.

The alternative, of civil war and Commonwealth, is mentioned or alluded to in at least nine passages before the argument on government. The references range from the explicit description of ugly scars, dishonest to the sight, the memory of civil wars (lines 72-74), to the implications of Shimei's republicanism. One of the most telling reminders comes in line 292, where Dryden gives the rebels' "general Cry":

> Religion, Common-wealth, and Liberty.

The favourite slogan and rallying cry of the Whigs at the time, repeated over and over in their pamphlets and reflecting their fear of Roman Catholicism and arbitrary government, was "No Popery! No Slavery!"—much like the slogan scrawled on walls in Northern Ireland today: "No Popery! No Surrender!" John Caryll in his poem *Naboth's Vineyard* (1679) sought to ridicule the Whig slogan and so, first turning the negative terms into their positive counterparts—Religion and Liberty, he then added to them a satiric third term to complete the Whig cry and show his readers what it really meant:

> Some words there are which have a special charm
> To wind their fancies up to an alarm:
> Treason, Religion, Liberty are such;[1]

Dryden evidently saw how he could improve on Caryll. He retained the positive counterparts but modified the new third term to something

---

[1] John Caryll, *Naboth's Vinyard* (London: C. R., 1679), II, 165-67, in *Poems on Affairs of State*, II, 89.

more apparently moderate (but actually much more frightening) and slipped it in between the other two, to sit in quiet mock innocence: "Religion, Common-wealth, and Liberty." His readers would remember well that under the Commonwealth Anglicans had been severely restricted in the practice of their religion and the people in general had been oppressed by the puritanical Major-Generals, who had ruled in a most arbitrary manner.[2]

Dryden also took more direct ways of handling the Whig charges that Charles, of all people, aimed at absolutism and the return of Roman Catholicism. He insinuated, over and over again, that Charles's rule was mild: so how could it aim at absolutism? Right after an early reminder of the civil wars, he remarks:

> And David's mildness manag'd it so well,
> The Bad found no occasion to Rebell.
>
> (ll. 77-78)

David's "fatal mercy," already noted, was a form of mildness. Absalom is made to give extended praise for that quality in his father's rule, a quality David shares with God (lines 319-28). And even Achitophel is made to acknowledge David's mildness (line 381), which of course he promptly wishes to take advantage of, for his own personal gain. The other charge, of giving way to Popery, Dryden handles by putting it into the mouths of characters who have already been thoroughly discredited. It is Achitophel/Shaftesbury who claims that Charles is himself a Roman Catholic (line 213), and what reader is now prepared to believe him? The same character claims that fear of his brother makes Charles do what James wants him to do (line 469). Not only does the nature of the character making the claim seriously undermine its credibility, but the claim itself is contradicted by what another character says. According to Absalom/Monmouth, Charles's life is endangered by James and the Queen (lines 749-50): if Charles in fact did what James wished, what need would there be for James to kill him? But of course both conflicting claims are preposterous, the patent propaganda of discredited villains. The same Absalom it is who, straining hard to be a traitor to his father, claims that the King is "brib'd with petty summs of Forreign Gold," that he is overly influenced by his Papist whore, and that he allows the Roman Catholics to invade the "Sacred Rites" of the country's church (lines 706-10). What a conglomeration of charges, but what can one expect from such a fool?

For all the problems which Charles's failings made for Dryden, the King did have three qualities which helped his poetic defender. One of these was his position as the apparent underdog, which surely would appeal to the sympathies of most of the uncommitted Englishmen. In his "Declining Age," he is depicted by Achitophel (lines 267-91) as

[2] See Godfrey Davies, The Early Stuarts, 1603-1660, 2nd ed. (Oxford: Clarendon, 1959), pp. 179-80, 201-03, 240.

> setting in his Western Skies,
> The Shadows lengthning as the Vapours rise.

The "heaps of People" who at his restoration thronged to see him are now, thanks to the Plot, "Blown off and scatter'd by a puff of Wind," and he is now "Naked of Friends, and round beset with Foes." Assistance from foreign lands is out of the question, and at home Achitophel himself has estranged the "alter'd Hearts" of all sorts of Englishmen, turning them from "*David*'s Rule." Nor will David's beleagueredness stop here, for Achitophel promises (lines 389-400) that, by his cunning, he will proceed to remove from David even those few supporters who still stand by him, until "He shall be Naked left to publick Scorn." What Englishman, with any shred of Christian charity, could withhold his support?

Another asset Charles had was that he did represent stability. That was why, after all, as Dryden reminds his readers, England called him back from exile: the Commonwealth had not worked, and the country joyously returned to its monarch (lines 59-60, 270-73). The Roman Catholics, that potentially rebellious minority, were in submission to his government (line 93). And Absalom is made to reiterate the obvious:

> My Father Governs with unquestion'd Right;
> The Faiths Defender, and Mankinds Delight:
> Good, Gracious, Just, observant of the Laws;
> And Heav'n by Wonders has Espous'd his Cause.
>
> (ll. 317-20)

Who but a fool would want to exchange such beneficent stability for civil war?

The third attribute of Charles that assisted Dryden was the one he wished to emerge strongly at the end of his poem: the special relation of the King to God. Dryden is careful to build up to this relation slowly. In the opening lines, on David's "polygamy," he plays, ironically, with the concept of the King's being Vice-Regent of God. Implanting the idea at this early stage will of course help, but admittedly on any serious consideration, Charles in the opening lines comes across simply as a man all too human and all too sinful. By proceeding from Charles the impregnator to Charles the father in an indulgent relation to his son, Dryden is able, because the concept of father is common to all three, to proceed further to Charles the King: "While *David*, undisturb'd, in *Sion* raign'd" (line 42). Soon the concept of the parallel between God and King is reintroduced—"No King could govern, nor no God could please" (line 48)—and before long the parallel becomes something closer still, the "God's Anointed" of line 130. When Achitophel and Absalom discuss the King, he emerges even more strongly as the father both of Absalom and of his people, a father whose

principal attribute of mildness is shared with God and whose cause has
been espoused by heaven through its wonders. This King, so favoured
by God, is attacked by various bad people: cunning plotters designing
their own advancement, republicans taking the name of God in vain in
an effort to undermine the King, and a son who traduces his father in
public. The reaction in Dryden's readers against these evil actions, a
reaction strengthened by Dryden's argument about good government
(in which Kings are presented as "the Godheads Images"—lines 792),
would prepare those readers to look for, and welcome, a King who, in
order to preserve his loyal people, takes the sword of divine punishment in hand. And that is the kind of King who emerges: "Righteous
David," "too good a King" (lines 811-12), who consults with his wise
advisers and then

> With all these loads of Injuries opprest,
> And long revolving, in his carefull Breast,
> Th'event of things; at last his patience tir'd,
> Thus from his Royal Throne by Heav'n inspir'd,
> The God-like *David* spoke: with awfull fear
> His Train their Maker in their Master hear.
>
> (ll. 933-38)

The speech of David/Charles is itself carefully designed to display
attractive qualities. The mildness, of which the reader has been reminded throughout the poem, is still present, and is in fact confirmed
in the opening of the speech, for there mercy and forbearing, forgiveness and clemency are very much to the fore:

> Thus long have I, by native mercy sway'd,
> My wrongs dissembl'd, my revenge delay'd:
> So willing to forgive th'Offending Age,
> So much the Father did the King asswage.
> But now so far my Clemency they slight,
> Th'Offenders question my Forgiving Right.
>
> (ll. 939-44)

And even as he prepares to punish by the law, the King again expresses
his innate mildness:

> Oh that my Power to Saving were confin'd:
> Why am I forc'd, like Heaven, against my mind,
> To make Examples of another Kind?
> Must I at length the Sword of Justice draw?
> Oh curst Effects of necessary Law!
> How ill my Fear they by my Mercy scan,
> Beware the Fury of a Patient Man.
>
> (ll. 999-1005)

These qualities of mildness and mercy are extended to Monmouth, as Charles the King remains very much Charles the loving father and calls upon his son to repent (ll. 955-70). At the same time the fatherly concern extends to all his people, as he reminds Monmouth:

> Whence comes it that Religion and the Laws
> Should more be *Absalom*'s than *David*'s Cause?

The special position of the King is likewise reiterated and re-emphasized. He exists "to Rule, for that's a Monarch's End" (line 946); "A King's," Charles remarks wryly, "at least a part of Government" (line 977); and so great is his power and so elevated his position, that Charles may say,

> For Gods, and Godlike Kings their Care express,
> Still to Defend their Servants in distress.
>
> (ll. 997-98)

Two new qualities of Charles as King emerge in his speech, both further reflecting his sublime position. One is a magisterial wit. Already seen in the wry comment about a King's being at least a part of government, it crackles through his comment about the petitioners who sought to change the course of government by the sheer weight of numbers and reiteration:

> True, they Petition me t'approve their Choise,
> But *Esau*'s Hands suite ill with *Jacob*'s Voice.
> My Pious Subjects for my Safety pray,
> Which to Secure they take my Power away.
> From Plots and Treasons Heaven preserve my years,
> But Save me most from my Petitioners.
> Unsatiate as the barren Womb or Grave;
> God cannot Grant so much as they can Crave.
>
> (ll. 981-88)

The other quality is an awesomeness producing terror in wrong-doers. Just as Dryden interlaced the lines of wit with references to the Bible so as to elevate the wit itself and make it magisterial, so he turns to a passage in Exodus (33:17-23) for an image of the most sublime terror. The Lord, in graciously allowing Moses to see his glory, stationed him so that he might see the "back parts" of the Lord as he passed by, but not his face, for no man might see his face and live. So Charles, most reluctantly taking up the sword of Justice, with which to smite the rebels, says,

> Law they require, let Law then shew her Face;
> They coud not be content to look on Grace,
> Her hinder parts, but with a daring Eye
> To tempt the terror of her Front, and Dye.
>
> (ll. 1006-09)

Admittedly the inclusion of "Grace,/Her hinder parts" adds a tone of sexual wit, even humour, and potentially bathos. It is but a touch, however, and we are immediately reminded of the awesome power that is associated with this ironically humorous image. The final effect may well vary with individual readers, but in the amalgam of tones the lower one can readily, through contrast, strengthen the grandeur of the higher one. In fact, by introducing the mystery, inexplicable to man, of the Lord's wishing to have his majesty conveyed to Moses through a glimpse of his divine "back parts," Dryden manages to remind his readers of the other mystery before them: that a very human individual, the King, may, while retaining an appreciation of those aspects of sexuality often considered baser, continue to function, thanks to his having been anointed by God, as the Lord's vice-regent in the realm, wielding the power of life and death with divine sanction. Some Whigs saw only the witty lecher, and some Tories saw only the office. Dryden sees both, and invites his readers to do likewise.

Of Every Royal Virtue

Charles's brother and heir apparent, James, presented far more liabilities than assets to Dryden.

To begin with, he was as notorious for his lechery as was Charles. In fact the two were linked together in the pamphlet by Stephen Colledge (quoted earlier) in which Charles is called the manager of a raree (or peep) show:

> Raree show in French lap,
> Is gone to take a nap,
> And successor has the clap,

All the other charges that were made against James and that we of a later era might find credible, are summed up in this paragraph from *A Just and Modest Vindication of the proceedings of the Two last Parliaments*:

The violence of his natural temper is sufficiently known: His vehemence in exalting the Prerogative (in his Brothers time) beyond its due bounds, and the principles of his Religion which carry him to all imaginable excesses of cruelty, have convinced all mankind that he must be excluded, or the Name of King being left unto him, the power put into the hands of another. The Parliament [actually, the House of Commons] therefore considering this, and observing the precedents of former ages, did wisely choose rather to exclude him, than to leave him the Name, and place the power in a Regent. For they could not but look upon it as folly, to expect that one of his temper, bred up in such principles in politicks, as made him in love with Arbitrary power, and bigotted in that Religion, which allewise propagates it self by Blood, would patiently bear these shackles, which would be very disgustful unto a Prince of the most meek disposition.[3]

Other charges were made, not so credible to us, but still of bearing on the poem, such as these three from the twenty which Robert Ferguson made:

5. It was this darling and beloved one, that authorised the burning of London [in 1666], and not only made his own palace a sanctuary to the villains, who were suspected as instruments of that dreadful conflagration, but rescued and discharged divers who were apprehended in the very fact....

. . . .

9. He hath not only maintained correspondence with foreign princes, to the betraying of the king's counsels, but hath confederated with them for the extirpation of our religion, and overthrowing our legal government.

10. He was consenting to and hath co-operated in the whole popish plot; for both his confessor and secretary did, with his knowledge and approbation, seal the resolves for the king's death.[4]

Of special concern to those attacking James was his temper. One of his defenders complained that James's enemies had fabricated "the inexorableness of the duke's temper, if once offended: a groundless and malicious scandal; an opinion that, being generally spread abroad, has already begot many great evils."[5] In a footnote to this passage Sir Walter Scott illustrated the prevalent fear of James's temper thus:

The opinion of James's obstinacy was deeply rooted among the people, who compared his temper with that of his brother. "Do you not know," said he to one of the numerous state criminals of his time, from whom he wished to extort a confession, "do you not know that it is in my power to pardon you?" "It may be in your power," retorted the condemned person, "but it is not in your nature."

Even James's virtues his enemies could make appear to be dangerous. Being convinced that he should restore Roman Catholicism, he would (they said) use those virtues to do a more effective job of trying to restore it than a weak king would—and of course Roman Catholicism meant complete tyranny.

His Fortitude . . . makes him the more daring in the Cause of Rome; his Justice makes it a point of Conscience to deliver us up to the Pope; his Temperance in the government of his Passions, makes him more close and steady; and

---

[3] *A Just and Modest Vindication of the proceedings of the Two last Parliaments* (London, 1681), pp. 30-31.

[4] [Robert Ferguson], *A Letter to a Person of Honour concerning the King's disavowing the having been married to the Duke of Monmouth's Mother* (London, 1680), in Somers' *Tracts*, VIII, 205.

[5] *England's Concern in the Case of his Royal Highness James Duke of York and Albany* (London, 1680), in Somers' *Tracts*, VIII, 178.

his *Prudence crowns the work by the assistance it gives him in the management of his Policies and Conduct.* . . . What boots it in a Popish Heir to say, he's
the truest Friend, the greatest of Hero's, the best of Masters, the justest Judge,
and the honestest of Men? All meer treacherous Quick-sands for a People to
repose the least glimps of Safety in, or build the least Hopes upon.[6]

With even his virtues turned against him, what was a defender of
James to do? Thomas D'Urfey in his poem *The Progress of Honesty*
tried to put a bold front on it. He praised James's constancy,

> Positive fixt and setled to his Will,
> And dares to do anything but Ill,[7]

extolled his bravery in battle,

> Bravest in danger, valiant but not rash:
> For when the Belgian Streamers brav'd the British Cross,
> Then on the bloody Deck he seem'd to grow,
> Whilst Fate affrighted aim'd the Shot too low,
> Aw'd with the Terror of his dauntless Brow.

and then took the high road concerning his arrogance and religion:

> His haughty Soul ne'er understood
> To humour the Mechanick Brood.
> The People like rough Waters are to him,
> On which he swims against the Stream,
> Nor fears the danger of the wildest storm;
> His courage and his Fate contemns all harm.
> In his Religion firm, but not precise,
> Admires the Counsel of the Wise,
> But cares not to be Catechis'd,
> Or new untrodden paths be shown,
> As if the way to Heaven he had not known,
>   Or that his Soul were not his own;
> His Conscience will be guided by his sense,
>   Not by the vulgar's impudence.
> So th'Roman Heroes rather chose to die
> By their own noble hands than by an Enemy.

Such an approach might work with a few Tory readers, but certainly
the moderates would only be led to believe that the Whigs were right
about the danger James represented to the country. Put a man like that
on the throne and be prepared for trouble. He would rather die a Roman
hero, would he, and take the country with him?

Dryden's approach is much more low-keyed. He ignores James's
sexual immorality and almost ignores both his religion and his arbi-

---

[6] [Elkanah Settle], *The Character of a Popish Successour Compleat* (London, 1681),
p. 1.

[7] *Progress of Honesty*, sec. IX, p. 9. Succeeding quotations are from pp. 9-10.

trary qualities, thereby implying that all the talk about these qualities is merely a Whig ruse to cover their lust for power. He disposes of three charges in the way he disposed of charges against Charles: he puts them in the mouths of characters already discredited. To Monmouth is attributed the charge that James plotted against his brother's life (lines 749-50), and Shaftesbury is made to admit that it is he himself who, through his propaganda, has created the popular dislike of James (lines 401-04). It is also Shaftesbury who charges James with vengefulness and then is made to show the emptiness of the charge by offering as his reason for it the observation "He meditates Revenge who least Complains" (line 446). Those who practise Christian charity and turn the other cheek to their tormentors must then, in Shaftesbury's way of thinking, be riddled with vengefulness. Immediately after committing the illogic of his observation, Shaftesbury is made to offer an image for James that actually works counter to his intent:

> And like a Lyon, Slumbring in the way,
> Or Sleep-dissembling, while he waits his Prey,
> His fearless Foes within his Distance draws;
> Constrains his Roaring, and Contracts his Paws;
> Till at the last, his time for Fury found,
> He shoots with suddain Vengeance from the Ground:
> The Prostrate Vulgar, passes o'r, and Spares;
> But with a Lordly Rage, his Hunters teares.
>
> (ll. 447-54)

Though vengefulness is repeated in the image, it is subsumed in the lordly and regal nature of the lion, long a symbol of royalty and even, in Hosea 11:10, associated with the Lord in his perfectly justified anger.

James's few assets Dryden makes Absalom/Monmouth admit to: legitimacy, bravery, loyalty, and (most of all) mercy:

> His Brother, though Opprest with Vulgar Spight,
> Yet Dauntless and Secure of Native Right,
> Of every Royal Vertue stands possest;
> Still Dear to all the Bravest, and the Best.
> His Courage Foes, his Friends his Truth Proclaim;
> His Loyalty the King, the World his Fame,
> His Mercy even th'Offending Crowd will find,
> For sure he comes of a Forgiving Kind.
>
> (ll. 353-60)

Even this listing of favourable qualities is low-keyed. While Dryden has certainly not chosen to say as little as possible about James, he has still kept him in the background, especially compared to Charles. In doing so, he of course implies two things about the Whigs; it is they who have fabricated the problem about James and then magnified it out of all proportion, and they have done so in order to cover up their real aim

—to reduce the kingly power of the monarch already reigning, Charles II.

There may still be another passage in which James is concerned, but, since scholars have not read it that way, I should like to consider it separately.

Agag

It will be remembered that when describing Titus Oates under the name of Corah, Dryden writes:

> His Zeal to heav'n, made him his Prince despise,
> And load his person with indignities:
> But Zeal peculiar priviledg affords;
> Indulging latitude to deeds and words.
> And *Corah* might for *Agag*'s murther call,
> In terms as course as *Samuel* us'd to *Saul*.
>
> (ll. 672-77)

The Biblical Agag (1 Samuel 15) was the King of the Amalekites, a people hostile to the Israelites. The prophet Samuel commanded King Saul to slay all the Amalekites (including women and children) and all their cattle. When Saul killed all the subjects but spared Agag himself and some of the better cattle, Samuel berated Saul and hacked Agag to pieces personally. In Dryden's sentence containing the reference to Agag, there are established three categories which must be filled by anyone answering to the identity of Agag: (1) Agag was the leader of a people hostile to the Israelites, (2) his murder was *called for* by Corah (Oates)—not, here, actually brought about, and (3) Corah called for that murder in coarse language. In addition there is a fourth category created by the parallelism between this sentence and the preceding one (so close is the parallelism, in fact, that many modern editors replace the separating period with a joining semi-colon): viz., (4) the calling for the murder is in some manner related to the fact that Oates despised his prince and loaded his person with indignities.

To the present, scholars have put forward three contenders for the person of Agag. Sir Edmund Berry Godfrey is the oldest claimant, but, especially since he was a Protestant, he does not fit any of the categories, unless one believes that Dryden accepted the extreme Tory charge that Oates was responsible for Godfrey's murder—and even if one does, Godfrey would still not fit categories one and four. Lord Chief Justice Sir William Scroggs has been suggested:[8] Oates certainly attacked him verbally, no doubt in a coarse manner, and tried to have him convicted of "high misdemeanour"; the third category would be filled, and, with some stretching, so would the second; but not the first,

[8] See E. S. de Beer, "Literary and Historical Notes," p. 309.

and the relation of the fourth would be vague indeed. Lord Stafford is the third person put forward.[9] As a Roman Catholic peer he would come close to fitting the first category, being, not *the* leader, but *a* leader of a people supposedly hostile to the Anglicans of England. Oates called for Stafford's murder inasmuch as he accused him of treason and gave evidence against him at his trial. But I have been unable to find any written record of Oates's having used coarse or abusive language towards him—though there is ample evidence of his having used such language towards others. As with the other contenders, Stafford's relation to the fourth category would appear to be vague.

To these three contenders I would re-introduce a fourth, originally suggested in *A Key (With the Whip)*: James, Duke of York, who fits all four categories. He was *the* leader of the Roman Catholics within England. Oates repeatedly called for his murder or execution for treason. Oates is furthermore on record as having, on several occasions, spoken violently against the Duke: three times he is recorded as having called James a traitor, he compared him to a scavenger and to the Devil, and three times he said that he would see James hanged.[10] Edmund Warcup testified that a gentleman "told me Oates had said the Duke had betrayed the nation & wished, if the devill had a hotter place in hell than [any] other, that he would reserve it for the duke."[11] Obviously three of the four categories of identification are filled, and, I should think, with a better fit than with the other claimants. There is, moreover, a relation between the call for Agag's murder and Corah's despising of his prince and loading his person with indignities. If "Prince" refers to Charles, the call for his brother's murder is an intensified parallel to the other indignities heaped on the King. If "Prince" refers to James himself (and the term was often used for both Prince James and his deceased cousin, Prince Rupert), and James is then the one on whose person Oates loaded indignities, the coarsely phrased call for his murder is even more closely related.

Admittedly there remains a bit of a puzzle: why would Dryden choose a name, like Agag, which would call attention to the supposed hostility of the Roman Catholics to the Anglicans of England? The answer would appear to lie in the fact that it was Corah/Oates who, in calling for the murder of his victim, gave that victim the name of Agag. In other words, the choice of name reflects, not Dryden the narrator's view of Roman Catholics, but Oates's ludicrously exaggerated view—as if the true-born Englishmen who happened to be Roman Catholic could properly be compared to the separate race of Amalekites who had ac-

[9] See Kinsley, "Historical Allusions," pp. 295-96.
[10] *State Trials*, X, 134-39.
[11] Keith Feiling and F. R. D. Needham, "The Journals of Edmund Warcup, 1676-84," *English Historical Review*, 40 (1925), 260.

tively fought against the Israelites and who remained openly hostile to them. (To compare English Roman Catholics with Jebusites is one thing, but with Amalekites is quite another.) What Dryden is doing in this passage is something he has done elsewhere, with a further twist. He attributes the charge of treason against James (for heading the Papists and being part of the Plot) to a character whom he has just finished thoroughly discrediting—as he attributes other charges to Monmouth and Shaftesbury. With this particular charge, however, he so phrases the attribution as to solicit greater sympathy for the innocent victim. Corah does not call righteously for the legal execution of a man convicted of a crime: instead Corah blackens his victim with a name most unfairly exaggerated, he calls for his "murther," and he does so in terms that are "coarse" and (with the Biblical story in mind) downright bloodthirsty. With such a man calling in such a way for the murder of one of the embodiments of legitimate kingship and succession, should not all loyal Englishmen rally to the royalist cause?

Fortunately for Charles and James, and of course for England, there were already some valuable supporters of the royal pair, though they were few.

8

THIS SHORT FILE

Shaftesbury was right about one thing: in 1681 the range of active supporters of Charles was rather limited. There had been a fairly rapid turnover in the leading ministers of the crown in the years immediately preceding, and both Sunderland and Godolphin, able ministers who were to rise to eminence under later monarchs, had just fallen from favour. Sir William Temple, who had acquired some reputation as diplomat and constitutionalist, had just retired from politics to return to his domestic and literary pursuits. Of those currently regarded as the predominant ministers, moreover, all presented some difficulties. Viscount Halifax had just recently been restored to Charles's favour, after having for some time supported Shaftesbury and some of his policies. The Earl of Conway, according to a modern historian, was "notoriously stupid."[1] Sir Leoline Jenkins was a faithful drudge and a stickler for form—obviously not one to use in an appeal to the uncommitted.[2] Laurence Hyde was young and not particularly experienced. And Edward Seymour had been a most arrogant speaker of the House of Commons and had, furthermore, recently been charged by it with malfeasance in the discharge of his current duties as the person responsible for the navy.

A few others who were associated with the court, though not active in it, were available for use. The Duke of Ormonde was widely respected for his courage, upright character, and steadfastness. His son, the Earl of Ossory, had become a national hero because of his martial exploits and had consolidated his fame and good-will by dying not long before. The Earl of Mulgrave had likewise gained military fame and was currently in the public eye. Similarly the leaders of the Church of England (the Archbishop of Canterbury, the Bishop of London, and the Dean of Westminster) might be used to impress Dryden's readers with their support for Charles.

[1] Jones, *The First Whigs*, p. 140.
[2] James McMullen Rigg, "Jenkins, Sir Leoline," *DNB*, X, 741.

In view of what he had available to him, Dryden evidently chose to present the King's supporters in four different ways. He made the fullest use of those who were highly esteemed in the nation—and, incidentally, not closely associated with the court. He isolated desirable qualities in a group of the supporters rather than presenting those supporters as well-rounded individuals. He said nothing at all about those people, like Conway and Jenkins, who were not attractive. And he made a very special use of Seymour, the former speaker of the House of Commons.

Friends in Distress

He began with the DUKE OF ORMONDE.[3] Since the Duke had served Charles I and had gone into exile with Charles II, where he gave his King comfort and assistance, it is fitting that Dryden should have assigned him the name of Barzillai, the aging man who helped David in his exile (2 Samuel 17:27). But since two others are named in the same Biblical passage for helping David in the same way, we may wonder why Dryden chose the name he did from the three available to him. One reason could be that Barzillai is mentioned again (praisingly and, curiously, in close conjunction with Shimei—1 Kings 2:7-8) and the others are not. Another reason could readily be the meaning of the name Barzillai ("as hard as iron"), for Ormonde was outstandingly steadfast. In addition to maintaining the purity of his morals within an immoral world, he had served Charles faithfully for many years as Lord Lieutenant of Ireland. During that time he had been schemed against and intrigued against by courtiers like Buckingham and Lady Castlemaine. He was almost assassinated by the ruffian Thomas Blood, who may in fact have been hired for the job by Buckingham—a thought that gains some credence from the fact that when Blood was captured, Charles personally asked Ormonde to pardon him. When for seven years Ormonde was removed from the lord lieutenancy (in an effort by Charles to please courtiers), he remained loyal to his sovereign. In fact he remained so loyal, so stubbornly loyal, that when Charles was about to reappoint him Lord Lieutenant, the King said to his courtiers as Ormonde approached: "Yonder comes Ormonde; I have done all I can to disoblige that man, and to make him as discontented as others; but he will not be out of humour with me; he will be loyal in spite of my teeth; I must even take him in again, and he is the fittest person to govern Ireland." A man of iron character, indeed. And one who was greatly respected by the moderates. During his period of disfavour at court, he was chosen Chancellor of Oxford and he saw the freedom of

---

[3] Biographical details are drawn from Osmund Airy, "Butler, James," *DNB*, III, 504-12. The speech of Charles is quoted from p. 511.

Dublin conferred on his eldest son, with an address composed chiefly of compliments to himself. When the Popish Plot broke, he acted swiftly, but without panic, to make sure that it did not spread to Ireland. All in all he was abundantly a man for Dryden to parade before his moderate readers, as a man both greatly esteemed for his integrity and firmly in support of his liege lord, the King:

> In this short File *Barzillai* first appears;
> *Barzillai* crown'd with Honour and with Years:
> Long since, the rising Rebells he withstood
> In Regions Waste, beyond the *Jordans* Flood:
> Unfortunately Brave to buoy the State;
> But sinking underneath his Masters Fate:
> In Exile with his Godlike Prince he Mourn'd;
> For him he Suffer'd, and with him Return'd.
> The Court he practis'd, not the Courtier's art:
> Large was his Wealth, but larger was his Heart:
> Which, well the Noblest Objects knew to choose,
> The Fighting Warriour, and Recording Muse.
>
> (ll. 817-28)

Ormonde's son, the EARL OF OSSORY, had become a national hero through the martial exploits he had performed while fighting against his country's enemies.[4] In fact, so highly regarded was he that when he died a few months before *Absalom and Achitophel* was written, no fewer than five long and fulsome elegies were published in his praise.[5] So to remind the public that this hero was a supporter of the King would indeed help Dryden's cause. In fact Ossory had been so much a supporter of the King that he had been appointed a member of the Privy Council not long before his death,[6] and had even more recently been made commander of the expedition destined for Tangier and the relief of the English garrison there undergoing siege. Dryden evidently felt no need to mention these circumstances specifically: presumably he felt that his readers knew well who and what Ossory had been, knew of his death and the loss it represented, and probably also knew of the many and lengthy elegies that had been published in his honour. So

[4] Biographical details are drawn from Osmund Airy, "Butler, Thomas," *DNB*, III, 533-37.

[5] *An Elegy to the Memory of the Right Honorable Thomas, Earl of Ossory, who departed this Life, July the 30th, 1680* (1680), *A Second Elegy on that Incomparable Heroe, Thomas Earl of Ossory* (1680), Thomas Flatman's *A Pindarique Ode on the Death of the Right Honourable Thomas Earl of Ossory* (1681), Elkanah Settle's *An Heroick Poem on the Right Honourable, Thomas Earl of Ossory* (1681), and Knightley Chetwood's *An Ode in Imitation of Pindar on the Death of the Right Honourable Thomas Earl of Ossory* (1681). In addition, there was *A Brief Compendium of the Birth, Education, Heroick Exploits and Victories of the Truly Valorous and Renowned Gentleman, Thomas Earl of Ossory* (1680).

[6] Luttrell, I, 40.

Dryden could afford merely to touch lightly on these matters in what is in effect a eulogy, and the desired amount of response would be forthcoming. Consequently he expresses grief at the Earl's death, "snatcht in Manhoods prime,"

> Yet not before the Goal of Honour won,
> All parts fulfill'd of Subject and of Son;
> Swift was the Race, but short the Time to run.
> Oh Narrow Circle, but of Pow'r Divine,
> Scanted in Space, but perfect in thy Line!
> By Sea, by Land, thy Matchless Worth was known;
> Arms thy Delight, and War was all thy Own:
> Thy force, Infus'd, the fainting *Tyrians* prop'd:
> And Haughty *Pharaoh* found his Fortune stop'd.
> Oh Ancient Honour, Oh Unconquer'd Hand,
> Whom Foes unpunish'd never coud withstand!
>
> (ll. 835-45)

There is one hope left, that from heaven

> thy kindred legions mayst thou bring
> To aid the guardian Angel of thy King.
>
> (ll. 852-53)

It is also worth remarking that the person who had written the longest and the most fulsome elegy on Ossory was Elkanah Settle, the noted writer for the Whigs (who in a few months was to be pilloried as Doeg in the Second Part of the poem). Here in the first part Dryden uses him, implicitly, to implement one of the most telling devices of the skilled polemicist, for it would appear that Dryden is in effect saying to his moderate reader: here in the Earl of Ossory was a man on whom even the Whigs heaped praise and who of course chose to support the King.

After the much esteemed father and son, Dryden turns to the Church, to remind his readers that its worthy leaders are in support of the King. First is WILLIAM SANCROFT, whom Dryden describes thus:

> *Zadock* the Priest, whom, shunning Power and Place,
> His lowly mind advanc'd to *David*'s Grace:
>
> (ll. 864-65)

The name Zadoc in Dryden's day was recognized as the name of the High Priest among the Hebrews, although in literal fact the Zadoc of the Biblical David's acquaintance had not become High Priest till after the episode with Absalom—another little indication of the independent nature of Dryden's fictional construct. Sancroft must have startled both the court and the ecclesiastical world when in September of 1668 he declined promotion from the deanship of St. Paul's to the bishopric of Chester, because he wished to stay at St. Paul's and remain closely involved in the rebuilding of the cathedral.[7] Hence Dryden's ascription to him of a "lowly mind," "shunning Power and Place." Actually one month after this "shunning," Sancroft became Archdeacon of Canterbury, and when in 1677 he was chosen Archbishop of Canterbury (over the likely candidate, Henry Compton, Bishop of London), he was so elevated because James preferred him over the violently Protestant Compton and because, Burnet says, the court thought that it could control him. Dryden of course mentions nothing of this, saying only that he had a "lowly mind" and implying that Charles showed his grace in advancing him to the power and place he had previously shunned.

Next to Zadoc/Sancroft was

> The *Sagan* of *Jerusalem*,
> Of hospitable Soul and noble Stem;
>
> (ll. 866-67)

This was HENRY COMPTON, the man whom Sancroft defeated for the Archbishopric of Canterbury.[8] Compton had owed his rapid rise in the church to three things: his high birth—Dryden's "noble Stem" (Compton was the sixth son of the second Earl of Northampton), the influence of his intimate friend, the Earl of Danby, and his bold avowal of hostility to the Papists. This last quality, however, caused him to come into contention with James and so be denied the highest post. As Bishop of London he remained in second position, reflected in the name Dryden gave him, Sagan, a name that Dryden found, not in the Bible, but in a contemporary description of Hebrew ecclesiastical offices.[9]

Following Compton, Dryden presented JOHN DOLBEN, Dean of Westminster, who had been noted during the Commonwealth for daringly and illegally conducting secret and underground Church of England services and who was later noted as Dean of Westminster for his pulpit oratory.[10] This the church historian Overton has described as clear and plain in content, pure and terse in style—famous for its raciness and practicality. Hence Dryden's couplet:

> Him of the Western dome, whose mighty sense
> Flows in fit words and heavenly eloquence.
>
> (ll. 868-69)

And look: such a man as he supports the King—of course.

[7] Biographical details are drawn from William Holden Hutton, "Sancroft, William," *DNB*, XVII, 733-38.

[8] Biographical details are drawn from Sidney Lee, "Compton, Henry," *DNB*, IV, 899-903.

[9] T. Godwin, *Moses and Aaron: Civil and Ecclesiastical Rites, Used by the ancient Hebrews* (1625), referred to by de Beer, "Literary and Historical Notes," p. 303n.

[10] Biographical details are drawn from Edmund Venables, "Dolben, John," *DNB*, V, 1094-97. Overton is quoted on p. 1096.

Proceeding easily from the Church to the Universities (where learning and loyalty are taught), Dryden then makes his pitch to them, reminding them that

> *Colleges* on bounteous Kings depend,
> And never Rebell was to Arts a friend.
>
> (ll. 872-73)

Nor does the royal support end there. A few temporal lords of the realm stayed at Charles's side—while he allowed them to do so. John Sheffield, the EARL OF MULGRAVE, was one. Dryden begins by reminding his readers of Mulgrave's intelligence (he was, after all, a poet of some renown) and his loyalty:

> Sharp judging *Adriel* the Muses friend,
> Himself a Muse—In Sanhedrins debate
> True to his Prince; but not a Slave of State.
>
> (ll. 877-79)

The next couplet (the last of this brief description of Mulgrave)—

> Whom *David*'s love with Honours did adorn,
> That from his disobedient Son were torn.—

refers to the transfer to Mulgrave which Charles had just made of the honours and commands Monmouth had enjoyed. The Earl had deserved these, and it was very politic of Charles to recognize him in this way, because he had recently acquired fame while serving in a campaign with the French army in Turenne and still more recently had been appointed to command the expedition for the relief of Tangier —the expedition which the hero, Ossory, was to have commanded.[11] In fact this latest command may well have been what Dryden had in mind when he gave Mulgrave the name Adriel. There appears to be no connection between Mulgrave and the circumstances of the Biblical character Adriel, who received one of Saul's daughters in marriage (1 Samuel 18:19). But since the name Adriel means "flock of God," Dryden could well have applied it to the shepherd who was about to lead the English flock to Tangier. It was of course astute of Dryden to remind his readers, as he appears to be doing with both Ossory and Mulgrave, of the fact that the Whigs in the House of Commons had tried to prevent the relief expedition from setting out for Tangier (and rescuing the British troops there) until they had had their way with the King.

The next peer described also calls to mind the Whigs in Parliament. George Savile, VISCOUNT HALIFAX, Dryden describes as

> *Jotham* of ready wit and pregnant thought,
> Indew'd by nature, and by learning taught
> To move Assemblies. . . .
>
> (ll. 882-84)

---

[11] Edward Irving Carlyle, "Sheffield, John," *DNB*, XVIII, 13.

Halifax, who was indeed noted for his intelligence, wit, and persuasive speech, presented to Dryden a potential difficulty and a very useful asset.[12] For some time he had been a most effective opponent of the government and close associate of Shaftesbury—so much so, in fact, that he won Charles's disfavour even more thoroughly than Shaftesbury had. But then when Charles appointed him to the Privy Council (in an attempt to reconcile opposition), his suavity so fascinated Charles that he became a prime favourite with the King. Not only that, but in the Exclusion Crisis, Halifax separated from Shaftesbury and sought to preserve stability. When the House of Commons passed the Exclusion Bill and it came before the House of Lords, Halifax came down firmly on the King's side and in a debate that went on for ten hours spoke sixteen times, answering the arguments of Shaftesbury and Essex. Thanks to his eloquence (and to the presence of Charles throughout the debate), the House of Lords rejected the Bill 63-30. As a result, the Whig-controlled House of Commons immediately called upon the King to dismiss Halifax from his councils forever: the wishes of the lowest third of Parliament were evidently not to be thwarted in this manner, nor was the world to see that the upper two-thirds of Parliament were for legitimate succession. These two aspects of Halifax, his former opposition to Charles and his recent triumph on his behalf, Dryden was able to turn to his use and to phrase most happily:

> who but onely try'd
> The worse awhile, then chose the better side;
> Nor chose alone, but turn'd the balance too;
> So much the weight of one brave man can doe.
>
> (ll. 884-87)

From the ministers of the crown Dryden then selects only two —judiciously ignoring the others as not being attractive to the moderate readers. LAURENCE HYDE, second son of the Earl of Clarendon, had served as the King's ambassador in a number of missions on the continent.[13] In 1679 (at the age of 37) he had become one of the lords of the commission administering the treasury, and in November of that year he became the first lord of the Treasury, and shortly afterwards one of a triumvirate of ministers still predominant when Dryden wrote *Absalom and Achitophel*. To him Dryden ascribes not only the necessary quality of frugality (to explain how Charles could live on no funds from the House of Commons, simply on import duties) but also the Biblical name of Hushai. The name was appropriate in part, in that the Biblical Hushai had been the "King's companion" to David (1 Chronicles 27:33), evidently the principal royal advisor. The meaning of the name, "hasting," was also appropriate (whether intended or not), for

[12] Biographical details are drawn from Thomas Seccombe, "Savile, George," *DNB*, XVII, 845-53.

[13] Biographical details are drawn from James McMullen Rigg, "Hyde, Laurence," *DNB*, X, 394-400.

Hyde had moved swiftly up to the highest offices and honours and had reached them at such an early age that he and his coeval ministers were called "The Chits."

> *Hushai* the friend of *David* in distress,
> In publick storms of manly stedfastness;
> By foreign treaties he inform'd his Youth;
> And join'd experience to his native truth.
> His frugal care supply'd the wanting Throne,
> Frugal for that, but bounteous of his own:
> 'Tis easy conduct when Exchequers flow,
> But hard the task to manage well the low:
> For Soveraign power is too deprest or high,
> When Kings are forc'd to sell, or Crowds to buy.
>
> (ll. 888-97)

(The appeal in the last couplet to the golden mean of the moderate reader will not have escaped notice.)

The other minister, SIR EDWARD SEYMOUR, was actually the minister in charge of the navy, but Dryden refers only to his earlier role as Speaker of the House of Commons.[14] His overweening pride is shown in his reply to Prince William of Orange, who had asked him whether he was of the Duke of Somerset's family. In fact Seymour was the head of the elder branch of the Seymours, in the younger branch of which the Duke of Somerset found himself. So Seymour replied to William: "Pardon me, sir, the Duke of Somerset is of *my* family." His arrogance is shown in his action when his carriage broke down one day at Charing Cross. He had the beadles stop the next gentleman's coach to come along, ejected the owner, and drove off in the commandeered coach, saying merely that it was fitter for the other man to walk in the streets than for the Speaker of the House of Commons to do so. His contemporary Burnet described him thus:

> The ablest man of his party was Seymour, that was the first Speaker of that house that was not bred to the law. He was a man of great birth, being the elder branch of the Seymour family, and was a graceful man, bold and quick, but was the most immoral and impious man of the age. He had a sort of pride so peculiar to himself that I never saw anything like it. He had neither shame nor decency with it. And in all private as well as in public dealings he was the unjustest and blackest man that has lived in our time. He was violent against the court, till he forced himself into good posts. He was the most assuming speaker that ever sate in the chair. He knew the house and every man in it so well [at a time when parties were still amorphous and shifting], that by looking about he could tell the fate of any question. So if any thing was put when the court party were not well gathered together, he would have held the house from doing anything, by a wilful mistake or mistating the question, so that he

---

[14] Biographical details are drawn from Thomas Seccombe, "Seymour, Sir Edward," *DNB*, XVII, 1250-53.

gave time to those who were appointed for that mercenary work, to go about and gather in all their party. And he would discern when they had got the majority, and then he would very fairly state the question, when he saw he was sure to carry it.[15]

In the closing days of the Cavalier Parliament, Seymour had quarrelled with Danby, so that when the House of Commons in the first Exclusion Parliament presented him to the King as its choice of speaker, Charles refused to accept him: it would be much too dangerous to allow so skilful a man to occupy such a position when he was disaffected. Charles's rejection of him led to a row with the House of Commons, finally resolved in the compromise election as Speaker of Serjeant Gregory, described as a "mild and sympathetic Speaker." The House of Commons in the next two Parliaments exercised its right and chose as Speaker the partisan Whig and exclusionist, William Williams. Meanwhile Seymour re-entered the royal employ as treasurer of the navy. In this position he was accused by the House of Commons on 17 November 1680 with having illegally transferred a large sum from the funds appropriated by the House of Commons for the navy to the army so that certain units could continue in existence, even though by law they should have been disbanded. When the Parliament was dissolved, the articles of impeachment were dissolved with it.[16] Many of these circumstances surrounding Seymour were well known, but Dryden is careful to ignore them and to concentrate instead on his family and personal greatness and on his ability (partisanly presented) as Speaker of the House.

> Of ancient race by birth, but nobler yet
> In his own worth, and without Title great;
> The Sanhedrin long time as chief he rul'd,
> Their Reason guided and their Passion coold;
> So dexterous was he in the Crown's defence,
> So form'd to speak a Loyal Nation's Sense,
> That as their band was *Israel*'s Tribes in small,
> So fit was he to represent them all.
> Now rasher Charioteers the Seat ascend,
> Whose loose Carriers his steady Skill commend:
> They like th'unequal Ruler of the Day,
> Misguide the Seasons and mistake the Way;
> While he withdrawn at their mad Labour smiles,
> And safe enjoys the Sabbath of his Toyls.
>
> (ll. 900-13)

Here is the reason why the later Houses of Commons proved so rebellious: their factiousness needed the loyal restraint of the dextrous Seymour. When he was gone, chaos was returned again.

[15] Burnet, II, 79-80.

[16] For most of the political details, see Jones, *The First Whigs*, pp. 49-50, and Ogg, II, 604.

Dryden has been most selective in his presentation of the King's friends. He has omitted the games of politics they played, the internecine warfare they indulged in, their seeking for power, and their occasional obsequiousness, as well as their individual idiosyncracies—precisely all the sorts of things which in the Whigs he had fastened on satirically. Instead he has presented the loyal supporters as a small band, appealing to the readers chiefly because of the qualities they represent en masse: loyalty, nobility, courage, eloquence, perspicacity, steadfastness, frugality, and capability. These are the qualities evident in those people who have chosen to support the King: these are the qualities evident in the King's government. Nonetheless, this band, though worthy, is small. Its members need all the support and assistance which the moderate readers can render them and the King.

Men of Jebus

Strikingly absent from the list of the King's supporters are any Roman Catholics. Were not these the people who, the Whigs charged, were far too supportive and influential in the court circles, people who would naturally be supporters because they were the ones who benefitted from the court's policies? This charge undoubtedly had much to do with the way Dryden handled the Roman Catholics, whom he called Jebusites, the original inhabitants of Jerusalem.

There had been Roman Catholics among Charles's ministers in the days of the Cabal (Clifford and Arlington in particular), but since them no Roman Catholic had been a minister of any significance. The Test Act of 1678, moreover, had effectively removed all Roman Catholics (except the Duke of York) from both Houses of Parliament.[17] These facts would be known to Dryden's readers, and he adds the overt observation that (because of the Test Acts) the Roman Catholics were "depriv'd of all Command" (line 94) in the armed forces. Furthermore, as he points out (line 95), their taxes were double those of other citizens; so, all in all,

> worn and weaken'd, well or ill content,
> Submit they must to *David*'s Government:
>
> (ll.92-93)

How then could this weakened, impoverished, and submissive group represent a threat to the country? Dryden tacitly admits that a few Catholic extremists were involved in what was called the Popish Plot, but having admitted that (a good polemical ploy), he proceeds to ridicule the excessive charges levelled against the Catholics by attributing them, as was his wont, to characters who have been discredited. It is Monmouth who says that the Jebusites have invaded the rites of the

[17] Ogg, II, 517; Clark, *The Later Stuarts*, p. 96.

Church of England (line 706), and it is Titus Oates (Dryden implies) who says that the country is "groaning under Jebusitic Crimes" (line 663).

The attitude that emerges of Dryden the narrator towards the Catholics is appropriately ambivalent. In a manner that is in keeping with the anticlericalism in the opening lines of the poem, he scoffs at those aspects of the Roman Catholics that set them off from their fellow Englishmen: their images ("Their Gods disgrad'd, and burnt like common wood"—line 97), their doctrine of transubstantiation ("Deities... serv'd at once for Worship and for Food"—lines 120-21), and the proselytizing carried out by their priests:

> Their busie Teachers mingled with the *Jews*;
> And rak'd, for Converts, even the Court and Stews:
> (ll. 126-27)

Apart from these divisive aspects, however, Dryden the narrator finds much in the plight of the Catholics over which to be sympathetic. As he notes, they simply carry on the faith that all Englishmen had held to before the Reformation, and the change that took place at the Reformation was basically political, not really altering the validity of their religion:

> Th'inhabitants of old *Jerusalem*
> Were *Jebusites*: the Town so call'd from them;
> And their's the Native right——
> But when the chosen people grew more strong,
> The rightfull cause at length became the wrong:
> (ll. 85-89)

Worse than that, the more victorious the Protestants (especially the Dissenters) became, the more they accused the Catholics of evil:

> And every loss the men of *Jebus* bore,
> They still were thought God's enemies the more.
> (ll. 90-91)

So Dryden the narrator (whatever Dryden the man may have felt) is able to continue projecting the kind of image calculated to win his moderate readers: he deplores (and lightly mocks) the divisive aspects of Roman Catholicism, but sympathizes humanely with those of his fellow Englishmen whom political circumstances have put in an unfortunate position.

In Midst of Health

To the support which the King's friends and well-wishers give Charles, Dryden adds the support of a reasoned argument about government. Being a poet, he leaves much to implication and conveys much through images.

He introduces his argument with a shake of the head:

> Oh foolish *Israel*! never warn'd by ill,
> Still the same baite, and circumvented still!
>
> (ll. 753-54)

"Baite" is evidently a variant of "bate," and means "contention, strife, and discord"; "circumvented" similarly means "encompassed with enmity." This is the sad state of Israel/England, which never learns its lesson and is always embroiled in strife.

> Did ever men forsake their present ease,   [755]
> In midst of health Imagine a desease;
> Take pains Contingent mischiefs to foresee,
> Make Heirs for Monarks, and for God decree?

Taking care to foresee contingent mischiefs of course refers to the attempt to exclude James in case he should, if he came to the throne, restore popery and bring about arbitrary government. In these opening lines Dryden introduces, in varying degrees of completeness, each of the three pairs of images which will be central to his argument. Obvious is the contrasting pair of health and disease, suggesting the great perversity of those who see ills in a government that functions perfectly well: the imagining of disease is itself a disease and evidently afflicts those who complain about the government. The paralleling and implicit equating of King and God establishes another image, one we can refer to as God-King. It reminds Dryden's readers of the concept of kingship as devolving from God, not the people, and of kings' being vice-regents of God. Its opposite image, not yet made concrete, is implicit in the "men" who dare to try to make heirs for monarchs and to decree for God. In that word "decree" is the third image: it is still rather embryonic, but it does clearly imply the role of law, and in the actions of the men who dare to decree for God is implied the opposite of rightful law—arbitrariness.

Having established his images, and have reminded his readers through one of them of the divine origin of kingship, Dryden begins his argument by looking at one form of the contract theory of government, that which pictured the people of a nation giving all power to a king, without reserve:

> What shall we think! can People give away
> Both for themselves and Sons, their Native sway?   [760]

The results are disastrous:

> Then they are left Defensless, to the Sword
> Of each unbounded Arbitrary Lord:
> And Laws are vain, by which we Right enjoy,
> If Kings unquestiond can those laws destroy.

In this concept, the absolute king (unlike England's royal monarch—a distinction discussed in the first chapter) proves arbitrary, and the law is unable to protect the people's rights—rights which are in fact protected by a royal monarch, who rules by law (as currently in England, where "we Right enjoy"). The pair of imagistic concepts, law and arbitrariness, have emerged from their embryo.

Now as he turns to the other form of contract theory, in which the people reserve a right to remove their king, Dryden makes concrete the image opposite to his God-King:

> Yet, if the Crowd be Judge of fit and Just,   [765]
> And Kings are onely Officers in trust.

"Crowd" is indeed for Dryden, and most of his contemporary readers, the opposite of King: they are the populace, the mob, whom both Shaftesbury and Monmouth courted. When the "Crowd" determine whether the King should be removed or not (and the specific current situation in England would come to mind), the King himself is reduced to a trustee, something much less than vice-regent of God. But this is not the only objection Dryden has to this particular form of the contract theory: if there were a clause reserving to the people the right of removing their King, then that clause must have been public knowledge from the very beginning:

> Then this resuming Cov'nant was declar'd
> When Kings were made, or is for ever bard:

Of course no such declaration had ever been made in English history. If it be objected that a preceding generation cannot bind a succeeding one, then the whole basis of law is undermined, for what do legal deeds do, what do entails in wills do, what did Adam do, but bind succeeding generations to the terms stipulated in the deed?

> If those who gave the Scepter, coud not tye
> By their own deed their own Posterity,
> How then coud *Adam* bind his future Race?   [770]
> How coud his forfeit on mankind take place?

With the mention of Adam there enters, of course, not only human law, but also divine law, which sanctioned the fastening on succeeding generations of the consequences of what Adam had done:

> Or how coud heavenly Justice damn us all,
> Who nere consented to our Fathers fall?

So few of Dryden's readers would have questioned the rightness of their suffering for what Adam did, that Dryden can afford to use this argument as a parallel and analogy. At the same time, of course, he makes further use of the God-King image, in the function of judge—a function which, by the end of the poem, King David/Charles will also assume. This present part of the argument Dryden then rounds off in a couplet full of antitheses that show how very much counter to nature is the theory of contract and trusteeship:

> Then Kings are slaves to those whom they Command,   [775]
> And Tenants to their Peoples pleasure stand.

This same couplet, as is typical with Dryden, serves as a smooth transition to the next topic. The Whigs claimed that the source of government and its power should be based more on the possession of property than it was, and they also insisted that, since now the bulk of property was owned by the middle class, that middle class itself should control the government, through the House of Commons.[18] Dryden puts the concept thus:

> That Pow'r, which is for Property allowd,
> Is mischeivously seated in the Crowd:

The term "Crowd" has evidently expanded, to include, now, not only the populace but also the middle class. Dryden himself, being of the middle class, would be a member of that "Crowd," and, what is initially more strange, so would most of his moderate readers. Yet he lumps them in with the proletarian mob in his term "the Crowd." Not only that, he says that theorists ask for trouble when they would give power to that "Crowd." Would he not antagonize and perhaps alienate his readers at this point? That appears to be his calculated gamble. He appears to be saying, in effect, "You and I, dear reader, for we are in this together, are not the ones to have governmental power: for our own sake and for the sake of the nation as a whole, we must leave that power with the King." He must indeed have good support for his argument if, instead of alienating his readers, he is to convince them. The first form of support he offers is the claim that only the King's power can protect the rights of the individual (rights which Englishmen now enjoy) from attack by the crowd:

> For who can be secure of private Right,
> If Sovereign sway may be dissolv'd by might?   [780]

Dryden's readers would remember what happened to individual liberties when the Puritans' army triumphed in the Civil War. To this memory Dryden adds a general reason:

> Nor is the Peoples Judgment always true:
> The most may err as grossly as the few,
> And faultless Kings run down, by Common Cry,
> For Vice, Oppression, and for Tyranny.

These of course were the complaints about Charles I (whom the "People" martyred), and these have likewise been the complaints about

---

[18] See *Works*, II, 273, quoting Henry Neville, *Plato Redivivus*, p. 35.

Charles II, against whom, as King, his opposites—the crowd, the people—have again railed in common cry. Their error is understandable, for they have no judgement: how can they?—

> What Standard is there in a fickle rout,   [785]
> Which, flowing to the mark, runs faster out?

It would appear that the simplest way of reading this couplet is as follows: what standard or criterion, especially one implying constancy (as the *OED* observes for "standard," citing this couplet), is there in a milling mob, fickle to begin with and behaving like the tide, which, as soon as it flows up to the high-water mark, runs out (or at least appears to run out) faster than it moved when coming in?[19] The point of the image is in the agitated motion of the mob, always in flux, in contrast to constancy, which stands firm like a King. This is strong stuff for his readers to take, but the truly moderate reader would have to admit that, within the history of England over the preceding forty years, there had been ample evidence of precisely the flux in people's judgement to which Dryden points. In this flux, in the agitation of the metaphor Dryden uses, the tidal image becomes a variant of the image of disease, especially since, earlier in the poem (lines 136-41), Dryden had characterized the raging fevers within the body politic as being full of agitation—boiling the blood, bubbling over, and working up to foam. Another aspect of the tidal image, the fact that the motion is controlled by the moon, allows him to proceed to another form of disease:

> Nor only Crowds, but Sanhedrins may be
> Infected with this publick Lunacy:
> And Share the madness of Rebellious times,
> To Murther Monarchs for Imagin'd crimes.   [790]

Parliament had in fact murdered Charles I; by removing James from the succession, Parliament would in effect murder him as King; and the implication is even stronger (as seen also in other parts of the poem) that the present Parliament would not be averse to removing Charles II himself: and all because of "Imagin'd crimes," the product of a crazed imagination. Again the moderate reader would have to concede that, as much as it hurts, Dryden is right: for a nation's people and for that people's Parliament to abolish the monarchy and quite literally to kill the King and then, within eleven years, to re-establish the monarchy and to restore to it the son of the man they killed does not argue for

---

[19] A. W. Verrall, in a passage often cited by editors, offers a more complex reading: "The higher the tide and consequently the greater the distance between high and low watermark (the interval of time between tides remaining the same), the more rapid is the fall of the water at the ebb" (*Lectures on Dryden* [Cambridge: Cambridge University Press, 1914], p. 87). Verrall may well be right, but of course the point of the image remains the agitated motion of the mob.

sanity. Having repeated the concept of King, Dryden at once couples it again with that of God:

> If they may Give and Take when e'r they please,
> Not Kings alone, (the Godheads Images,)
> But Government it self at length must fall
> To Natures state; where all have Right to all.

This is the third reference to "Right," and here "Right" is associated with property, for in "Natures state" everyone has a claim to everyone else's property. Only law (maintained by a royal monarch) can protect the right of the individual to his own property, just as only law (maintained by the same kind of God-King) can protect the liberty of the individual. The Whigs had been protesting that Charles's government threatened both liberty and property. Dryden in reply asserts the very opposite: it is the giving of power to the "Crowd," even when that "Crowd" is assembled in the House of Commons, that would threaten liberty and property (as witnessed by the way the Commonwealth Parliament seized property and suppressed individual liberties), and the only protection against the arbitrariness of the "Crowd" is to be found in maintaining the law so effectively safeguarded by England's royal monarch.

Whatever view of the origin of government one may take, contract or patriarchic, who in his right mind would attempt to tamper with a government that was working as well as any government can work?

> Yet, grant our Lords the People Kings can make,   [795]
> What Prudent men a setled Throne woud shake?
> For whatsoe'r their Sufferings were before,
> That Change they Covet makes them suffer more.
> All other Errors but disturb a State;
> But Innovation is the Blow of Fate.   [800]

Again, we have agitation, increasing this time, from "shake" through "disturb" to the fatal "Blow" delivered by "Innovation," which here means insurrection. The same kind of diseased agitation finds a parallel in another variant:

> If ancient Fabricks nod, and threat to fall,
> To Patch the Flaws, and Buttress up the Wall,
> Thus far 'tis Duty. . . .

But there is a difference within this parallel, for inside the ancient fabric of the state is the holy of holies, something awesomely mysterious and beyond the understanding of man—certainly beyond his tinkering. For an image to express this concept Dryden goes to the story of Uzzah in 2 Samuel 6:2-7. When King David sought to move the ark of God (the most holy chest in the tabernacle, representing the presence of God himself) from one location to another, he received assistance from Uzzah and others, who carefully placed the ark (without touching it) on a newly made cart, drawn by oxen. At one point the oxen shook the ark so much that Uzzah, fearing it would fall, reached out and touched it, so as to steady it. For his impiety (in spite of his intentions which were otherwise good) God struck him dead. So it is, says Dryden, with trying to reform the government: patch up the flaws and buttress up the walls, but beyond that, leave all agitation and its cure to God:

> ... but here fix the Mark:
> For all beyond it is to touch our Ark.

The image of God-King has returned: to it are added once again the images of diseased motion and steadfast laws:

> To change Foundations, cast the Frame anew,   [805]
> Is work for Rebels who base Ends pursue:
> At once Divine and Humane Laws controul;
> And mend the Parts by ruine of the Whole.

As Dryden began his discourse with the image of disease, so he ends it, in a couplet containing two words with meanings slightly different from those of the present day ("tampering" meant "meddling with medically" and "to physick" meant "to doctor"):

> The Tampering World is subject to this Curse,   [810]
> To Physick their Disease into a worse.

To avoid disease in the body politic, to avoid arbitrary measures that would limit his liberty and his property, the moderate reader must avoid lending support to the crowd; instead he must do everything he can to support his divinely anointed King, who alone can preserve the health of the body politic and who alone, through the laws of state, can safeguard the liberty and property of the individual.

The Way of Majesty

In the praise heaped on the King's supporters, and in the imagistic argument on government, it may appear that Dryden has departed a long way from satire. Actually, with regard to theme, he has only (as noted earlier) been practising what he was to preach in his essay on satire: he seeks to inculcate the one virtue (loyalty) that is the opposite of the one vice (treason) that he has sought to make repulsive. But what about tone? Is there not a marked difference between what we would call the satiric parts of *Absalom and Achitophel* and those parts we have been examining in this and the preceding chapter? When Dryden turns from the villains and ridicule to the heroes and support, is there not a distinct change of tone, and does he not, in this regard at least, depart a long way from satire?

Not according to his own view of satire. In his essay he was to argue vehemently that we should not regard Horace's rather low manner in satire as the only kind possible or desirable. Instead we should accept as an alternative (at least as worthy) the manner of Persius and Juvenal. By taking pains with their versification and by using lofty images, Juvenal achieved the sublime and Persius the *grande sophos*, which can be translated as the loud bravo. Each thus achieved "the majestic way" or manner in satire.[20] Evidently it is this majestic manner which he himself deliberately used in those portions of the poem that are supportive of the King.

Nor there alone. Throughout the poem he makes use of the Biblical element for at least a background of majesty. When he wishes to elevate, as with his reader's view of the role of the King, he stresses the close similarity between the Biblical element and the English, showing how close are the roles of the divinely anointed David and the equally divinely anointed Charles—and how close both are to God in his dealings with the nations involved. And when Dryden wishes to belittle or to mock, he often bounces his satire off the backdrop of the Biblical element. When, for instance, he has Achitophel hail Absalom as the Saviour long foretold, he invites his reader to observe how petty Monmouth is in comparison with the Biblical character of Christ. Even when Dryden wishes to be merely witty, without necessarily being satiric as well, he will still often invite his reader to compare something English with something Biblical, as in the opening lines of the poem, "In pious times, e'r Priestcraft did begin." Whether used seriously or comically, directly or ironically, for its similarity or for its contrast, the Biblical element pervades the poem and provides an almost constant element of majesty.

The same kind of pervasive constancy—in fact the same kind of majesty (or at least weighty significance)—can be seen in Dryden's use of imagery. As already noted, he uses the image of grave disease in the same singleminded direct way, when he is arguing against inconstancy in government as when he points satirically to the dangers inherent in the agitation of the Whigs. Similarly there is no essential difference in his handling of the image of the God-King when he says, "Make Heirs for Monarks, and for God decree" (line 758) than when he says much earlier, "No King could govern, nor no God could please" (line 48). When he does make use of difference, it is a difference added to the basic similarity. The image of lunacy, for instance, can be used for both serious and comic purposes. When serious, it is presented in formal terms, with its shocking effects presented with solemn pointing:

> Nor only Crowds, but Sanhedrins may be
> Infected with this publick Lunacy:
> And Share the madness of Rebellious times,
> To Murther Monarchs for Imagin'd crimes.

(ll. 787-90)

[20] *Discourse concerning the Original and Progress of Satire*, II, 101.

When he wishes the lunacy to be applied satirically, in a comic and belittling manner, he writes:

> If *David's* Rule *Jerusalem* Displease,
> The *Dog-star* heats their Brains to this Disease.
> Why then shoud I, Encouraging the Bad,
> Turn Rebell, and run Popularly Mad?
>
> (ll. 333-36)

Here derisiveness increases steadily through various phrases: "Dog-star," "heats their Brains," "Turn Rebell," and "run Popularly Mad" like a human dog, slavering his speeches and fawning on the mob. When the monarch is harmed by the lunacy, the poetic treatment is solemn; when a born fool is harmed, it is derisive—but the basic image is the same.

The same kind of fundamental constancy, with only an occasional difference added, can be seen in Dryden's handling of rhetoric. The most entertaining passages of satire abound in balance and antithesis, the smooth control of rhythm and the sudden reversal of direction, as in the lines on Shimei

> whose early Youth did Promise bring
> Of Zeal to God, and Hatred to his King;
> Did wisely from Expensive Sins refrain,
> And never broke the Sabbath, but for Gain:
>
> (ll. 585-88)

The more serious passages can still have balance and even antithesis, for often irony is at work there too, as in Charles's speech when he observes, "My Rebel ever proves my Peoples Saint" (line 974). But when a change of direction occurs, usually a whole line is given to the new direction:

> From Plots and Treasons Heaven preserve my years,
> But Save me most from my Petitioners.
>
> (ll. 985-86)

And when the medial pause is delayed (as it was for Shimei), it is usually employed, not to change direction, but to reinforce the same direction and tone, as when Dryden has Charles speak of Law and those who seek

> with a daring Eye
> To tempt the terror of her Front, and Dye.
>
> (ll. 1008-09)

The pace is more measured for majesty, but basically the rhythm is the same, just as the images and the Biblical element are the same; and the poem as a whole, satiric and not so obviously satiric, is of a piece, a varied piece, but still a single piece.

Some Let Me Name

Of considerable importance to the build-up of the majestic manner has been the use of the Biblical element, and within that element the use of Biblical names has been prominent, especially for the King's supporters (whom to name is to praise). But the significance of the names has not been confined to the supporters: throughout the entire poem we have had repeated need to look closely at what Dryden was doing with specific names. This is a convenient place to pull together his various uses, reviewing some and examining others for the first time, so as to see the full range of what he does with them. In the process we should find a little more light appearing on the canvas.

On occasion Dryden wished his readers to have in mind virtually all the circumstances surrounding the Biblical character whose name he has applied to one of his own characters. He obviously wished most of what was involved with the Biblical Achitophel to be applied to Shaftesbury: the facts that Achitophel had been an esteemed adviser to David, that he had traitorously joined Absalom in his rebellion, and that he continued to give advice to his King's son. Dryden even wished the ending of the Biblical story to be borne in mind. In the Bible, "when Achitophel saw that his counsel was not followed, he saddled his ass, and arose, and gat him home to his house, to his city, and put his household in order, and hanged himself" (2 Samuel 17:23). In his prefatory remarks to the poem, Dryden professed that he was charitably disposed towards Achitophel, "For which reason, in this *Poem*, he is neither brought to set his House in order, nor to dispose of his Person afterwards, as he in Wisedom shall think fit." Similarly Dryden evidently wished his readers to have all the aspects of Agag's situation in mind for Corah's identification of Agag with James to be made. Recognition of the appropriateness of calling Dissenting ministers Levites depended in the same way on his readers' realizing that the Levites were inferior ministers who could only assist the Hebrew priests and were not in themselves proper priests. The choice of the term Jebusites was likewise richly appropriate, for the Jebusites were a clan of the Canaanites, who held Jerusalem until the invading Hebrews captured it: so the Roman Catholics possessed London until the Church of England moved in.

At times, it would appear, Dryden rejoiced in the witty aptness of certain details, found in the Biblical story of course, but still at first glance such as one would think them tangential. The principal reason for referring to Halifax by the name of Jotham was that, like the Biblical Jotham, Halifax had spoken out against a potential usurper of the throne (Judges 9:7-21). But of course throughout the Bible various people spoke out against various usurpers: why choose Jotham? Because, evidently, the usurper whom Jotham denounced was the illegitimate son of his father's foreign concubine (Judges 8:31), circumstances beautifully parallelling those of Monmouth, who was born of the Welsh Lucy Walter.

On other occasions Dryden evidently wished to isolate certain aspects of a Biblical situation and to focus on those to the exclusion of all other aspects. We have already seen this with regard to choosing the name of Michal for David's Queen: certain aspects, her own royalty and her barrenness, allowed for an apt allusion to Charles's Queen, but several circumstances associated with the Biblical Michal Dryden evidently hoped his readers would overlook. He did much the same with the choice of Hushai for Laurence Hyde, the first lord of the Treasury. Hushai was indeed the chief governmental companion to David, and so, in that regard, the name would fit Laurence Hyde in 1681. But the Hushai of the Bible, on orders from David, associated himself with Absalom, served under him, and gave him specious advice that would actually assist David. Hyde did none of this. Presumably Hushai's position as foremost adviser was what led Dryden to choose the name—that and possibly the meaning of the name, "hasting," which certainly matched the quick ascent that Hyde had made through the ministerial ranks.

In fact it would appear that not infrequently did Dryden choose a Biblical name for the appropriateness of its meaning when translated into English. He and his readers had available to them a concordance, printed with the Geneva Bible (such as the London edition of 1600 and later), that provided, rather prominently, "the interpretation of the Hebrue, Caldean, Greeke, and Latine wordes and names scatteringly dispersed throughout the whole Bible."[21] (It makes interesting reading, differs in the meaning of some names from the twentieth-century concordance, and is of course the source for meanings offered in this study.) The author of the poem *A Key (With the Whip)*, written in reply to *Absalom and Achitophel*, was very much aware of the English meanings of the Hebrew names and frequently referred to them. So altogether it should not surprise us that Dryden was evidently alert to the possibilities they offered. As already noted, the choice of Barzillai from among the three men who helped David in exile is perhaps accounted for—and certainly the richness of appropriateness is intensified—by the fact that the meaning of Barzillai ("as hard as iron") well reflected the steadfastness of Ormonde's character. With two other characters there appears to be no reason other than the meaning of the names why they should have been assigned the names they were. Mulgrave did not marry a king's daughter as Adriel did, but since Adriel means "flock of God," Dryden may well have been referring to Mulgrave's appointment to command the relief army of Christian Englishmen that was to go to

---

[21] Title page to the concordance in *The Bible: Translated according to the Ebrew and Greeke . . .* (London: Robert Barker, 1600). The pages are unnumbered.

the relief of the garrison at Tangier, beleaguered by Pagan infidels. Similarly the Ammiel of the Bible has no recognizable similarity, in the very scanty detail provided (Numbers 13:12 and 1 Chronicles 26:5), to Edward Seymour, the former Speaker of the House of Commons—none, that is, unless through the meaning of the Biblical name, "people of God," which can be a very witty reference to the House of Commons itself, members of which thought very highly of themselves and included among their number many Dissenters who often referred to themselves as "saints," "the chosen people," and even "the people of God."

In view of this possibility that Dryden on occasion made use of the English meaning of the Hebrew names he chose, it may well be that the meaning of Amnon will allow us to confine the reference in lines 39-40 to one of Monmouth's major wrongdoings. The lines read, following on the "warm excesses" committed by Monmouth,

> And *Amnon*'s Murther, by a specious Name,
> Was call'd a Just Revenge for injur'd Fame.

Critics have tried to make use of Amnon's situation in the Bible—the facts that he was Absalom's half-brother, that he raped their mutual sister, and that in revenge Absalom killed him (2 Sam. 13:1-29). They have tried to apply these facts to Monmouth's dealings with his half-brothers and with the husband of his uterine sister, but have found no record of any serious injury done. So they have been left with two proffered readings, one a reference to Monmouth's murder of the beadle who arrested him in a brothel and the other a reference to an incident involving Sir John Coventry. When that Member of Parliament made slighting remarks about Charles and his liking for actresses, a group of Monmouth's troopers, presumably acting on his orders, lay in wait for Coventry and slit his nose. Of the circumstances associated with the Biblical Amnon, only one—admittedly the most important one and the one Dryden mentions—fits the poor murdered beadle, and none at all fit Coventry. Of the various parts of Dryden's phrasing, the reference to "Just Revenge for injur'd Fame" could refer equally well to the attack on Coventry for his remarks about Charles and to the punishment of the beadle for daring to arrest a royal duke. But of course the "Murther" of the first line of the couplet, while fitting the beadle, would have to be stretched a great deal to fit Coventry. Let us now add the meaning of the name Amnon: "faithful." It fits the beadle with an appropriateness that is devastating to Monmouth: the beadle was merely being faithful to his trust in arresting Monmouth, and his vicious murder has been speciously passed off as a "Just Revenge of [the] injur'd Fame" of a royal bastard. Evidently in choosing the character Amnon, Dryden has been concerned with only two things—from all the circumstances surrounding Amnon—merely the one fact of his murder by Absalom, and the meaning of the name.

With three other names, the meanings afford an added fillip to Dryden's use of them. (With each, the meaning in Dryden's day was different from what it is today.) The fact that Absalom meant "the father's peace" provides a fine note of irony to Monmouth's progress through the West and even to Dryden's summary line, "And Peace it self is War in Masquerade" (line 752). Similarly the fact that Achitophel meant "brother of ruine" adds something to the line in which Dryden summed up Shaftesbury's character: "Resolv'd to Ruine or to Rule the State" (line 174). And for those aware of it, the barrenness of poor Michal, that "Soyl ungratefull to the Tiller's care" (line 12), is nicely summed up in the meaning of her name, which, when translated, makes the question, "Who is perfect?"

One could well be pardoned for wondering just how many of Dryden's readers would actually be aware of the English meanings of the Hebrew names. Yet, as mentioned, the author of *A Key (With the Whip)* made considerable use of such meanings: he spelled out, in his verse, the meaning of five names, the meaning of which Dryden, it would appear, likewise made use of (Caleb, Barzillai, Adriel, Hushai, and Ammiel), and, for good measure, cited the meanings of three others (Achitophel, Zimri, and Jotham) and complained that the meanings did not fit the characters to whom Dryden had given the names.[22] Evidently there would be at least a few people among Dryden's readers who would in fact know the meanings, and for those, it is also evident, Dryden wrote as he did. Presumably he saw within his reading audience a considerable variety. There would be those who understood, and were content with, the bare outline of the story. There would be others conversant with the details of the Biblical situations alluded to. There would be those, however few, who knew the meanings of the names (or who would go and look them up). And there would be those who relished Dryden's wit in setting up the parallel between his English characters and either the situations of their Biblical counterparts or the meanings of their Biblical names.

Matching this variety within his readers is the variety within his poem, of theme and characters, of methods and manners. What genre would hold this variety of elements? What structure would present them most effectively to his readers?

---

[22] *A Key (With the Whip)*, pp. (in order of names cited in the text) 30, 36, 38, 40, 40, 24, 29, 38.

9

VARRONIAN SATIRE

Many Things Included

The great variety of elements within *Absalom and Achitophel* has no doubt been the reason why there have been so many conflicting views as to which genre the poem belongs to. Dryden himself referred to it as a satire,[1] his early editor Sir Walter Scott called it a political satire,[2] and sporadically since him other scholars, such as Mark Van Doren,[3] R. F. Jones,[4] and R. A. Brower,[5] have followed suit. But from about 1914 an increasing number of scholars have become dissatisfied and have not been willing to regard the poem as satire. They have two basic reasons. One is the fact that Dryden, although calling the work a satire in a later essay, called it a poem in the subtitle of the work itself and repeated the term in his prefatory remarks to the reader. The other reason is the presence, in such large proportion, of other elements which strike the scholars as non-satiric. Principally these elements are the heroic and the historical, and certainly they bulk large, so large that scholars such as Arthur W. Hoffman,[6] Earl Miner,[7] Bernard N. Schilling,[8] and H. T. Swedenberg, Jr.,[9] say, in one way or another, that the poem is more than satire.

[1] *Discourse concerning the Original and Progress of Satire*, II, 67; cf. II, 93.

[2] John Dryden, *Works*, ed. Sir Walter Scott (London: Miller, 1808), IX, 197.

[3] Mark Van Doren, *John Dryden: A Study of His Poetry* (Bloomington, Indiana: Indiana University Press, 1960 [1st ed. 1920]), p. 211.

[4] R. F. Jones, "The Originality of *Absalom and Achitophel*," *Modern Language Notes*, 46 (1931), 217.

[5] R. A. Brower, "Dryden's Epic Manner and Virgil," *PMLA*, 55 (1940), 132.

[6] Arthur W. Hoffman, *John Dryden's Imagery* (Gainesville, Fla.: University of Florida Press, 1962), p. 89.

[7] Earl Miner, *Dryden's Poetry* (Bloomington and London: Indiana University Press, 1967), 141.

[8] Bernard N. Schilling, *Dryden and the Conservative Myth* (New Haven and London: Yale University Press, 1961), pp. 262-63.

[9] *Works*, II, 234. Mention should be made of Charles H. Cable, who sees the poem as epic satire ("*Absalom and Achitophel* as Epic Satire," in *Studies in Honor of John Wilcox* [Detroit: Wayne State University Press, 1958], pp. 51-60).

The alternatives which these and other scholars offer are basically three, although each has sub-varieties. One of these is simply to call the work a "big" poem, containing many genres,[10] or, more simply still, to disregard the question altogether, on the assumption, presumably, that Dryden did not have a specific genre in mind either—this in spite of his calling it a satire.

Another alternative is to regard the poem as some kind of epic: miniature epic, epic fragment, and epyllion have been terms used.[11] There are certainly reasons for holding to this view. There is a large heroic element in the content of *Absalom and Achitophel*, and much of its manner (as well as all its versification) is heroic. In addition, in his essay on satire, Dryden praised Boileau's satiric poem *Le Lutrin*, likewise written in heroic verse, as "undoubtedly a species" of heroic poetry. However, there are at least two strong reasons against regarding *Absalom and Achitophel* as primarily some kind of epic. One is of course that Dryden said it was a satire, and the other is the effect that such a view has on the way one regards the structure of the poem. The term "epic fragment" in itself indicates the effect. Especially since the action appears to be incomplete, broken off before it could end, the poem (as some kind of epic) has often been regarded as broken-backed or abortive. This judgement, in fact, illustrates the reason for being concerned with finding the right genre to which the poem belongs, for from the view of genre flows the view of structure, and from the view of structure flows much of one's appraisal of the quality of the poem as a whole.

The third alternative is to view the work as some kind of historical poem. Ian Jack calls it a "narrative poem" and a "historical poem."[12] Alan Roper has retained the "historical" while rejecting the "narrative,"[13] and Earl Miner sees it as partisan history.[14] Again there are certainly reasons for looking on *Absalom and Achitophel* as a historical poem. It is, after all, very much concerned with Absalom's rebellion and through that with Monmouth's virtual rebellion. And Dryden himself, in his prefatory remarks, observed, "Were I the Inventour, who am only the Historian, I shoud certainly conclude the Piece, with the Reconcilement of *Absalom* to *David*."

---

[10] E.g., Schilling, p. 11.

[11] By Morris Freedman, "Dryden's Miniature Epic," *JEGP*, 48 (1957), 211-19; E. M. W. Tillyard, *Poetry Direct and Oblique* (London: Chatto and Windus, 1934), pp. 81-82; Verrall, p. 59.

[12] Ian Jack, *Augustan Satire* (Oxford: Clarendon, 1952), pp. 53, 71.

[13] Alan Roper, *Dryden's Poetic Kingdoms* (London: Routledge & Kegan Paul, 1965), p. 195.

[14] Miner, p. 141.

As with the other alternatives, however, there are also reasons against this one. Dryden's remark about being "the Historian" cannot bear much weight, for another remark he made, in his *Life of Plutarch*, would appear to show that he did not mean by it what the proponents of the historical alternative would like him to. In that *Life*, while lamenting the fact that England could boast no truly good historian, he said that Buchanan "might be placed among the greatest, if he had not too much leaned to prejudice, and too manifestly declared himself *a party of a cause, rather than an historian of it.*"[15] This declared need for freedom from partisanship in an historian bears directly on Dryden's own ready admission, in his prefatory remarks to *Absalom and Achitophel*, that in writing that poem he drew "his Pen for one Party" and so "must expect to make Enemies of the other." Evidently we should interpret his word "Historian" in the same prefatory remarks either as irony or in such a way that his sentence can be understood to mean, "If I had invented the piece, instead of merely relating it, I should certainly conclude with the reconcilement of Absalom to David." So read, the sentence would then not conflict with his statement that *Absalom and Achitophel* is a satire, which is, of course, another reason against reading the poem as primarily historical. There is furthermore the same objection concerning the effect on one's view about the structure of the poem as there is for the epic alternative. In fact Professor Miner himself points to certain difficulties: neither the opening nor the closing of the poem fits the historical structure particularly well; the historical metaphor that is supposed to control the poem has to be seen as coasting along at times, with neither vehicle nor tenor operating; and the narrative element poses a further problem in that, on the one hand, it appears to be so slight that it calls the historical nature of the poem into question and yet, on the other hand, it is present to a greater degree "in the English tenor than the poem's structure in fact allows."[16] When the poem appears to have both too little narrative and too much, something is wrong with the view of genre which prompts such a view of structure.

Let us reconsider viewing the poem as satire. The fact that Dryden called it a poem in the subtitle and in the prefatory remarks does not really preclude its being satire. In those prefatory remarks he twice refers to satire. The first time is when he says that he has rebated the satire and kept it from carrying too sharp an edge: here, admittedly, he appears to be speaking of satire as an element within his poem. But the other time is when he begins his final paragraph by saying, "The true end of *Satyre*, is the amendment of Vices by correction." Especially since he goes on to speak of his purpose as a whole (like that of a physi-

---

[15] *Works* (ed. Scott), XVII, 58. (Italics mine.)
[16] Miner, pp. 113, 140-42.

cian to his patient), it would appear that, in this instance, the odds are very much in favour of his having had his whole poem in mind when he wrote of "Satyre." Certainly in his later essay on satire there is no doubt. In one sentence which says a number of things to our purpose in this study of Absalom and Achitophel, Dryden remarked that "Satire is a poem of a difficult nature in itself, and is not written to vulgar readers."[17] The matter of difficulty (implying a need for explanation) and the select nature of the audience will not escape notice, but most pertinent at the moment is the clear indication that, at the very least, Dryden had no difficulty in seeing his work as both a satire and a poem, since one category fitted inside the other.

The kind of satire Dryden saw his poem belonging to should also remove any remaining difficulties about the inclusion in it of what appear to be non-satiric elements. He says that Absalom and Achitophel is a Varronian satire and quotes Varro himself (through Tully) as he described his kind of satire: ". . . those pieces of mine, wherein I have imitated Menippus, though I have not translated him, are sprinkled with a kind of mirth and gaiety, yet many things are there inserted, which are drawn from the very entrails of philosophy, and many things severely argued; which I have mingled with pleasantries on purpose, that they may more easily go down with the common sort of unlearned readers."[18] Although Varro speaks of his "pieces," it is evident from what he says, and especially from the words "inserted" and "mingled," that, when he speaks of the variety in his satires, he means each of his satires, or certainly each of most of them. It is this variety which allows us to resolve an apparent contradiction between the statement of Varro, quoted approvingly here and indicating an audience (in part) of "unlearned readers," and Dryden's own statement, quoted in the preceding paragraph, that satire "is not written to vulgar readers." Within the variety of Varronian satire are difficult elements for the learned and amusing elements for the vulgar. In this way Varronian satire operates in much the same way as allegory, according to the conventional view as expressed by Sir John Harington in 1591. In a remark that has special relevance to Absalom and Achitophel in view of its Biblical element, Harington compared allegory to a kind of meat that can feed different tastes. Weaker capacities will feed themselves on the pleasantness of the story and the sweetness of the verse; those that have stronger stomachs will take a further taste of the moral sense; and a third sort, "more high conceited than they," will digest the allegory.[19] As in al-

---

[17] Discourse concerning the Original and Progress of Satire, II, 74. (The title will be shortened to Discourse hereafter.)

[18] Discourse, II, 65.

[19] Sir John Harington, "Preface" to his translation of Ludovico Ariosto's Orlando Furioso, ed. Robert McNulty (Oxford: Clarendon, 1972), pp. 5-6.

legory, where only a few elements need to be allegorical, so in Varronian satire: it is capacious and varied enough to contain many non-satirical elements without losing the nature of satire.

There remains the relation, in Dryden's mind, of satire to heroic poetry, especially in view of what he said about Boileau's *Lutrin*. Actually a fuller indication of what he says will resolve any problem. *Le Lutrin* he believes was modelled on an Italian poem, itself an example of Varronian satire. Boileau calls his poem heroic because it is written in heroic verse, but Dryden says that it is "the most beautiful and most noble kind of satire. Here is the majesty of the heroic, finely mixed with the venom of the other; and raising the delight which otherwise would be flat and vulgar, by the sublimity of the expression." Because of the heroic expression, Dryden goes on to remark, as quoted earlier, this satire is "undoubtedly a species" of heroic poetry.[20] As with the relation between satire and poem, in which "satire" fits as a sub-category, within the category "poem," so here it is evident that, as the most beautiful and noble kind of satire, *Le Lutrin* fits into the larger category of *heroic* poetry as well, without for a moment losing its nature as satire. In fact, especially since Dryden in the same essay distinguishes between the "tragical satire" of Juvenal and the "comical" of Horace,[21] we can certainly be pardoned for presuming that he regarded his own *Absalom and Achitophel* as a form of Varronian satire that could be called heroic satire, following, for its expression, in the majestic way of Juvenal and Persius.

Absalom and Achitophel is certainly a poem, as Dryden called it in his prefatory remarks. More specifically, within the general category "poem," it is more precisely a heroic poem, like *Le Lutrin*, evincing the same kind of "majesty of the heroic" and "sublimity of the expression" as the French poem. More specifically still, within the sub-category of "heroic poem," *Absalom and Achitophel*, like Boileau's poem, is still more precisely a satire, as Dryden called it, a heroic satire made heroic largely because of its majestic expression.

About the peculiar nature of the most specific sub-category, satire, Dryden has more to say in the same essay. There he gives a further description of satire, this one much longer and of even more detailed application to *Absalom and Achitophel*. Dryden quotes it from Heinsius, but, since he says that Heinsius "makes it for me," it is obvious that Dryden accepts it as his own, modifying it in only one respect, so as to include "the *grande sophos* of Persius, and the sublimity of Juvenal."[22] The definition begins: "Satire is a kind of poetry, without a series of action...." As Dryden himself says, this qualifying phrase "distin-

[20] *Discourse*, II, 108.
[21] *Discourse*, II, 96.
[22] *Discourse*, II, 100-01.

guishes satire properly from stage-plays, which are all of one action, and one continued series of action." (Presumably, to judge from Dryden's careful insistence on unity—"one action" and "one continued series"—he did not feel that the phrase "without a series of action" prohibited the inclusion of discontinuous narrative segments within a satire.) The definition next rounds on the purpose of satire: ". . . invented for the purging of our minds; in which human vices, ignorance, and errors, and all things besides, which are produced from them in every man, are severely reprehended . . . . " That much is clear; the section following needs interpretation: ". . . partly dramatically, partly simply, and sometimes in both kinds of speaking; but, for the most part, figuratively, and occultly . . . " In view of the meanings current in Dryden's day, it would appear that Dryden is here concerned with the *method* of reprehending vice, ignorance, and error: this may be done in part "dramatically"—e.g., through speeches given by characters, in part through unadorned description (which is how I would read "simply"), but for the most part "figuratively, and occultly," i.e., through metaphor and indeed allegory. The next section appears to be concerned with the *manner* of presenting the material: " . . . consisting in a low familiar way, chiefly in a sharp and pungent manner of speech; but partly, also, in a facetious and civil way of jesting. . ."; to which Dryden shortly adds "the *grande sophos* of Persius, and the sublimity of Juvenal." Apparently any number of the three manners may be used: the low and familiar, the civil and jesting (i.e., raillery), and the majestic. The definition then concludes with the effect of these methods and manners: ". . . by which either hatred, or laughter, or indignation, is moved."

Not surprisingly, all the parts of this description of satire are illustrated in *Absalom and Achitophel*. That work is a kind of poetry, not "all of one action" or "one continued series of action"—a fact that bedevils any attempt to view the poem, structurally, as primarily heroic or historical. It was invented to purge the minds of Dryden's readers of certain ideas concerning Shaftesbury and the other Whigs. In it the vices, ignorance, and errors of those opposing the King are severely reprehended, through each of the three methods noted: dramatic speeches, simple description (as in the character sketches of the Whig leaders), and both recurring metaphor and pervasive allegory. Even all three of the different manners are represented. The low and familiar appears more strikingly in the characters of Og and Doeg in the Second Part, e.g.:

> A Monstrous mass of foul corrupted matter,
> As all the Devils had spew'd to make the batter.
>
> (ll. 464-65)

But it is still present in various phrases throughout the poem we are concerned with, as in "well hung *Balaam*," "Cool was his Kitchen, tho his Brains were hot," and "Erect thy self thou Monumental Brass." Raillery is to be found at its finest, as Dryden observed in the same essay, in the character sketch of Zimri.[23] (And raillery, perhaps it should be noted, is what provides only "the nicest and most delicate touches of satire":[24] all the other multitudinous undelicate touches are still satire.) And the third manner, the majestic way, is to be found in most of the versification throughout the poem and, par excellence, both in the description of the King's supporters and in the speech of David himself. By means of these methods and manners, each of hatred, laughter, and indignation is aroused in the reader, depending on which kind of royal opponent is satirized. In the two paragraphs following this description, Dryden emphasized the need for unity in satire, which should give (as we have noted earlier) "one precept of moral virtue" and caution against "one particular vice or folly." In this regard, too, *Absalom and Achitophel* illustrates Dryden's view of satire, recommending loyalty and support for the King and his government and cautioning against the disloyalty and factiousness of the Whigs. All in all, the various pertinent descriptions of satire that Dryden gives in his essay fit *Absalom and Achitophel* like a glove. Perhaps he had his poem in mind when setting down the various descriptions.

There is still, however, a major aspect of the nature of *Absalom and Achitophel* as a satiric poem that has not been examined in the present argument. We have seen that Dryden probably regarded his satiric poem as a *heroic* satiric poem, but that heroic aspect of the nature derives, not nearly so much from the method of proceeding as from the manner of expression. The question is still unanswered: what kind of satire is *Absalom and Achitophel* with regard to method, its way of proceeding, its structure? Is it a dramatic satire, a narrative satire, a descriptive satire, a discursive satire, or what? Fortunately, both the genesis of the poem in the pamphlet warfare of the day and Dryden's preliminary remarks to the reader make it clear what kind of satire it is. Since it is addressed to the "more Moderate sort," seeking to win their approbation for one party to the dispute and their detestation for the other, it is evidently a polemical satire, an argumentative satire. It includes narrative, but it does not proceed primarily by narrative: its method, its structure, is not narrative. Similarly it includes drama, but it does not proceed by dramatic action; it includes character-pieces and other forms of description, but it is not primarily descriptive. Rather it turns all these different methods—narrative, dramatic, descriptive, and the rest—to the purpose and indeed function of argument. *Absalom*

[23] *Discourse*, II, 93-94.
[24] *Discourse*, II, 92.

and Achitophel is a satiric poem, heroic in manner, polemical in intent, and argumentative in method.

What it is that provides a structure to the argument and allows it to proceed in the peculiar way it does is the remaining consideration to which we must now turn our attention.

Perfecting the Design

The variety of elements we have already seen within the argumentative method is only part of the total variety of *Absalom and Achitophel*, a Varronian variety that is not only multifold but also apparently disparate. To begin with, there is of course the pervasive Biblical element. There is also a more conventional kind of literary parallel: it consists of various classical personifications such as Virtue, Fortune, and Folly; epic elements such as similes, harangues, and heroic style; and also the Messianic and Satanic elements which, although derived ultimately from other parts of the Bible, enter the poem from Milton's epics. There are the character sketches of individuals and groups, and copious dramatic conversation, especially as this is used to reveal weaknesses in opponents' arguments. There are analytic descriptions of current events, such as the use made of the Popish Plot, and there is even a closely argued though imagistic discourse on government. As if these were not enough, there is also (incongruously?) a eulogy of a loyal servant, and there are repeated references to English history, contained, not only in the account of the Jebusites, but also in the frequent reminders of the Commonwealth that was and might again be.

As has been noted in the earlier chapters, each of these elements had formed the subject matter of at least one pamphlet (and usually more) in that part of the passage of pens over the Exclusion Crisis that had occurred before Dryden wrote *Absalom and Achitophel*. He had accordingly been able to see, at least in general terms, what sort of effect could be created on his readers by including each subject. There had also been pamphlets which successfully combined a number of the elements. *Naboth's Vineyard* (1679) had combined Biblical allegory with satiric character (including one of Oates as Malchus) and had presented them in heroic verse. *The Waking Vision* (1681) had combined, in verse, the Biblical names of Absalom and Achitophel, dramatic harangue, and references to Commonwealth history. In addition there existed a tradition of "Advice to a Painter" poems, which had flourished just a few years earlier and which had made a practice of mingling several such elements.[25] These poems had been concerned with commenting on a number of events that had occurred recently —and on the people responsible for them—and so very naturally in-

[25] See *Poems on Affairs of State*, I, 20-21.

cluded a wide variety of subjects. One of the best, *The Last Instructions to a Painter*, which was probably written by Andrew Marvell in 1667 and which Dryden could well have seen in manuscript, offers a number of parallels to *Absalom and Achitophel*.[26] Besides being of much the same length as Dryden's poem, it has satiric character sketches, analysis of current events, two lengthy narrative episodes, and a conclusion that focuses directly on the King. It uses the figure of parading troops for political supporters (as Dryden does in the phrase "this short File"), it alludes to the work of earlier English poets, and it even interrupts a description for a eulogy of a brave hero. All in all, as one looks at many of the pamphlets, it is evident that polemical writers of the time were accustomed to mingling and perhaps even combining a number of disparate elements.

But a particular reason for Dryden's combining the specific elements he chose to may be found in a poem that had appeared just a year before his. *The Progress of Honesty*, by Thomas D'Urfey, makes use of Biblical analogies, calling Shaftesbury *Achitophel* and a *Rabbi* (stanzas 14 and 15), and referring to Eli and Jacob (stanza 4), the Old Testament idols (stanza 16), and Absalom (stanza 17). It makes use, too, of a more conventional, semi-classical kind of allegory, calling Charles *Titus*, James *Resolution*, and the King's supporters by such names as *Clitus* and *Cleon*, and providing *Discord* and *Treason* with a Spenserian Grott for their home (stanza 10). It presents character sketches of many of the people Dryden was to portray and provides long speeches for some of the characters. It analyzes current events, making a judgement on the Popish Plot remarkably similar to Dryden's, and refers to the "Good Old Cause" (stanza 10) and the "Yoke of impudent Presbytery" (stanza 15). And it does all this in a verse form that is elevated enough to warrant the subtitle "A Pindarique Poem." The differences in the elements of subject matter and methods between *The Progress of Honesty* and *Absalom and Achitophel* are actually few. D'Urfey does not present a eulogy of a loyal servant, and he introduces two elements Dryden does not make use of: the elaborate framework of an overheard conversation and an extended satire of vice in general—though Dryden's description of the Jews in general may in fact be a counterpart. All in all, differences are so few and the similarities are so many and so striking that it would indeed appear that Dryden had read D'Urfey's poem carefully and had seen in it an epitome of almost all the elements appearing in other contributions to the warfare that he himself could handle well. Presumably Dryden then decided (for his own poem) to discard D'Urfey's framework and his satire of vice in general, to reverse the prominence given to the two kinds of allegory (Biblical and semi-classical), and to add a eulogy on Ossory, but otherwise to use

[26] *Poems on Affairs of State*, I, 97-139; cf. I, 34.

D'Urfey's poem as a sort of model for all the other kinds of subject matter he thought of including.

To whatever extent it may have served as a model for what to include, however, it nevertheless lacked one thing which Dryden evidently looked for earnestly and valued greatly: a unifying structural principle which would bring all the varied elements together and make fully felt the sense of total unity, a unity that was required, as he was to observe in his essay, "for perfecting the design of true satire."[27] Within his frame, D'Urfey had alternated repeatedly between praising the heroes and satirizing the villains, between dealing with specifics and commenting in general. His structure had accommodated a large variety of elements, but made for little cohesion and therefore little cumulative impact. The "Advice to a Painter" poems usually had even less to offer by way of structural direction. Especially since they often parallelled actual historical pictures (one of which is reproduced in *Poems on Affairs of State*[28]), in which various inserts are added around the perimeter, they often abounded in digressions and usually relied, as did Marvell's *Last Instructions*, on a simple narrative progression from event to event to provide whatever feeling there was of cohesion.

When, in writing his character description of Zimri, Dryden was faced with a similar problem of somehow unifying elements so disparate that they threatened to go flying off in several directions at once, he turned for assistance (as we have seen) to a device from rhetoric. The use of chiasmus allowed him to retain the disparateness of the elements and yet arrange them in such a way that he was able to proceed in the most effective manner from one element to the next. Not only that: he also freely modified the specific terms of chiasmus so as to provide greater rhetorical and poetic variety in his description, and he even proceeded to elaborate on those terms—to such an extent that they were not immediately recognizable as chiastic terms—and to use them to provide a structure for the whole of his character of Zimri, the passage which he felt made the entire poem worthwhile. Was there any other device of rhetoric to which he could turn for assistance in organizing the whole of his lengthy poem, his argumentative, polemical satire?

Yes: there was the structure of the classical oration. Undoubtedly while at Westminster School Dryden had studied Cicero and Quintilian, the advocates of that kind of oration,[29] and Halifax's *Seasonable Address to Both Houses of Parliament* (1681) would have reminded him (if he had needed reminding) of the advantages inherent in the

---

[27] *Discourse*, II, 104.

[28] *Poems on Affairs of State*, opp. I, 124.

[29] See Charles E. Ward, *The Life of John Dryden* (Chapel Hill, N.C.: University of North Carolina Press, 1961), pp. 10-11.

classical structure. There is in it, not only a remarkable cohesive power, but also an expansive freedom: there is virtually a place for everything, and everything can be put in its place. Halifax had not made the divisions of his pamphlet obvious, but one can still see that he followed the classical order, to good effect. After an *exordium* concerning the sickness of the body politic, with which Dryden would certainly have agreed, and which incorporated the *propositio* that the cause of the sickness was wicked and ambitious men and the consequence was the danger of civil war, he proceeded through a *narratio* of the times preceding 1641, to a *confutatio* in which he disposed of Whig arguments and fears concerning Popery and arbitrary government. From there he proceeded through a *confirmatio* (the major part of the pamphlet) discussing the various dangers from the wrong-headed and ambitious Whigs, to a *peroratio* in which he expressed the hope that the next Parliament would be a healing Parliament.[30]

Dryden himself was later, as Professor Roper has shown, to structure *The Medall* in the manner of a classical forensic oration,[31] and in *Absalom and Achitophel* itself, as Professor Lillian Feder has shown, he uses, in addition to chiasmus, many other of the classical rhetorical devices, with the result that the poem has "the liveliness of a great oration."[32] It will accordingly come as no surprise that I suggest that Dryden turned to a rhetorical device for assistance, as he had to chiasmus to help him with Zimri, and structured the whole of *Absalom and Achitophel* itself in the manner of a classical oration. In addition to the organizing assistance it could give him in general, there were at least two especially appropriate reasons for him to turn to this device in particular. As Professor Feder has pointed out, Dryden remarked in one of his poems, "*Satire* is our Court of Chancery"[33]—a court which would be equivalent, with us, to the court of appeals, the court concerned with equity and conscience, and the figurative court to which he was, in *Absalom and Achitophel*, appealing for a decision against the Whigs and in favour of the King. Consequently it would be appropriate for him to use the structure of the classical forensic oration, the one followed by Roman lawyers when they spoke in the courts of law. This

---

[30] The one part of Halifax's pamphlet which might appear to depart from the classical structure is that, towards the end, which returns to the kind of arguments disposed of in the *confutatio* (pp. 14-17 of the original edition and pp. 233-35 of the version printed in vol. VIII of *Somers' Tracts*). Since, however, those arguments are here recapitulated so as to be applied to the situation of the Duke of York, one can see these pages as constituting a *digressio*, at an appropriate position, concerning the succession to the throne.

[31] Roper, pp. 101-02.

[32] Lillien Feder, "John Dryden's Use of Classical Rhetoric," *PMLA*, 69 (1954), 1275-77.

[33] Feder, p. 1275. The poem is "Epistle the Eleventh, to Henry Higden, Esq.," *Works* (ed. Scott), XI, 55.

structure is closely similar to that of the classical deliberative oration, in which the speaker asks his hearers to choose between two courses of action, and this is, of course, precisely what Dryden asks of his readers, that they choose between supporting the Whigs and supporting the King. What better organization, then, for his polemical poem than this most successful of polemical structures?

Especially since only a few elements of the poem are expository, I do not suggest that Dryden made of *Absalom and Achitophel* a classical forensic oration in verse: merely that, as he elaborated the terms of a chiasmus and used them in that modified form to provide the structure for his character of Zimri, so he arranged the parts of the whole poem in the order of a classical oration. What I suggest is somewhat similar to what Professor Ian Jack has suggested. Being impressed with the fact that the poem is crowded with figures divided into two opposing groups and painted both in suitable poses and varying perspectives, Professor Jack suggested that the "poem as a whole may be compared to a masterpiece of 'historical painting.' "[34] He did not claim that it was an "Advice to a Painter" poem, but he did imply that, without using the overt terminology of that genre, Dryden used its organizing principles. Likewise I suggest that Dryden used the structural principles of the classical oration, which would have suited his polemical purpose and his desire to have a unified design much more than would the sprawling nature of the "Advice to a Painter" genre. He used the principles, but not the terminology: he avoided the names of the various parts of the oration (as he avoided naming the chiasmus) but used the essential nature of those parts and arranged them in the order in which they usually appear. It would, presumably, not have been necessary for anyone else to have recognized the presence of those principles and to have identified the parts by name: it would instead have been sufficient for the comprehensive, cohesive, and unifying effect of the oratorical structure to be felt, and for his satirical and polemical design to be thereby perfected.

The test of a theory is of course in its application; so we can now see how well the oratorical structure accounts for the onward movement of *Absalom and Achitophel*. In the process an answer should appear to a question which may well have been forming: how nonexpository passages of a poem may be used for the purposes of argument. At the same time we shall be able to see how the various parts of the poem, which we have examined individually, fit together and function in the way Dryden planned.

[34] Jack, p. 73.

10

OUR COURT OF CHANCERY

To the Reader

On his title page Dryden wrote the encouraging motto (from Horace),

⸻Si Propriùs stes
Te Capiet Magis⸻

"If you stand closer, it will charm you more." (What better justification
could there be for a close reading?) Then, by way of further preparing
his reader for the poem, he inserted three paragraphs of prose and
entitled them "To the Reader."

The opening sentences place the poem in the context of the pamphlet warfare raging between the two opposing sides:

'T is not my intention to make an Apology for my *Poem*: Some will think it
needs no Excuse; and others will receive none. The Design, I am sure, is honest:
but he who draws his Pen for one Party, must expect to make Enemies of the
other. For, *Wit* and *Fool*, are Consequents of *Whig* and *Tory*: And every man is a
Knave or an Ass to the contrary side. There's a Treasury of Merits in the
Phanatick Church, as well as in the *Papist*; and a Pennyworth to be had of
Saintship, Honesty and Poetry, for the Leud, the Factious, and the Blockheads:
But the longest Chapter in *Deuteronomy*, has not Curses enow for an
Anti-*Bromingham*.[1]

Dryden conjectures the response to his poem from the opposition and,
in doing so, indulges (perhaps deliberately) in the wishful thinking of
the artist who thinks that his excellence will triumph over political
prejudice:

My Comfort is, their manifest Prejudice to my Cause, will render their Judgment of less Authority against me. Yet if a *Poem* have a *Genius*, it will force its
own reception in the World. For there's a sweetness in good Verse, which
Tickles even while it Hurts: And, no man can be heartily angry with him, who

---

[1] An Anti-Bromingham was a Tory, an anti-Whig, one opposed to "Bromingham (or
Birmingham—i.e., counterfeit) Protestants."

pleases him against his will. The Commendation of Adversaries, is the greatest Triumph of a Writer; because it never comes unless Extorted.

He is actually more concerned, however, with the moderates in between the two parties:

But I can be satisfied on more easy termes: If I happen to please the more Moderate sort, I shall be sure of an honest Party; and, in all probability, of the best Judges; for, the least Concern'd, are commonly the least Corrupt: And, I confess, I have laid in for those, by rebating the *Satyre*, (where Justice woud allow it) from carrying too sharp an Edge. They, who can Criticize so weakly, as to imagine I have done my Worst, may be Convinc'd, at their own Cost, that I can write Severely, with more ease, than I can Gently. I have but laught at some mens Follies, when I coud have declaim'd against their Vices; and, other mens Vertues I have commended, as freely as I have tax'd their Crimes.

He turns again to his opponents, ostensibly, though still (indirectly) appealing to the moderates:

And now, if you are a Malitious *Reader*, I expect you should return upon me, that I affect to be thought more Impartial than I am. But, if men are not to be judg'd by their Professions, God forgive you *Common-wealths-men*, for professing so plausibly for the Government. You cannot be so Unconscionable, as to charge me for not Subscribing of my Name; for that woud reflect too grossly upon your own Party, who never dare, though they have the advantage of a Jury to secure them. If you like not my *Poem*, the fault may, possibly, be in my Writing: (though 'tis hard for an Authour to judge against himself;) But, more probably, 'tis in your Morals, which cannot bear the truth of it.

Having spoken about his poem as a whole, and in general terms, Dryden then comments on the characterization of the principals mentioned in the title. First is Absalom, whose character he pretends to have drawn far more favourably than he really has:

The Violent, on both sides, will condemn the Character of *Absalom*, as either too favourably, or too hardly drawn. But, they are not the Violent, whom I desire to please. The fault, on the right hand, is to Extenuate, Palliate and Indulge; and, to confess freely, I have endeavour'd to commit it. Besides the respect which I owe his Birth, I have a greater for his Heroique Vertues; and, *David* himself, coud not be more tender of the Young-man's Life, than I woud be of his Reputation. But, since the most excellent Natures are always the most easy; and, as being such, are the soonest perverted by ill Counsels, especially when baited with Fame and Glory; 'tis no more a wonder that he withstood not the temptations of *Achitophel*, than it was for *Adam*, not to have resisted the two Devils; the Serpent, and the Woman. The conclusion of the Story, I purposely forbore to prosecute; because, I coud not obtain from my self, to shew *Absalom* Unfortunate. The Frame of it, was cut out, but for a Picture to the Wast; and, if the Draught be so far true, 'tis as much as I design'd.

Were I the Inventour, who am only the Historian, I shoud certainly conclude the Piece, with the Reconcilement of *Absalom* to *David*. And, who knows but this may come to pass? Things were not brought to an Extremity where I left the Story: There seems, yet, to be room left for a Composure; hereafter, there may only be for pity.

With the character of Achitophel, Dryden has it both ways. He reminds his reader of the fact that the Biblical Achitophel hanged himself and associates him with Satan, and yet (for the benefit of the moderates, no doubt) he professes to have only charitable wishes for him:

I have not, so much as an uncharitable Wish against *Achitophel*, but, am content to be Accus'd of a good natur'd Errour; and, to hope with *Origen*, that the Devil himself may, at last, be sav'd. For which reason, in this *Poem*, he is neither brought to set his House in order, nor to dispose of his Person afterwards, as he in Wisedom shall think fit. God is infinitely merciful; and his Vice-regent is only not so, because he is not Infinite.

The image of the King as Vice-Regent of God will not have escaped notice, and Dryden proceeds, as he turns to the conclusion of these prefatory remarks, to introduce another major image which will recur repeatedly in the poem, that of disease:

The true end of *Satyre*, is the amendment of Vices by correction. And he who writes Honestly, is no more an Enemy to the Offendour, than the Physician to the Patient, when he prescribes harsh Remedies to an inveterate Disease: for those, are only in order to prevent the Chyrurgeon's work of an *Ense rescindendum*,[2] which I wish not to my very Enemies. To conclude all, If the Body Politique have any Analogy to the Natural, in my weak judgment, an Act of *Oblivion* were as necessary in a Hot, Distemper'd State, as an *Opiate* woud be in a Raging Fever.

Exordium

When one's audience is weary—as Dryden's moderate readers would be of the pamphlet warfare, Cicero's advice was to "open with something that may provoke laughter—a fable, a plausible fiction, a caricature, an ironical inversion of the meaning of a word, an ambiguity, innuendo, . . . an exaggeration, . . . an unexpected turn, a comparison, a novel tale, a historical anecdote. . . ."[3] Dryden makes use of all of these, with his fabulous tale of "polygamy" in a never-never land where David ruled "e'er Priest-craft did begin" and performed feats of astonishing verility as, "wide as his Command," he "Scatter'd his Maker's Image through the Land." There was further reason for such a devious beginning to his *exordium* or introduction: "if there is some-

---

[2] A reference to Ovid, *Metamorphoses*, I, 190-91: sed inmedicabile corpus / ense recidendum. (Loeb trans.: "But that which is incurable must be cut away with the knife.")

[3] Cicero, *Rhetorica ad Herennium*, tr. Harry Caplan, Loeb Classical Library (London and Cambridge, Mass.: Heinemann and Harvard University Press, 1954), I.vi.10.

thing scandalous in the case," Cicero advised proceeding through insinuation.[4] As we have seen, there certainly was something scandalous to the moderate readers: Charles's promiscuity and his apparent lack of concern for the immorality that pervaded his court. The first cause of scandal Dryden handles in precisely the way Cicero advised: the Roman had said, "substitute for the person at whom offence is taken another who is favoured, or for a thing at which offence is taken, another which is approved,"[5] and Dryden slyly substitutes King David for Charles and patriarchal polygamy for Restoration wenching.

> In pious times, e'r Priest-craft did begin,
> Before *Polygamy* was made a sin;
> When man, on many, multiply'd his kind,
> E'r one to one was, cursedly, confind:
> When Nature prompted, and no law deny'd   [5]
> Promiscuous use of Concubine and Bride;
> Then, *israel*'s Monarch, after Heaven's own heart,
> His vigorous warmth did, variously, impart
> To Wives and Slaves: And, wide as his Command,
> Scatter'd his Maker's Image through the Land.   [10]
> *Michal*, of Royal blood, the Crown did wear,
> A Soyl ungratefull to the Tiller's care:
> Not so the rest; for several Mothers bore
> To Godlike *David*, several Sons before.
> But since like slaves his bed they did ascend,   [15]
> No True Succession could their seed attend.

The other source of scandal, laxity at court, Dryden will handle a few lines later, but immediately his task, while still in the *exordium*, is to move from his opening attention-grabber to the subject at hand—the bad character of the King's opponents. Again his performance parallels Cicero's advice: "by working imperceptibly, as far as possible to win the good-will of the audience away from your opponents."[6] Dryden turns deftly from Charles to Monmouth:

> Of all this Numerous Progeny was none
> So Beautifull so brave as *Absolon*:

After thus reminding his readers of Monmouth's illegitimacy, Dryden centres first on the Duke's admirable traits, but then glides unobtrusively towards his faults—"for who from faults is free?"

> Whether, inspir'd with some diviner Lust,
> His Father got him with a greater Gust;   [20]

---

[4] Cicero, *De Inventione*, tr. H. M. Hubell, Loeb Classical Library (London and Cambridge, Mass.: Heinemann and Harvard University Press, 1960), I.xvii.23.
[5] *De Invent.*, I.xvii.24.
[6] *De Invent.*, I.xvii.24.

Or that his Conscious destiny made way
By manly beauty to Imperiall sway.
Early in Foreign fields he won Renown,
With Kings and States ally'd to *Israel*'s Crown:
In Peace the thoughts of War he coud remove,   [25]
And seem'd as he were only born for love.
What e'r he did was done with so much ease,
In him alone, 'twas Natural to please.
His motions all accompanied with grace;
And *Paradise* was open'd in his face.   [30]
With secret Joy, indulgent *David* view'd
His Youthfull Image in his Son renew'd:
To all his wishes Nothing he deny'd,
And made the Charming *Annabel* his Bride.
What faults he had (for who from faults is free?)   [35]

"Good-will," Cicero remarked, "is acquired from the person of the opponents if we can bring them into hatred, unpopularity, or contempt. They will be hated if some act of theirs is presented which is base, haughty, cruel, or malicious; they will become unpopular if we present their power, political influence, wealth, family connexions, and their arrogant and intolerable use of these advantages, so that they seem to rely on these rather than on the justice of their case."[7] Monmouth was known to have been responsible for slitting the nose of Sir John Coventry and to have murdered the beadle: Dryden accordingly glances at these (and probably other wrongdoings) as illustrations of the faults which

His Father coud not, or he woud not see.
Some warm excesses, which the Law forbore,
Were constru'd Youth that purg'd by boyling o'r:
And *Amnon*'s Murther, by a specious Name,
Was call'd a Just Revenge for injur'd Fame.   [40]
Thus Prais'd, and Lov'd, the Noble Youth remain'd,
While *David*, undisturb'd, in *Sion* raign'd.

Monmouth has taken gross advantage of who he is, but Charles has simply proved paternally indulgent—not unconcerned, merely indulgent. Thus most of the odium for promiscuity, illegitimacy, and wild immorality is unobtrusively transferred from Charles to Monmouth, and by line 44 Dryden's *exordium* is complete. He then slides through a transition couplet.

But Life can never be sincerely blest;
Heaven punishes the bad, and proves the best.

and his reader is ready for his *narratio*.

[7] *De Invent.*, I.xvi.22.

Narratio

This part of the classical oration, according to Cicero, "is an exposition
of events that have occurred or are supposed to have occurred," and
that have produced the situation about which the argument is to be
made.[8] Of the three kinds of exposition Cicero lists, the second is that
"in which a digression is made beyond the strict limits of the case for
the purpose of attacking somebody, or of making a comparison, or of
amusing the audience in a way not incongruous with the business at
hand. . . ." At the same time Cicero advised that the "mental attitude"
be portrayed of any person or group attacked. Dryden does this and
achieves all three purposes of the "digression," which is not at all
incongrous with the business at hand. That business is to explain how
the Exclusion Crisis came about, and Dryden begins, not unreasonably,
by portraying the "mental attitude" of the group of people, the Whigs,
who were responsible for that crisis coming about.

> The *Jews*, a Headstrong, Moody, Murmuring race,   [45]
> As ever try'd th'extent and stretch of grace;
> God's pamper'd people whom, debauch'd with ease,
> No King could govern, nor no God could please;
> (Gods they had tri'd of every shape and size
> That God-smiths could produce, or Priests devise.)   [50]
> These *Adam*-wits, too fortunately free,
> Began to dream they wanted libertie,
> And when no rule, no president was found
> Of men, by Laws less circumscrib'd and bound,
> They led their wild desires to Woods and Caves   [55]
> And thought that all but Savages were Slaves.

With this strange philosophy in their minds, it is no wonder that the
Whigs thought it was they who, when Cromwell died, made his son
leave the Protectorate and brought back Charles as King, figuratively
from Scotland where he had been crowned King before, though literally from Brussels where he had been living in exile. And having
thought this, it is not surprising that they should think more:

> They who when *Saul* was dead, without a blow,
> Made foolish *Isbosheth* the Crown forgo;
> Who banisht *David* did from *Hebron* bring,
> And, with a Generall Shout, proclaim'd him King: [60]
> Those very *Jewes*, who, at their very best,
> Their Humour more than Loyalty exprest,
> Now, wondred why, so long, they had obey'd
> An Idoll Monarch which their hands had made.
> Thought they might ruine him they could create;   [65]
> Or melt him to that Golden Calf, a State.

[8] *De Invent.*, I.xix.27.

Parallelling Cicero's advice (after attacking somebody, to make a comparison), Dryden then compares the factious Whigs with the "sober part" of England, the "moderate sort of Men":

> But these were randome bolts: No form'd Design,
> Nor Interest made the Factious Croud to joyn:
> The sober part of *Israel*, free from stain,
> Well knew the value of a peacefull raign: [70]
> And, looking backward with a wise afright,
> Saw Seames of wounds, dishonest to the sight;
> In contemplation of whose ugly Scars,
> They Curst the memory of Civil Wars.
> The moderate sort of Men, thus qualifi'd, [75]
> Inclin'd the Ballance to the better side:
> And *David*'s mildness manag'd it so well,
> The Bad found no occasion to Rebell.

There being no occasion at hand, one had to be made: for the "Good old Cause" of republicanism there had to be a plot, and the "carefull Devil" will supply—perhaps, in view of the satanic name of Achitophel in the title of the poem, an early reference to Shaftesbury himself:

> But, when to Sin our byast Nature leans,
> The carefull Devil is still at hand with means; [80]
> And providently Pimps for ill desires:
> The Good old Cause reviv'd, a Plot requires.
> Plots, true or false, are necessary things,
> To raise up Common-wealths, and ruin Kings.

In providing Ciceronian amusement, Dryden has ridiculed the Whiggish Dissenters, who were an extreme on one side of the moderate, middle position of the royalist Church of England. He now turns his attention to the opposite extreme, the Roman Catholics, especially since it was claimed that from their number came the Plot.

> Th' inhabitants of old *Jerusalem* [85]
> Were *Jebusites*: the Town so call'd from them;
> And their's the Native right————
> But when the chosen people grew more strong,
> The rightfull cause at length became the wrong:
> And every loss the men of *Jebus* bore, [90]
> They still were thought God's enemies the more.
> Thus, worn and weaken'd, well or ill content,
> Submit they must to *David*'s Government:
> Impoverisht, and depriv'd of all Command,
> Their Taxes doubled as they lost their Land, [95]
> And, what was harder yet to flesh and blood,
> Their Gods disgrac'd, and burnt like common wood.
> This set the Heathen Priesthood in a flame;

> For Priests of all Religions are the same:
> Of whatsoe'r descent their Godhead be,   [100]
> Stock, Stone, or other homely pedigree,
> In his defence his Servants are as bold
> As if he had been born of beaten gold.
> The *Jewish Rabbins* thô their Enemies,
> In this conclude them honest men and wise;   [105]
> For 'twas their duty, all the Learned think,
> T'espouse his Cause by whom they eat and drink.

With nice ambiguity Dryden returns to the Plot and presents his balanced view, which, presumably, would impress his moderate reader:

> From hence began that Plot, the Nation's Curse,
> Bad in it self, but represented worse.
> Rais'd in extremes, and in extremes decry'd;   [110]
> With Oaths affirm'd, with dying Vows deny'd.
> Not weigh'd, or winnow'd by the Multitude;
> But swallow'd in the Mass, unchew'd and Crude.
> Some Truth there was, but dash'd and brew'd with Lyes;
> To please the Fools, and puzzle all the Wise.   [115]
> Succeeding times did equal folly call,
> Believing nothing, or believing all.

But Dryden does not rest with his balanced view: he proceeds instead, while talking further about the Roman Catholics, to insinuate that they really did not have what it takes to put together the kind of plot they were accused of:

> Th' *Egyptian* Rites the *Jebusites* imbrac'd;
> Where Gods were recommended by their Tast.
> Such savory Deities must needs be good,   [120]
> And serv'd at once for Worship and for Food.
> By force they could not Introduce these Gods;
> For Ten to One, in former days was odds.
> So Fraud was us'd, (the Sacrificers trade,)
> Fools are more hard to Conquer than Perswade.   [125]
> Their busie Teachers mingled with the *Jews*;
> And rak'd, for Converts, even the Court and Stews:
> Which *Hebrew* Priests the more unkindly took,
> Because the Fleece accompanies the Flock.
> Some thought they God's Anointed meant to Slay   [130]
> By Guns, invented since full many a day:
> Our Authour swears it not; but who can know
> How far the Devil and *Jebusites* may go?

In effect Dryden has been doing two things covertly in this "exposition of events that have occurred or are supposed to have occurred." By insinuating that the Roman Catholics could not really have been responsible for the Popish Plot as published by Titus Oates and sub-scribed to by the Whigs, he suggests that much of it owes its existence to the Whigs themselves, which, after all, is not surprising, inasmuch as they were in need of a plot to further the "Good old Cause." At the same time, just as he has made an explicit comparison of the Whigs with the moderates, so does he here make an implicit comparison of the Roman Catholics with the sensible, moderate group of Englishmen, who will be able to weigh the evidence and come to the same conclu-sion he has. Nowhere in his analytic exposition does Dryden mention or even hint at the fuss over Exclusion—for good reason, for the whole point of his argument (and his poem) is that the Exclusion Crisis, like much of the Popish Plot, has been fabricated by the Whigs as a means of undermining royal power and moving the country closer to repub-licanism. As he goes on to say:

> This Plot, which fail'd for want of common Sense,
> Had yet a deep and dangerous Consequence: [135]
> For, as when raging Fevers boyl the Blood,
> The standing Lake soon floats into a Flood;
> And every hostile Humour, which before
> Slept quiet in its Channels, bubbles o'r:
> So, several Factions from this first Ferment,   [140]
> Work up to Foam, and threat the Government.

Propositio and Partitio

This last phrase, "and threat the Government," serves the function in *Absalom and Achitophel* that the *propositio*, or statement of the thesis to be argued, serves in the classical oration. This is the burden of the whole poem: the factiousness and rebelliousness of the Whigs threaten to bring about, not a change in elected government, but the violent overthrow of all government and the plunging of the country into a civil war such as England had endured not long before, and such as had resulted in the truly arbitrary rule of the puritanical Commonwealth. Often at this point in the classical oration the speaker would make a *partitio*, an indication of how he was going to proceed through the various headings of his *confutatio*, in which he would dispose of the arguments that ran counter to his thesis, and of his *confirmatio*, in which he would present those arguments that supported his thesis. In the eight lines immediately following the *propositio* about the threat to the government, Dryden provides what is, in effect, a *partitio*, not of all the rest of the work, but of the *confutatio*, which is by far the largest part of the work. He quickly indicates the kinds of people who pose the threat and, in doing so, he indicates, in thumbnail fashion, a variety of motives behind the threat:

Some by their Friends, more by themselves thought wise,
Oppos'd the Power, to which they could not rise.
Some had in Courts been Great, and thrown from thence,
Like Feinds, were harden'd in Impenitence.   [145]
Some by their Monarch's fatal mercy grown,
From Pardon'd Rebels, Kinsmen to the Throne;
Were rais'd in Power and publick Office high:
Strong Bands, if Bands ungratefull men could tye.

Confutatio

What is virtually the *confutatio* of the poem is divided into three sections: the gallery of Whig leaders, who are analyzed either directly by the narrator or through self-revelation in their speeches; the progress of Absalom/Monmouth through the West; and, in the discourse on government, the narrator's analysis of the philosophic basis for the Whig's arguments. Throughout the *confutatio* Dryden in effect combines qualities of the forensic oration and the deliberative oration (both of which, as noted earlier, have similar structures to begin with). Since the Whigs are virtually on trial in the poem for what is at least morally a crime —intending to rebel or "threatening" the Government, the tone of accusation and charge and the bringing to light of criminal motivation are of course appropriate. Since at the same time Dryden is asking his readers to choose between two courses of action, supporting the King and supporting the Whigs, it is also appropriate that he employ elements of the deliberative oration as presented by Cicero in his *Rhetorica ad Herennium* (III.ii.2-iii.7). Accordingly Dryden based his arguments, as Cicero advised, on the matter of the security of the state (here threatened by the Whigs) and on the matter of honour—what is right and praiseworthy; at the same time, he pointed to the Ciceronian qualities of wisdom, justice, courage, and temperance (here seen in the King, the Duke of York, and their supporters) and to the absence of those qualities—often to a startling degree—in the various Whig leaders. Though Shaftesbury has courage, he lacks all the other qualities, and each of Monmouth, Buckingham, Bethel, and Oates lacks two, three, or even four of the virtues.

(a) Gallery

The analytic descriptions of these people likewise parallel the observations of Cicero, those he made in his *De Inventione* (I.xxiv.35-xxv.36) concerning the nature of persons to be discussed in the *confutatio* and *confirmatio*. Cicero listed as topics such aspects as a person's birth and family, the advantages and disadvantages he possessed in mind and body (in the *Rhetorica* Cicero detailed beauty, strength, and health[9]),

---

[9] *Rhetorica*, III.vii.14.

his manner of personal and home life, his conduct as an official with authority, the purpose behind his actions, the things he did, the things that happened to him, and the things he said. All of the major character descriptions in *Absalom and Achitophel* are concerned with most of these topics, often in the order in which Cicero listed them, as can be seen first in the character sketch of Shaftesbury, under the damning name of Achitophel.

By saying "Of these" Achitophel was first, Dryden links him to the "Pardon'd Rebels" elevated to be "Kinsmen to the Throne" and so refers to his social status, modest at birth but since raised to the peerage. Immediately following is a quick summary of his qualities of mind:

> Of these the false *Achitophel* was first: [150]
> A Name to all succeeding Ages Curst.
> For close Designs, and crooked Counsell fit;
> Sagacious, Bold, and Turbulent of wit:
> Restless, unfixt in Principle and Place;
> In Power unpleas'd, impatient of Disgrace.   [155]

While glancing at the ill health of his body, Dryden elaborates on the wit and ambition of his mind:

> A fiery Soul, which working out its way, ⎫
> Fretted the Pigmy Body to decay: ⎬
> And o'r inform'd the Tenement of Clay.   ⎭
> A daring Pilot in extremity;
> Pleas'd with the Danger, when the Waves went high   [160]
> He sought the Storms; but for a Calm unfit,
> Would Steer too nigh the Sands, to boast his Wit.

Dryden becomes more critical of Shaftesbury's ambition, even relating it to his home life (in the person of his son) as Cicero had recommended, and then pinpointing the danger of his ambition:

> Great Wits are sure to Madness near ally'd;
> And thin Partitions do their Bounds divide:
> Else, why should he, with Wealth and Honour blest,   [165]
> Refuse his Age the needful hours of Rest?
> Punish a Body which he coud not please;
> Bankrupt of Life, yet Prodigal of Ease?
> And all to leave, what with his Toyl he won,
> To that unfeather'd, two Leg'd thing, a Son: [170]
> Got, while his Soul did hudled Notions try;
> And born a shapeless Lump, like Anarchy.
> In Friendship False, Implacable in Hate:
> Resolv'd to Ruine or to Rule the State.

Still following Cicero, both in his advice and in his order, Dryden then assesses Shaftesbury's conduct in public office, both bad (in foreign and domestic affairs) and good (in his conduct as a judge):

> To Compass this the Triple Bond he broke;[10] ⎫   [175]
> The Pillars of the publick Safety shook: ⎬
> And fitted *Israel* for a Foreign Yoke.   ⎭
> Then, seiz'd with Fear, yet still affecting Fame,
> Assum'd a Patriott's All-attoning Name.
> So easie still it proves in Factious Times,   [180]
> With publick Zeal to cancel private Crimes:
> How safe is Treason, and how sacred ill,
> Where none can sin against the Peoples Will:
> Where Crouds can wink; and no offence be known,
> Since in anothers guilt they find their own.   [185]
> Yet, Fame deserv'd, no Enemy can grudge;
> The Statesman we abhor, but praise the Judge.
> In *Israels* Courts ne'r sat an *Abbethdin*
> With more discerning Eyes, or Hands more clean:
> Unbrib'd, unsought, the Wretched to redress;   [190]
> Swift of Dispatch, and easie of Access.
> Oh, had he been content to serve the Crown,
> With vertues only proper to the Gown;
> Or, had the rankness of the Soyl been freed
> From Cockle, that opprest the Noble seed: [195]
> *David*, for him his tunefull Harp had strung,
> And Heaven had wanted one Immortal song.

Shaftesbury's actions since leaving public office are next analyzed, to show his criminal ambition still at work and the Whigs ready and foolish accomplices:

> But wilde Ambition loves to slide, not stand;
> And Fortunes Ice prefers to Vertues Land:
> *Achitophel*, grown weary to possess   [200]
> A lawfull Fame, and lazy Happiness;
> Disdain'd the Golden fruit to gather free,
> And lent the Croud his Arm to shake the Tree.
> Now, manifest of Crimes, contriv'd long since,
> He stood at bold Defiance with his Prince: [205]
> Held up the Buckler of the Peoples Cause,
> Against the Crown; and sculk'd behind the Laws.
> The wish'd occasion of the Plot he takes,
> Some Circumstances finds, but more he makes.
> By buzzing Emissaries, fills the ears   [210]
> Of listning Crowds, with Jealosies and Fears
> Of Arbitrary Counsels brought to light,

---

[10] Shaftesbury was in part responsible for breaking the Triple Alliance of England, the States General (Holland), and Sweden against France.

> And proves the King himself a *Jebusite*:
> Weak Arguments! which yet he knew fulwell,
> Were strong with People easie to Rebell. [215]
> For, govern'd by the *Moon*, the giddy *Jews*
> Tread the same track when she the Prime renews:
> And once in twenty Years, their Scribes Record,
> By natural Instinct they change their Lord.

Of these foolish accomplices one in particular is of special concern:

> *Achitophel* still wants a Chief, and none [220]
> Was found so fit as Warlike *Absolon*:
> Not, that he wish'd his Greatness to create,
> (For Politicians neither love nor hate:)
> But, for he knew, his Title not allow'd,
> Would keep him still depending on the Crowd: [225]
> That Kingly power, thus ebbing out, might be
> Drawn to the dregs of a Democracy.
> Him he attempts, with studied Arts to please,
> And shed his Venome, in such words as these.

The inclusion of dramatic speeches designed to further the author's argumentative purposes was condoned, indeed recommended, by Quintilian. ". . . entreaty, statement, and argument . . . are all of frequent occurrence in *forensic, deliberative,* or *demonstrative* subjects . . . and we often introduce fictitious speeches of historical persons, whom we select ourselves. Cicero for instance in the *pro Caelio* makes both Appius Caecus and her brother Clodius address Clodia, the former rebuking her for her immorality, the latter exhorting her thereto."[11] It should accordingly be no surprise to see Dryden varying the method of presenting his argument, by inventing speeches for his characters. This method serves the same purpose as his more direct analysis of character, for in the speeches of Achitophel and Absalom we see revealed, not only the motivation of the two Whig leaders, but also Monmouth's lack of intelligence, as witnessed by his acceptance of Shaftesbury's outrageous logic.

Achitophel/Shaftesbury begins by addressing Absalom/Monmouth in the most extravagant terms, comparing his listener first to Moses and then to Christ himself, all the while that listener, evidently, accepts the comparison:

> Auspicious Prince! at whose Nativity [230]
> Some Royal Planet rul'd the Southern sky;
> Thy longing Countries Darling and Desire;
> Their cloudy Pillar, and their guardian Fire:

[11] Quintilian, *Institutio Oratoria*, tr. H. E. Butler, Loeb Classical Library (London and Cambridge, Mass.: Heinemann and Harvard University Press, 1963), III.viii.53-54.

> Their second *Moses*, whose extended Wand
> Shuts up the Seas, and shews the promis'd Land: [235]
> Whose dawning Day, in every distant age,
> Has exercis'd the Sacred Prophets rage:
> The Peoples Prayer, the glad Deviners Theam,
> The Young-mens Vision, and the Old mens Dream!
> Thee, *Saviour*, Thee, the Nations Vows confess;   [240]
> And, never satisfi'd with seeing, bless:
> Swift, unbespoken Pomps, thy steps proclaim,
> And stammerring Babes are taught to lisp thy Name.

Absalom must not remain inactive, "Like one of Vertues Fools that feeds on Praise"—surprisingly like what Absalom has just been doing in listening to the egregious praise barely ended:

> How long wilt thou the general Joy detain;
> Starve, and defraud the People of thy Reign?   [245]
> Content ingloriously to pass thy days
> Like one of Vertues Fools that feeds on Praise;
> Till thy fresh Glories, which now shine so bright,
> Grow Stale and Tarnish with our daily sight.

Instead, Absalom must act immediately and seize the one opportunity which Fortune presents. (That that opportunity is the Exclusion Crisis, and that Absalom/Monmouth's action would be a form of treason against his father, Dryden's readers would recognize—and so would Absalom.)

> Believe me, Royal Youth, thy Fruit must be,   [250]
> Or gather'd Ripe, or rot upon the Tree.
> Heav'n, has to all allotted, soon or late,
> Some lucky Revolution of their Fate:
> Whose Motions, if we watch and guide with Skill,
> (For humane Good depends on humane Will,)   [255]
> Our Fortune rolls, as from a smooth Descent,
> And, from the first Impression, takes the Bent:
> But, if unseiz'd, she glides away like wind;
> And leaves repenting Folly far behind.
> Now, now she meets you, with a glorious prize,   [260]
> And spreads her Locks before her as she flies.

The implied action against the King leads Achitophel/Shaftesbury, typically, to invert a Biblical reference and to use the earlier experience of the King as a reason why Absalom/Monmouth should act in the manner he has just been urged to:

> Had thus Old *David*, from whose Loyns you spring,
> Not dar'd, when Fortune call'd him, to be King,
> At *Gath* an Exile he might still remain,
> And heavens Anointing Oyle had been in vain.   [265]

Let his successfull Youth your hopes engage,
But shun th'example of Declining Age:
Behold him setting in his Western Skies,
The Shadows lengthning as the Vapours rise.
He is not now, as when on *Jordan*'s Sand ⎫   [270]
The Joyfull People throng'd to see him Land, ⎬
Cov'ring the *Beach*, and blackning all the *Strand*: ⎭
But, like the Prince of Angels from his height,
Comes tumbling downward with diminish'd light;
Betray'd by one poor Plot to publick Scorn,   [275]
(Our only blessing since his Curst Return:)
Those heaps of People which one Sheaf did bind,
Blown off and scatter'd by a puff of Wind.

The moderate reader must wonder what kind of son Monmouth is to hear his father compared to Satan without protest, but wonder must turn to loathing when Monmouth listens without objection to the further use Shaftesbury makes of the King's current weakness:

What strength can he to your Designs oppose,
Naked of Friends, and round beset with Foes?   [280]
If *Pharaoh*'s doubtfull Succour he shoud use,
A Foreign Aid woud more Incense the *Jews*:
Proud *Egypt* woud dissembled Friendship bring;
Foment the War, but not support the King:
Nor woud the Royal Party e'r unite   [285]
With *Pharoah*'s Arms, t'assist the *Jebusite*;
Or if they shoud, their Interest soon would break,
And with such odious Aid make *David* weak.

Achitophel then concludes his first pitch with the marvellously illogical argument that Absalom should champion the cause of revolt and attempt to become the king of a republic:

All sorts of men by my successfull Arts,
Abhorring Kings, estrange their alter'd Hearts   [290]
From *David*'s Rule: And 'tis the general Cry,
Religion, Common-wealth, and Liberty.
If you as Champion of the publique Good,
Add to their Arms a Chief of Royal Blood;
What may not *Israel* hope, and what Applause   [295]
Might such a General gain by such a Cause?
Not barren Praise alone, that Gaudy Flower,
Fair only to the sight, but solid Power:
And Nobler is a limited Command,
Giv'n by the Love of all your Native Land,   [300]
Than a Successive Title, Long, and Dark,
Drawn from the Mouldy Rolls of *Noah*'s Ark.

The effects of this speech on Absalom/Monmouth Dryden presents in a most carefully ambiguous way. He begins:

> What cannot Praise effect in Mighty Minds,
> When Flattery Sooths, and when Ambition Blinds!

How "Mighty" Monmouth's "Mind" has been the reader can by now judge from the way he has accepted Shaftesbury's argument. "Flattery" today retains the pejorative connotations of the Restoration, but one must remember that "Ambition," today often regarded as a good thing, then was usually regarded as highly dangerous, something which tempted one to aspire beyond the rank and position in which he had been placed by God. Dryden elaborates by pinpointing "Desire of Power" as being at the centre of Absalom's "Ambition," and concerning that "Desire of Power" Dryden offers two sets of images: in heaven it is "Fire" and "Glory," but on earth, where, after all, Monmouth is operating, it is "a Vitious Weed."

> Desire of Power, on Earth a Vitious Weed,   [305]
> Yet, sprung from High is of Caelestial Seed:
> In God 'tis Glory: And when men Aspire,
> 'Tis but a Spark too much of Heavenly Fire.

Dryden proceeds in a similarly ambiguous way, appearing to excuse and condone but actually condemning, until in a parenthesis he puts the situation unambiguously:

> Th' Ambitious Youth, too Covetous of Fame,
> Too full of Angells Metal in his Frame;   [310]
> Unwarily was led from Vertues ways;
> Made Drunk with Honour, and Debauch'd with Praise.
> Half loath, and half consenting to the Ill,
> (For Loyal Blood within him strugled still)
> He thus reply'd————   [315]

In his dramatic reply Dryden makes Monmouth at once confess that he has no reason to rebel, not even the pretence he has used, that he seeks to protect the people's liberty:

> And what Pretence have I
> To take up Arms for Publick Liberty?

He has neither reason nor pretence because the King governs admirably, maintaining all the laws and practising both justice and mercy:

> My Father Governs with unquestion'd Right;
> The Faiths Defender, and Mankinds Delight:
> Good, Gracious, Just, observant of the Laws;
> And Heav'n by Wonders has Espous'd his Cause.   [320]
> Whom has he Wrong'd in all his Peaceful Reign?

Who sues for Justice to his Throne in Vain?
What Millions has he Pardon'd of his Foes,
Whom Just Revenge did to his Wrath expose?
Mild, Easy, Humble, Studious of our Good;   [325]
Enclin'd to Mercy, and averse from Blood.

Alluding to the Whig charges of laxity and arbitrary government (a
rather odd combination), Monmouth is then made to show how silly
they are:

If Mildness Ill with Stubborn *Israel* Suite
His Crime is God's beloved Attribute.
What could he gain, his People to Betray,
Or change his Right, for Arbitrary Sway?   [330]
Let Haughty *Pharaoh* Curse with such a Reign,
His Fruitfull *Nile*, and Yoak a Servile Train.
If *David*'s Rule *Jerusalem* Displease,
The *Dog-star* heats their Brains to this Disease.

What Monmouth should do is then clear: it would be insane of him to
turn rebel, and even if his father were arbitrary, it would be sacrilegious
of him as son to rebel:

Why then shoud I, Encouraging the Bad,   [335]
Turn Rebell, and run Popularly Mad?
Were he a Tyrant who, by Lawless Might,
Opprest the *Jews*, and Rais'd the *Jebusite*,
Well might I Mourn; but Natures Holy Bands
Woud Curb my Spirits, and Restrain my Hands: [340]
The People might assert their Liberty;
But what was Right in them, were Crime in me.
His Favour leaves me nothing to require;
Prevents my Wishes, and outruns Desire.

Then why does he listen to Achitophel/Shaftesbury and contemplate
rebellion? Because he longs for the crown, which must pass by legitimate succession to his uncle:

What more can I expect while *David* lives,   [345]
All but his Kingly Diadem he gives;
And that: But there he Paus'd; then Sighing, said,
Is Justly Destin'd for a Worthier Head.
For when my Father from his Toyls shall Rest,
And late Augment the Number of the Blest: [350]
His Lawfull Issue shall the Throne ascend,
Or the *Collateral* Line where that shall end.

The legitimate successor, Monmouth is made to admit, is entirely
worthy to succeed:

> His Brother, though Opprest with Vulgar Spight,
> Yet Dauntless and Secure of Native Right,
> Of every Royal Vertue stands possest;   [355]
> Still Dear to all the Bravest, and the Best.
> His Courage Foes, his Friends his Truth Proclaim;
> His Loyalty the King, the World his Fame.
> His Mercy even th'Offending Crowd will find,
> For sure he comes of a Forgiving Kind.   [360]

As Monmouth himself then asks,

> Why should I then Repine at Heavens Decree;
> Which gives me no Pretence to Royalty?

The answer is ambition, expressed in such a way, however, as to expose the meanness of his mind as he blames his mother for blighting his chances and merely repines instead of striving:

> Yet oh that Fate Propitiously Enclind,
> Had rais'd my Birth, or had debas'd my Mind;
> To my large Soul, not all her Treasure lent,   [365]
> And then Betray'd it to a mean Descent.
> I find, I find my mounting Spirits Bold,
> And *David*'s Part disdains my Mothers Mold.
> Why am I Scanted by a Niggard Birth,
> My Soul Disclaims the Kindred of her Earth: [370]
> And made for Empire, Whispers me within;
> Desire of Greatness is a Godlike Sin.

As Dryden makes the transition to Achitophel's next speech, he underlines the kind of morality to be found in the two Whig leaders: Monmouth's "Vertue" is indeed "fainting" and Shaftesbury serves the wrong master:

> Him Staggering so when Hells dire Agent found,
> While fainting Vertue scarce maintain'd her Ground,
> He pours fresh Forces in, and thus Replies: [375]

Achitophel resumes his outrageous flattery, unresisted:

> Th' Eternal God Supreamly Good and Wise,
> Imparts not these Prodigious Gifts in vain;
> What Wonders are Reserv'd to bless your Reign?
> Against your will your Arguments have shown,
> Such Vertue's only given to guide a Throne.   [380]

Monmouth's argument about Charles's mildness Shaftesbury seeks to counter thus:

> Not that your Father's Mildness I condemn;
> But Manly Force becomes the Diadem.
> 'Tis true, he grants the People all they crave;

And more perhaps than Subjects ought to have:
For Lavish grants suppose a Monarch tame,   [385]
And more his Goodness than his Wit proclaim.
But when shoud People strive their Bonds to break,
If not when Kings are Negligent or Weak?

An interesting statement, that last one: it implies that, in the Whig
view, the people are always opposed to the king and always seek to
increase their power in relation to his—a view that would not promise
much peace for the moderate reader if the Whigs made any gains at all,
or for Monmouth himself if he should become king, for he would
necessarily be a weak king, dependent on the people. The Whigs have
in fact been seeking to increase their power, especially in the House of
Commons, where they have sought to grant money (which the government needs to govern) only in return for a surrender of some further
aspect of the King's power, here called his "Prerogative":

Let him give on till he can give no more,
The Thrifty Sanhedrin shall keep him poor: [390]
And every Sheckle which he can receive,
Shall cost a Limb of his Prerogative.
To ply him with new Plots, shall be my care,
Or plunge him deep in some Expensive War;
Which when his Treasure can no more Supply,   [395]
He must, with the Remains of Kingship, buy.

The Whigs have already succeeded in weakening the King's support
and will continue trying to proceed in the same direction, until Monmouth is made King—at which time the Whigs will reign supreme:

His faithful Friends, our Jealousies and Fears,
Call *Jebusites*; and *Pharaoh*'s Pentioners:
Whom, when our Fury from his Aid has torn,
He shall be Naked left to publick Scorn.   [400]
The next Successor, whom I fear and hate,
My Arts have made Obnoxious to the State;
Turn'd all his Vertues to his Overthrow,
And gain'd our Elders to pronounce a Foe.
His Right, for Sums of necessary Gold,   [405]
Shall first be Pawn'd, and afterwards be Sold:
Till time shall Ever-wanting *David* draw,
To pass your doubtfull Title into Law:

"If not," Achitophel/Shaftesbury continues, and cites the Whig doctrine of the origin of government in a contract between a people and
their King. But much is implied in that phrase "If not": if David does
not pass Absalom's "doubtfull Title into Law," what then? Presumably
the only answer is open warfare, and this is what Achito-
phel/Shaftesbury seeks to justify by appealing to the contract theory:

If not; the People have a Right Supreme
To make their Kings, for Kings are made for them.   [410]
All Empire is no more than Pow'r in Trust,
Which when resum'd, can be no longer Just.
Succession, for the general Good design'd,
In its own wrong a Nation cannot bind:
If altering that, the People can relieve,   [415]
Better one Suffer, than a Million grieve.
The *Jews* well know their power: e'r *Saul* they Chose,
God was their King, and God they durst Depose.

Quite a leveller, that Shaftesbury: "Better one"—the rightful King—"Suffer," by being removed from kingship and possibly life itself, "than a Million grieve"—that million being subjects whose duty it is to obey their rightful King. And how casually sacrilegious Shaftesbury is, but no wonder: if he can dispose of God's vice-regent so calmly, using words, in fact, that recall Caiaphas's disposing of Jesus—"It is expedient for us, that one man should die for the people, and that the whole nation perish not" (John 11:50)—it is then only to be expected that he would dispose of God himself with little perturbation. And having done that, having practised impiety, he can now of course appeal to piety:

Urge now your Piety, your Filial Name,
A Father's Right, and fear of future Fame;   [420]
The publick Good, that Universal Call,
To which even Heav'n Submitted, answers all.

Next to be sundered by this Whig philosopher is filial devotion, which he seeks to subvert by appealing to ambition—again unopposed:

Nor let his Love Enchant your generous Mind;
'Tis Natures trick to Propagate her Kind.
Our fond Begetters, who woud never dye,   [425]
Love but themselves in their Posterity.
Or let his Kindness by th'Effects be try'd,
Or let him lay his vain Pretence aside.
God said he lov'd your Father; coud he bring
A better Proof, than to Anoint him King?   [430]
It surely shew'd he lov'd the Shepherd well,
Who gave so fair a Flock as *Israel*.
Woud *David* have you thought his Darling Son?
What means he then, to Alienate the Crown?
The name of Godly he may blush to bear: [435]
'Tis after God's own heart to Cheat his Heir.
He to his Brother gives Supreme Command;
To you a Legacy of Barren Land:
Perhaps th'old Harp, on which he thrums his Layes:
Or some dull *Hebrew* Ballad in your Praise.   [440]

If ambition needs an excuse for acting, it can be found in the argument of self-protection: Monmouth must protect himself against an attack that has never come (and never may):

> Then the next Heir, a Prince, Severe and Wise,
> Already looks on you with Jealous Eyes;
> See through the thin Disguises of your Arts,
> And markes your Progress in the Peoples Hearts.
> Though now his mighty Soul its Grief contains;   [445]
> He meditates Revenge who least Complains.
> And like a Lyon, Slumbring in the way,
> Or Sleep-dissembling, while he waits his Prey,
> His fearless Foes within his Distance draws;
> Constrains his Roaring, and Contracts his Paws;   [450]
> Till at the last, his time for Fury found,
> He shoots with suddain Vengeance from the Ground:
> The Prostrate Vulgar, passes o'r, and Spares;
> But with a Lordly Rage, his Hunters teares.
> Your Case no tame Expedients will afford;   [455]
> Resolve on Death, or Conquest by the Sword,
> Which for no less a Stake than Life, you Draw;
> And Self-defence is Natures Eldest Law.

Having provided Monmouth with this excuse, Shaftesbury then reminds him that his opportunity may well pass quickly: rebellion, which is now not regarded as a crime, may in time be so regarded (and of course morality is what people make it):

> Leave the warm People no Considering time;
> For then Rebellion may be thought a Crime.   [460]
> Prevail your self of what Occasion gives,
> But try your Title while your Father lives:
> And that your Arms may have a fair Pretence,
> Proclaim, you take them in the King's Defence:
> Whose Sacred Life each minute woud Expose,   [465]
> To Plots, from seeming Friends, and secret Foes.

Shaftesbury then clinches his argument by using the greatest perversity yet. He has already argued that Charles's fatherly love for Monmouth is of no account; now he uses Monmouth's remaining love for his father to argue that Monmouth will really please his father by rebelling against him—an argument whose nature is nicely exposed to the discerning reader in the image of the "pleasing Rape":

> And who can sound the depth of *David*'s Soul?
> Perhaps his fear, his kindness may Controul.
> He fears his Brother, though he loves his Son,
> For plighted Vows too late to be undone.   [470]
> If so, by Force he wishes to be gain'd,

> Like women's Leachery, to seem Constrain'd:
> Doubt not, but when he most affects the Frown,
> Commit a pleasing Rape upon the Crown.
> Secure his Person to secure your Cause;   [475]
> They who possess the Prince, possess the Laws.

In his description of Monmouth's acceptance of Shaftesbury's arguments, Dryden again has it both ways. He appears to hold Monmouth in high regard and yet at the same time he reminds his readers of what a blackguard he really is:

> He said, And this Advice above the rest,
> With *Absalom*'s Mild nature suited best;
> Unblam'd of Life (Ambition set aside,)
> Not stain'd with Cruelty, nor puft with Pride;   [480]

Was it not cruel of Monmouth to kill the beadle, and did he not do it out of his injured pride? And how can one set his ambition aside when it has led him into treason and rebellion against his King and father? Having thus set the tone of ambiguity for his apparent exculpation of Monmouth, Dryden is able to continue:

> How happy had he been, if Destiny
> Had higher plac'd his Birth, or not so high?
> His Kingly Vertues might have claim'd a Throne,
> And blest all other Countries but his own:
> But charming Greatness, since so few refuse;   [485]
> 'Tis Juster to Lament him, than Accuse.
> Strong were his hopes a Rival to remove,
> With blandishments to gain the publick Love;
> To Head the Faction while their Zeal was hot,
> And Popularly prosecute the Plot   [490]

Thus, through description and self-revealing speeches, Dryden has been able to show to his moderate reader the evil motivation and illogical arguments of the principal Whig leaders. What sort of people would accept these as leaders? The malcontents:

> To farther this, *Achitophel* Unites
> The Malecontents of all the *Israelites*;
> Whose differing Parties he could wisely Joyn,
> For several Ends, to serve the same Design.

Of these there were some who were simply mistaken, with the wrong view of government:

> The Best, and of the Princes some were such,   [495]
> Who thought the power of Monarchy too much:
> Mistaken Men, and Patriots in their Hearts;
> Not Wicked, but Seduc'd by Impious Arts.

By these the Springs of Property were bent,
And wound so high, they Crack'd the Government. [500]

But there were at least three other groups all eager to advance their own private fortunes at the expense of the country:

The next for Interest sought t' embroil the State,
To sell their Duty at a dearer rate;
And make their *Jewish* Markets of the Throne,
Pretending publick Good, to serve their own.
Others thought Kings an useless heavy Load, [505]
Who Cost too much, and did too little Good.
These were for laying Honest *David* by,
On Principles of pure good Husbandry.
With them Joyn'd all th'Haranguers of the Throng,
That thought to get Preferment by the Tongue. [510]

More dangerous than these are the Commonwealth men, who seek to restore their tyranny of old:

Who follow next, a double Danger bring,
Not only hating *David*, but the King,
The *Solymaean* Rout; well Verst of old,
In Godly Faction, and in Treason bold;
Cowring and Quaking at a Conqueror's Sword, [515]
But Lofty to a Lawfull Prince Restor'd;
Saw with Disdain an *Ethnick*[12] Plot begun,
And Scorn'd by *Jebusites* to be Out-done.
Hot *Levites* Headed these; who pul'd before
From th'*Ark*, which in the Judges days they bore, [520]
Resum'd their Cant, and with a Zealous Cry,
Pursu'd their old belov'd Theocracy.
Where Sanhedrin and Priest inslav'd the Nation,
And justifi'd their Spoils by Inspiration;
For who so fit for Reign as *Aaron*'s Race, [525]
If once Dominion they could found in Grace?
These led the Pack; tho not of surest scent,
Yet deepest mouth'd against the Government.

Associated with these were the far left wing of the Dissenters, the levellers:

A numerous Host of dreaming Saints succeed;
Of the true old Enthusiastick breed: [530]
'Gainst Form and Order they their Power employ,
Nothing to Build and all things to Destroy.

[12] *Ethnick* means, basically, gentile or heathen, i.e., of a race different from the Jews. If Dryden saw the word also as the adjectival form of Ethnan or Ethnei, he then implied that the Popish Plot was "a gift" to the Whigs.

And then the herd, chaos and anarchy:

> But far more numerous was the herd of such,
> Who think too little, and who talk too much.
> These, out of meer instinct, they knew not why,   [535]
> Ador'd their fathers God, and Property:
> And, by the same blind benefit of Fate,
> The Devil and the Jebusite did hate:
> Born to be sav'd, even in their own despight;
> Because they could not help believing right.   [540]
> Such were the tools; but a whole Hydra more
> Remains, of sprouting heads too long, to score.

These make up the malcontents: who in his right mind would wish to support them?

Having disposed of the followers, Dryden returns to the leaders and canvasses them from top to bottom, from Duke to weaver's issue. In presenting the sketch of Buckingham, Dryden again follows the order suggested by Cicero: from his high birth we proceed through the various qualities of his mind, see the variety of his personal life, observe that his purpose—"his peculiar Art"—appears to be "in squandring Wealth," and conclude with his political activities:

> Some of their Chiefs were Princes of the Land:
> In the first Rank of these did *Zimri* stand:
> A man so various, that he seem'd to be   [545]
> Not one, but all Mankinds Epitome.
> Stiff in Opinions, always in the wrong;
> Was every thing by starts, and nothing long:
> But, in the course of one revolving Moon,
> Was Chymist, Fidler, States-Man, and Buffoon: [550]
> Then all for Women, Painting, Rhiming, Drinking;
> Besides ten thousand freaks that dy'd in thinking.
> Blest Madman, who coud every hour employ,
> With something New to wish, or to enjoy!
> Rayling and praising were his usual Theams;   [555]
> And both (to shew his Judgment) in Extreams:
> So over Violent, or over Civil,
> That every man, with him, was God or Devil.
> In squandring Wealth was his peculiar Art: [560]
> Nothing went unrewarded, but Desert:
> Begger'd by Fools, whom still he found too late:
> He had his Jest, and they had his Estate.
> He laught himself from Court, then sought Releif
> By forming Parties, but coud ne're be Chief:
> For, spight of him, the weight of Business fell   [565]
> On *Absalom* and wise *Achitophel*:
> Thus, wicked but in will, of means bereft,
> He left not Faction, but of that was left.

Beneath Buckingham we descend through the ranks of leaders rather quickly, observing their vices along the way:

Titles and Names 'twere tedious to Reherse
Of Lords, below the Dignity of Verse.   [570]
Wits warriors Common-wealthsmen, were the best:
Kind Husbands and meer Nobles all the rest.
And, therefore in the name of Dulness, be
The well hung *Balaam* and cold *Caleb* free.
And Canting *Nadab* let Oblivion damn,   [575]
Who made new porridge for the Paschal Lamb.
Let Friendships holy band some Names assure:
Some their own Worth, and some let Scorn secure.
Nor shall the Rascall Rabble here have Place,
Whom Kings no Titles gave, and God no Grace: [580]
Not Bull-fac'd-*Jonas*, who could Statutes draw
To mean Rebellion, and make Treason Law.

And now we linger on that exemplar of Whig republicanism, Slingsby Bethel. Still following Cicero, we see Bethel emerge from the "Rascall Rabble," demonstrate his ruling passion even in his youth, and reveal his puritanical qualities of mind:

But he, tho bad, is follow'd by a worse,
The wretch, who Heavens Annointed dar'd to Curse.
Shimei, whose early Youth did Promise bring   [585]
Of Zeal to God, and Hatred to his King;
Did wisely from Expensive Sins refrain,
And never broke the Sabbath, but for Gain:
Nor ever was he known an Oath to vent,
Or Curse unless against the Government.   [590]

We are then treated to his hypocritical performance in public office:

Thus, heaping Wealth, by the most ready way
Among the Jews, which was to Cheat and Pray;
The City, to reward his pious Hate
Against his Master, chose him Magistrate:
His Hand a Vare of Justice did uphold;   [595]
His Neck was loaded with a Chain of Gold.
During his Office, Treason was no Crime.
The Sons of *Belial* had a glorious Time:
For *Shimei*, though not prodigal of pelf,
Yet lov'd his wicked Neighbour as himself: [600]
When two or three were gather'd to declaim ⎫
Against the Monarch of *Jerusalem*,   ⎬
Shimei was always in the midst of them.   ⎭
And, if they Curst the King when he was by,
Woud rather Curse, than break good Company.   [605]
If any durst his Factious Friends accuse,

> He pact a Jury of dissenting Jews:
> Whose fellow-feeling, in the godly Cause,
> Would free the suffring Saint from Humane Laws,
> For Laws are only made to Punish those,   [610]
> Who serve the King, and to protect his Foes.

His private life likewise bears witness to his ruling passion, republicanism:

> If any leisure time he had from Power,
> (Because 'tis Sin to misimploy an hour;)
> His business was, by Writing, to Persuade,
> That Kings were Useless, and a Clog to Trade: [615]

But capping even his republicanism is another characteristic that can be seen in both his private and his public life:

> And, that his noble Stile he might refine,
> No *Rechabite* more shund the fumes of Wine.
> Chast were his Cellars, and his Shrieval Board
> The Grossness of a City Feast abhor'd:
> His Cooks, with long disuse, their Trade forgot;   [620]
> Cool was his Kitchen, tho his Brains were hot.
> Such frugal Vertue Malice may accuse,
> But sure 'twas necessary to the Jews:
> For Towns once burnt, such Magistrates require
> As dare not tempt Gods Providence by fire.   [625]
> With Spiritual food he fed his Servants well,
> But free from flesh, that made the Jews Rebel:
> And *Moses*'s Laws he held in more account,
> For forty days of Fasting in the Mount.

Who could take seriously the Whig appeal for support when they have as a leader such a clown as this?

Another leader was taken seriously, much too seriously. But then Titus Oates put on a good front:

> To speak the rest, who better are forgot,   [630]
> Would tyre a well breath'd Witness of the Plot:
> Yet, *Corah*, thou shalt from Oblivion pass;
> Erect thy self thou Monumental Brass:
> High as the Serpent of thy mettall made,
> While Nations stand secure beneath thy shade.   [635]

Again the Ciceronian pattern, with first the subject's birth:

> What tho his Birth were base, yet Comets rise
> From Earthy Vapours ere they shine in Skies.
> Prodigious Actions may as well be done
> By Weavers issue, as by Princes Son.
> This Arch-Attestor for the publick Good,   [640]

By that one Deed Enobles all his Bloud.
Who ever ask'd the Witnesses high race,
Whose Oath with Martyrdom did *Stephen* grace?

Then his physical appearance and phenomenal memory:

Ours was a *Levite*, and as times went then,
His Tribe were Godalmightys Gentlemen.   [645]
Sunk were his Eyes, his Voyce was harsh and loud,
Sure signs he neither Cholerick was, nor Proud:
His long Chin prov'd his Wit; his Saintlike Grace
A Church Vermilion, and a *Moses*'s Face;
His Memory, miraculously great,   [650]
Could Plots, exceeding mans belief, repeat;
Which, therefore cannot be accounted Lies,
For humane Wit could never such devise.
Some future Truths are mingled in his Book;
But, where the witness faild, the Prophet Spoke: [655]
Some things like Visionary flights appear;
The Spirit caught him up, the Lord knows where:
And gave him his *Rabinical* degree
Unknown to Foreign University.

All his qualities of mind are applied to his performance in quasi-public
office as Saviour of the Nation:

His Judgment yet his Memory did excel;   [660]
Which peic'd his wondrous Evidence so well:
And suited to the temper of the times;
Then groaning under Jebusitick Crimes.

His purpose, protecting his trade, was implicit and is now made inescapable:

Let *Israels* foes suspect his heav'nly call,
And rashly judge his writ Apocryphal;   [665]
Our Laws for such affronts have forfeits made:
He takes his life, who takes away his trade.
Were I my self in witness *Corahs* place,
The wretch who did me such a dire disgrace,
Should whet my memory, though once forgot,   [670]
To make him an appendix of my plot.

His general performance thus discredited, his specific charges against
James are then dismissed and he himself is allowed to face his appropriate future:

His Zeal to heav'n, made him his Prince despise,
And load his person with indignities:
But Zeal peculiar priviledg affords;
Indulging latitude to deeds and words.   [675]

> And *Corah* might for *Agag*'s murther call,
> In terms as course as *Samuel* us'd to *Saul*.
> What others in his Evidence did Joyn,
> (The best that could be had for love or coyn,)
> In *Corah*'s own predicament will fall: [680]
> For *witness* is a Common Name to all.

Thus is the gallery of Whigs complete, leaders and followers, with their motives and purposes exposed, their arguments and performances discredited. One performance is now to be examined in detail, to show further how dangerous are the Whigs and their actions:

(b) Progress

In presenting his account of Monmouth's progress through the West of England, Dryden provides, not so much a narrative, as an analysis of what went on at that time and what it meant. He first describes Monmouth's approach to the people, emphasizing three things: that he dissembles, that he is courting the plebeians, and, through the image of Hybla drops, that he is base within:

> Surrounded thus with Freinds of every sort,
> Deluded *Absalom*, forsakes the Court:
> Impatient of high hopes, urg'd with renown,
> And Fir'd with near possession of a Crown,   [685]
> Th'admiring Croud are dazled with surprize,
> And on his goodly person feed their eyes:
> Dissembling Joy, he sets himself to show;
> On each side bowing popularly low:
> His looks, his gestures, and his words he frames,   [690]
> And with familiar ease repeats their Names.
> Thus, form'd by Nature, furnish'd out with Arts,
> He glides unfelt into their secret hearts:
> Then with a kind compassionating look,
> And sighs, bespeaking pity ere he spoak: [695]
> Few words he said; but easy those and fit:
> More slow than Hybla drops, and far more sweet.

The inner baseness is then made manifest in a speech of Monmouth's that is presented as typical. The dissembler begins by mouthing falsehoods about arbitrary laws and lost liberties:

> I mourn, my Countrymen, your lost Estate;
> Tho far unable to prevent your fate:
> Behold a Banisht man, for your dear cause   [700]
> Expos'd a prey to Arbitrary laws!
> Yet oh! that I alone cou'd be undone,
> Cut off from Empire, and no more a Son!

That last line almost gives the show away, for what "Empire" does Monmouth have any legitimate claim to? Having further discredited Monmouth by having him mouth such lies, Dryden can then afford to let him repeat the usual charges about Charles's government, for who will believe him now?

> Now all your Liberties a spoil are made; ⎫
> Ægypt and Tyrus intercept your Trade, ⎬   [705]
> And Jebusites your Sacred Rites invade. ⎭
> My Father, whom with reverence yet I name,
> Charm'd into Ease, is careless of his Fame:
> And, brib'd with petty summs of Forreign Gold,
> Is grown in Bathsheba's Embraces old: [710]
> Exalts his Enemies, his Freinds destroys:
> And all his pow'r against himself employs.
> He gives, and let him give my right away:
> But why should he his own, and yours betray?

A lot of twaddle, all that, and to make sure that his readers realize it, Dryden then has Monmouth expose himself again, by referring to his "revenge" (for what?), by wiping his eyes of crocodile's tears, and by being coyly ambiguous about who the "next Successor" is:

> He only, he can make the Nation bleed,   [715]
> And he alone from my revenge is freed.
> Take then my tears (with that he wip'd his Eyes)
> 'Tis all the Aid my present power supplies:
> No Court Informer can these Arms accuse,
> These Arms may Sons against their Fathers use, [720]
> And, tis my wish, the next Successors Reign
> May make no other Israelite complain.

The reception which Monmouth received in the West Dryden undermines in two ways: he ascribes it to the crowd's wrongheadedness, and he mockingly exaggerates the reception itself, pretending that the crowd regarded Monmouth as a messiah, Moses, and a household god, and then further deflating their attitude in the ironic reference to the ass who couched down between two burdens, "Wise Issachar":

> Youth, Beauty, Graceful Action, seldom fail:
> But Common Interest always will prevail:
> And pity never Ceases to be shown   [725]
> To him, who makes the peoples wrongs his own.
> The Croud, (that still believes their Kings oppress)
> With lifted hands their young Messiah bless:
> Who now begins his Progress to ordain;
> With Chariots, Horsemen, and a numerous train: [730]
> From East to West his Glories he displaies:
> And, like the Sun, the promis'd land survays.

> Fame runs before him, as the morning Star;
> And shouts of Joy salute him from afar:
> Each house receives him as a Guardian God;   [735]
> And Consecrates the Place of his aboad:
> But hospitable treats did most Commend
> Wise *Issachar*, his wealthy western friend.

What Monmouth's progress and his reception meant Dryden then makes manifest. Shaftesbury has used the situation to determine what support the Whigs have before they turn to open warfare:

> This moving Court, that caught the peoples Eyes,
> And seem'd but Pomp, did other ends disguise: [740]
> *Achitophel* had form'd it, with intent
> To sound the depth, and fathom where it went:
> The Peoples hearts, distinguish Friends from Foes;
> And try their strength, before they came to blows:
> Yet all was colour'd with a smooth pretence   [745]
> Of specious love, and duty to their Prince.
> Religion, and Redress of Grievances,
> Two names, that always cheat and always please,
> Are often urg'd; and good King *David*'s life
> Indanger'd by a Brother and a Wife.   [750]
> Thus, in a Pageant Show, a Plot is made;
> And Peace it self is War in Masquerade.

The Whig leaders and their followers, their statements and their actions, all threaten civil war. And what justification have they? All they can produce is a doctrinaire view of the origin of government. By way of completing his *confutatio*, Dryden accordingly turns to an analysis of that view which will show how foolish it is.

(c) Discourse

Diseased imagination and overweening pride mark the assumptions of the Whigs:

> Oh foolish *Israel*! never warn'd by ill,
> Still the same baite, and circumvented still!
> Did ever men forsake their present ease,   [755]
> In midst of health Imagine a desease;
> Take pains Contingent mischiefs to foresee,
> Make Heirs for Monarks, and for God decree?

One form of the contract theory of the origin of government that the Whigs propound would indeed lead to the very kind of arbitrary, lawless rule they profess to fear:

What shall we think! can People give away
Both for themselves and Sons, their Native sway? [760]
Then they are left Defenceless, to the Sword
Of each unbounded Arbitrary Lord:
And Laws are vain, by which we Right enjoy,
If Kings unquestiond can those laws destroy.

The other form of contract theory, in which Kings are merely trustees,
is shown to be invalid by the experience not only of the English nation
but also of mankind at large:

Yet, if the Crowd be Judge of fit and Just, [765]
And Kings are onely Officers in trust,
Then this resuming Cov'nant was declar'd
When Kings were made, or is for ever bard:
If those who gave the Scepter, coud not tye
By their own deed their own Posterity, [770]
How then coud *Adam* bind his future Race?
How coud his forfeit on mankind take place?
Or how coud heavenly Justice damn us all,
Who nere consented to our Fathers fall?
Then Kings are slaves to those whom they Command, [775]
And Tenants to their Peoples pleasure stand.

The Whig theory is not only invalid: it is also highly dangerous, for the
greatest source of arbitrariness is, not Kings who rule by law (as does
England's), but the "Crowd" that usurps royal power and never knows
its mind:

That Pow'r, which is for Property allowd,
Is mischeivously seated in the Crowd:
For who can be secure of private Right,
If Sovereign sway may be dissolv'd by might? [780]
Nor is the Peoples Judgment always true:
The most may err as grossly as the few.
And faultless Kings run down, by Common Cry,
For Vice, Oppression, and for Tyranny.
What Standard is there in a fickle rout, [785]
Which, flowing to the mark, runs faster out?

Nor is Parliament, as the representative of the "Crowd", any better able
to rule well, as witnessed by what they did to the Martyr King and to
the property and liberty of individuals during the Commonwealth:

Nor only Crowds, but Sanhedrins may be
Infected with this publick Lunacy:
And Share the madness of Rebellious times,
To Murther Monarchs for Imagin'd crimes. [790]
If they may Give and Take when e'r they please,
Not Kings alone, (the Godheads Images,)

> But Government it self at length must fall
> To Natures state; where all have Right to all.

Even if there were any validity to the Whigs' theory, who in his right mind would put the implementing of a theory ahead of maintaining a stable government which is governing well and which, after all, has received divine sanction?

> Yet, grant our Lords the People Kings can make,   [795]
> What Prudent men a setled Throne woud shake?
> For whatsoe'r their Sufferings were before,
> That Change they Covet makes them suffer more.
> All other Errors but disturb a State;
> But Innovation is the Blow of Fate.   [800]
> If ancient Fabricks nod, and threat to fall,
> To Patch the Flaws, and Buttress up the Wall,
> Thus far 'tis Duty; but here fix the Mark:
> For all beyond it is to touch our Ark.
> To change Foundations, cast the Frame anew,   [805]
> Is work for Rebels who base Ends pursue:
> At once Divine and Humane Laws controul:
> And mend the Parts by ruine of the Whole.
> The Tampering World is subject to this Curse,
> To Physick their Disease into a worse.   [810]

Diseased, perverse, and impious are the Whig goals, the fabrication of evil men motivated by private ambition and set on gaining arbitrary rule. Who would support them? On the other hand, there have been many reasons implicit throughout the *confutatio* for supporting the King: he is the legitimate and divinely sanctioned ruler, he has maintained peace in the nation (apart from the turbulence caused by the Whigs), and he has protected the liberty and property of the individual. There is consequently no need for a lengthy *confirmatio*, presenting the reasons why the moderate reader should support the King; but there are reasons, not yet touched upon, why he should lend his assistance to those specific individuals who have chosen to support the King in his government. Accordingly Dryden turns to a brief *confirmatio*.

Confirmatio (with Digressio)

The supporters are few but brave and worthy:

> Now what Relief can Righteous *David* bring?
> How Fatall 'tis to be too good a King!
> Friends he has few, so high the Madness grows;
> Who dare be such, must be the Peoples Foes:
> Yet some there were, ev'n in the worst of days;   [815]
> Some let me name, and Naming is to praise.

First are the two most esteemed men in England, both of them moral and courageous, competent and admired: the Duke of Ormonde and his late son, the Earl of Ossory. Ormonde in particular displays long-lasting loyalty in the most trying of circumstances:

> In this short File *Barzillai* first appears;
> *Barzillai* crown'd with Honour and with Years:
> Long since, the rising Rebells he withstood
> In Regions Waste, beyond the *Jordans* Flood: [820]
> Unfortunately Brave to buoy the State;
> But sinking underneath his Masters Fate:
> In Exile with his Godlike Prince he Mourn'd;
> For him he Suffer'd, and with him Return'd.
> The Court he practis'd, not the Courtier's art: [825]
> Large was his Wealth, but larger was his Heart:
> Which, well the Noblest Objects knew to choose,
> The Fighting Warriour, and Recording Muse.[13]
> His Bed coud once a Fruitfull Issue boast:
> Now more than half a Father's Name is lost. [830]

"His Eldest Hope," Dryden continues, and then breaks off his argument to sing a eulogy, for that eldest hope, the Earl of Ossory. This eulogy is in effect a *digressio*, and its timing and occasion parallel the example of a digression given by Quintilian, when he cited "the famous recital of the virtues of Gneius Pompeius in the *pro Cornelio* [by Cicero and now lost], where the great orator, as though the course of his eloquence had been broken by the mere mention of the general's name, interrupts the topic on which he had already embarked and digresses forthwith to sing his praises."[14] Since Ossory has been very highly regarded and praised, even by the Whigs, it is of course to Dryden's benefit that he elaborate on the virtues of this admired man who had been a loyal and active supporter of the King:

> His Eldest Hope, with every Grace adorn'd,
> By me (so Heav'n will have it) always Mourn'd,
> And always honour'd, snatcht in Manhoods prime
> By' unequal Fates, and Providences crime:
> Yet not before the Goal of Honour won, [835]
> All parts fulfill'd of Subject and of Son;
> Swift was the Race, but short the Time to run.
> Oh Narrow Circle, but of Pow'r Divine,
> Scanted in Space, but perfect in thy Line!

[13] The "Fighting Warriour" may be the Earl of Mulgrave soon to be described as Adriel, and the "Recording Muse" may be Dryden himself (presumably as Historiographer Royal), inasmuch as Ormonde's biographer includes these two men among the small group of men whom Ormonde used to invite to dine with him, in a party, every quarter. See *Works*, II, 275.

[14] *Institutio*, IV.iii.13.

By Sea, by Land, thy Matchless Worth was known;   [840]
Arms thy Delight, and War was all thy Own:
Thy force, Infus'd, the fainting *Tyrians* prop'd:
And Haughty *Pharaoh* found his Fortune stop'd.
Oh Ancient Honour, Oh Unconquer'd Hand,
Whom Foes unpunish'd never coud withstand!   [845]
But *Israel* was unworthy of thy Birth;
Short is the date of all Immoderate Worth.
It looks as Heaven our Ruine had design'd,
And durst not trust thy Fortune and thy Mind.
Now, free from Earth, thy disencumbred Soul   [850]
Mounts up, and leaves behind the Clouds and Starry Pole:
From thence thy kindred legions mayst thou bring
To aid the guardian Angel of thy King.
Here stop my Muse, here cease thy painfull flight;
No Pinions can pursue Immortal height: [855]
Tell good *Barzillai* thou canst sing no more,
And tell thy Soul she should have fled before;
Or fled she with his life, and left this Verse
To hang on her departed Patron's Herse?
Now take thy steepy flight from heaven, and see   [860]
If thou canst find on earth another *He*,
Another he would be too hard to find,
See then whom thou canst see not far behind.

Having thus returned to earth (after enlisting further divine aid for the King), Dryden resumes his argument, pointing to the pious leaders of the Church, the learned leaders of the colleges, and the judicious leaders of the law, all of whom support the King:

Zadock the Priest, whom, shunning Power and Place,
His lowly mind advanc'd to *David's* Grace: [865]
With him the *Sagan* of *Jerusalem*,
Of hospitable Soul and noble Stem;
Him of the Western dome, whose weighty sense
Flows in fit words and heavenly eloquence.
The Prophets Sons by such example led,   [870]
To Learning and to Loyalty were bred:
For *Colleges* on bounteous Kings depend,
And never Rebell was to Arts a friend.
To these succeed the Pillars of the Laws,
Who best cou'd plead and best can judge a Cause.   [875]

Two noble courtiers, currently very much in the public eye, may now be paraded, one for his sharp judgement and the other for his "ready wit and pregnant thought"—both, of course, staunch supporters (now) of the King:

Next them a train of Loyal Peers ascend:
Sharp judging *Adriel* the Muses friend,

> Himself a Muse—In Sanhedrins debate
> True to his Prince; but not a Slave of State.
> Whom *David*'s love with Honours did adorn, [880]
> That from his disobedient Son were torn.
> *Jotham* of ready wit and pregnant thought,
> Indew'd by nature, and by learning taught
> To move Assemblies, who but onely try'd
> The worst awhile, then chose the better side; [885]
> Nor chose alone, but turn'd the balance too;
> So much the weight of one brave man can doe.

Two nagging questions may well linger in the moderate reader's mind about Charles's government. One is, how did Charles manage to continue financing his government when the House of Commons had put an end to his income deriving from internal taxes and all he was left with was (to public knowledge) the income from import duties? A further implied question is, of course, is there any truth to the Whig charge that Charles must be receiving money from Louis of France? The answer (to both) is in the "frugal care" of Laurence Hyde, the lord treasurer:

> *Hushai* the friend of *David* in distress,
> In publick storms of manly stedfastness;
> By foreign treaties he inform'd his Youth; [890]
> And join'd experience to his native truth.
> His frugal care supply'd the wanting Throne,
> Frugal for that, but bounteous of his own:
> 'Tis easy conduct when Exchequers flow,
> But hard the task to manage well the low: [895]
> For Soveraign power is too deprest or high,
> When Kings are forc'd to sell, or Crowds to buy.

The other nagging question could be phrased thus: How is it that the "Crowd" in the House of Commons had been so fractious in the Exclusion Parliaments when it was not that way in the preceding Parliaments? Again there is an implied question: might not the later Houses have had reason to be fractious? The answer (to both) is in the dextrous skill of Sir Edward Seymour, the man who had cooled the passion of earlier Houses—when he was gone, the fractiousness emerged unchecked:

> Indulge one labour more my weary Muse,
> For *Amiel*, who can *Amiel*'s praise refuse?
> Of ancient race by birth, but nobler yet [900]
> In his own worth, and without Title great:
> The Sanhedrin long time as chief he rul'd,
> Their Reason guided and their Passion coold;
> So dexterous was he in the Crown's defence,
> So form'd to speak a Loyal Nation's Sense, [905]

> That as their band was *Israel*'s Tribes in small,
> So fit was he to represent them all.
> Now rasher Charioteers the Seat ascend,
> Whose loose Carriers his steady Skill commend:
> They like th'unequal Ruler of the Day,   [910]
> Misguide the Seasons and mistake the Way;
> While he withdrawn at their mad Labour smiles,
> And safe enjoys the Sabbath of his Toyls.

Here are the reasons for lending assistance to the supporters of the King: they demonstrate the admirable and very necessary qualities (Ciceronian, of course) of loyalty and courage, of nobility and steadfastness, of perspicacity and eloquence, of frugality and capability. In these qualities, and the assistance which the moderates can render their possessors, lies the only hope for England. There now remains the effective integration and rounding off of Dryden's argument.

Peroratio

According to Cicero, the *peroratio* has three parts: "the summing up, the *indignatio* or exciting of indignation or ill-will against the opponent, and the *conquestio* or the arousing of pity and sympathy."[15] In Dryden's poem the King's supporters provide such a summing up, after a typically smooth transition from the preceding section:

> These were the chief, a small but faithful Band ⎫
> Of Worthies, in the Breach who dar'd to stand,   ⎬   [915]
> And tempt th'united Fury of the Land.   ⎭
> With grief they view'd such powerful Engines bent,
> To batter down the lawful Government.
> A numerous Faction with pretended frights,
> In Sanhedrins to plume the Regal Rights.   [920]
> The true Successour from the Court remov'd:
> The Plot, by hireling Witnesses improv'd.
> These Ills they saw, and as their Duty bound,
> They shew'd the King the danger of the Wound:
> That no Concessions from the Throne woud please,   [925]
> But Lenitives fomented the Disease:
> That *Absalom*, ambitious of the Crown,
> Was made the Lure to draw the People down:
> That false *Achitophel*'s pernitious Hate,
> Had turn'd the Plot to Ruine Church and State: [930]
> The Councill violent, the Rabble worse
> That *Shimei* taught *Jerusalem* to Curse.

In the transition to David's speech, Dryden begins to evoke both *indignatio* and *conquestio*, the one at the "loads of Injuries" heaped by

[15] *De Invent.*, I.lii.98.

the Whigs on the King, and the other by the "patience" demonstrated by the King who could so readily have swept his enemies from the face of the earth:

> With all these loads of Injuries opprest,
> And long revolving, in his carefull Breast,
> The'event of things; at last his patience tir'd, [935]
> Thus from his Royal Throne by Heav'n inspir'd,
> The God-like *David* spoke: with awfull fear
> His Train their Maker in their Master hear.

In the speech itself Dryden alternates between passages which excite indignation against the Whigs and passages that arouse sympathy for the King. First is a reminder of the folly and presumption of the Whigs: they forget that Charles forgave them all for the murder of his father, they challenge his right to grant mercy, they preach perverted theory, they malign the King, and they parade illegal petitions before him with demands that he do their bidding:

> Thus long have I, by native mercy sway'd,
> My wrong dissembl'd, my revenge delay'd: [940]
> So willing to forgive th'Offending Age,
> So much the Father did the King asswage.
> But now so far my Clemency they slight,
> Th'Offenders question my Forgiving Right.[16]
> That one was made for many, they contend, [945]
> But 'tis to Rule, for that's a Monarch's End.
> They call my tenderness of Blood, my Fear:
> Though Manly tempers can the longest bear.
> Yet, since they will divert my Native course,
> 'Tis time to shew I am not Good by Force. [950]
> Those heap'd Affronts that haughty Subjects bring,
> Are burthens for a Camel, not a King:

Then as Charles turns to the behaviour of Monmouth, there is evoked sympathy for Charles, and even pity, as he views his wayward son and would like to pardon him:

> Kings are the publick Pillars of the State,
> Born to sustain and prop the Nations weight:
> If my Young *Samson* will pretend a Call [955]
> To shake the Column, let him share the Fall:
> But oh that yet he woud repent and live!
> How easie 'tis for Parents to forgive!
> With how few Tears a Pardon might be won
> From Nature, pleading for a Darling Son! [960]

[16] Evidently a reference to Bethel's challenging Charles's right to mitigate the execution of Stafford and also, probably, to the House of Commons's challenging his right to pardon the Earl of Danby the year before.

> Poor pitied Youth, by my Paternal care,
> Rais'd up to all the Height his Frame coud bear:
> Had God ordain'd his fate for Empire born,
> He woud have given his Soul another turn:
> Gull'd with a Patriots name, whose Modern sense   [965]
> Is one that would by Law destroy his Prince:
> The Peoples Brave, the Politicians Tool;
> Never was Patriot yet, but was a Fool.[17]
> Whence comes it that Religion and the Laws
> Should more be *Absalom*'s than *David*'s Cause?   [970]
> His old Instructor, e're he lost his Place,
> Was never thought indu'd with so much Grace.

Then back to indignation towards the Whigs for their folly and arrogance, their greed and perfidy:

> Good Heav'ns, how Faction can a Patriot Paint!
> My Rebel ever proves my Peoples Saint:
> Would *They* impose an Heir upon the Throne?   [975]
> Let Sanhedrins be taught to give their Own.
> A King's at least a part of Government,
> And mine as requisite as their Consent:
> Without my Leave a future King to choose,
> Infers a Right the Present to Depose: [980]
> True, they Petition me t'approve their Choise,
> But *Esau*'s Hands suite ill with *Jacob*'s Voice.
> My Pious Subjects for my Safety pray,
> Which to Secure they take my Power away.
> From Plots and Treasons Heaven preserve my years,   [985]
> But Save me most from my Petitioners.
> Unsatiate as the barren Womb or Grave;
> God cannot Grant so much as they can Crave.

In responding to this situation, Charles displays the two sides of mercy calculated to elicit sympathy and support: he will defend his kingship and his friends, and it is with reluctance that he feels compelled to exact justice on his enemies:

> What then is left but with a Jealous Eye
> To guard the Small remains of Royalty?   [990]
> The Law shall still direct my peacefull Sway,
> And the same Law teach Rebels to Obey:
> Votes shall no more Establish'd Pow'r controul,
> Such Votes as make a Part exceed the Whole:
> No groundless Clamours shall my Friends remove,   [995]
> Nor Crowds have power to Punish e're they Prove:[18]

[17] It should be remembered that "patriot" was often used at this time to mean, ironically, "a factious disturber of government" (*OED*, quoting Johnson and citing this line).

[18] Evidently a reference to the "Crowd" in the House of Commons who sentenced to the Tower, without trial, those to whom they took dislike.

For Gods, and Godlike Kings their Care express,
Still to Defend their Servants in distress.
Oh that my Power to Saving were confin'd:
Why am I forc'd, like Heaven, against my mind,   [1000]
To make Examples of another Kind?
Must I at length the Sword of Justice draw?
Oh curst Effects of necessary Law!
How ill my Fear they by my Mercy scan,
Beware the Fury of a Patient Man.   [1005]
Law they require, let Law then shew her Face;
They coud not be content to look on Grace,
Her hinder parts, but with a daring Eye
To tempt the terror of her Front, and Dye.

The King's enemies have of course deserved justice: in their factiousness and treason they have lived on innocent blood and have sought to
engulf the nation in the miseries of a civil war:

By their own arts 'tis Righteously decreed,   [1010]
Those dire Artificers of Death shall bleed.
Against themselves their Witnesses will Swear,
Till Viper-like their Mother Plot they tear:
And suck for Nutriment that bloody gore
Which was their Principle of Life before.   [1015]
Their *Belial* with their *Belzebub* will fight;
Thus on my Foes, my Foes shall do me Right:
Nor doubt th'event: for Factious crowds engage
In their first Onset, all their Brutal Rage;
Then, let 'em take an unresisted Course,   [1020]
Retire and Traverse, and Delude their Force:
But when they stand all Breathless, urge the fight,
And rise upon 'em with redoubled might:
For Lawfull Pow'r is still Superiour found,
When long driven back, at length it stands the ground.   [1025]

The argument is over, almost. We return to the beginning, to the
never-never land of long, long ago, where God's will prevailed:

He said. Th' Almighty, nodding, gave Consent;
And Peals of Thunder shook the Firmament.
Henceforth a Series of new time began,
The mighty Years in long Procession ran:
Once more the Godlike *David* was Restor'd,   [1030]
And willing Nations knew their Lawfull Lord.

Then, so long ago, the people of Israel and Judah had recognized the
King whom God had set over them, and they had rallied to his support.
In the day of Dryden's reader, the moderates of England and Scotland,
recognizing the divine lawfulness of their King, would likewise rally to
his support.

FINIS.

APPENDIX
PROPER NAMES AND THEIR COUNTERPARTS

In the left-hand column are listed those proper names that appear in Dryden's fictional construct. In the right-hand column are listed their counterparts in the political world to which he refers covertly.

Abbethdin	Judge
Absalom	Duke of Monmouth
Absolon (variant spelling of Absalom)	
Achitophel	Earl of Shaftesbury
Adriel	Earl of Mulgrave
Ægypt	France
Agag	James, Duke of York (see pp. 135-37)
Amiel	Sir Edward Seymour
Amnon	the beadle murdered by Monmouth (see pp. 160-61)
Annabel	Countess of Buccleuch (wife of Monmouth)
Balaam	Earl of Huntington
Barzillai	Duke of Ormonde
Bathsheba	Duchess of Portsmouth
Brother of David	James, Duke of York (brother of Charles)
Caleb	Lord Grey (see pp. 118-19)
Corah	Titus Oates
David	Charles II
Egypt	France
Egyptian	Roman (Catholic)
Ethnick	alien
Gath	Brussels
Hebrew(s)	Tory Anglican(s)
Hebrew Priests	Anglican clergy
Hebron	Scotland

Him of the Western Dome	Dean of Westminster
Hushai	Laurence Hyde, first lord of the Treasury
Isbosheth	Richard Cromwell (son of Oliver)
Israel	England
Israelite(s)	English
Issachar	Thomas Thynne
Jebus	the Pope
Jebusites	Roman Catholics (Papists)
Jerusalem	London
Jews	Whig Dissenters (see pp. 29-33)
Jewish Rabbins	Dissenting clergy (see p. 32)
Jonas (variant of Jonah)	Sir William Jones
Jordan (l. 270)	English Channel
Jordan (l. 829)	Irish Sea
Jotham	Viscount Halifax
Levites	Dissenting clergy (see p. 40)
Michal	Catherine, wife of Charles II
Nadab	Lord Howard
Nile	Seine
Pharaoh	Louis XIV, King of France
Prophets	faculty of the Universities
Sagan of Jerusalem	Bishop of London
Sanhedrin	House of Commons or House of Lords, depending on the context
Saul (ll. 57, 417)	Oliver Cromwell
Shimei	Slingsby Bethel
Sion	London
Son of Barzillai	Earl of Ossory
Solymaean Rout	London mob
Tyrians	Dutch
Tyrus	Holland
Zadock	Archbishop of Canterbury
Zimri	Duke of Buckingham

Biblical names with no counterparts noted should be read as referring directly to the persons described in the Bible, or on occasion being used as an open comparison for a character in the construct: Aaron, Adam, Belial, Belzebub, Esau, Jacob, Messiah, Moses, Rechabite, Samson, Samuel, Saul (l. 677), Saviour, Stephen.

INDEX

Notes

1. So that this index may also serve some of the functions of a bibliography, the titles of pamphlets that were part of the Exclusion Crisis and that are referred to in this study are listed under the heading "pamphlets"; likewise the names of scholars are grouped under "scholars, historical" and "scholars, literary."

2. For greater ease in reference, a guide to aspects of the crafting of the poem is given under the heading *Absalom and Achitophel*.